SPECIAL FORCES

SPECIAL FORCES

David Miller

PUBLISHED BY
SALAMANDER BOOKS LIMITED
LONDON

A Salamander Book
Published by Salamander Books Limited
8 Blenheim Court
Brewery Road
London N7 9NT

ISBN 1 84065 021 4

2 3 4 5 6 7 8 9

All correspondence concerning the content of this volume should be addressed to Salamander Books Ltd.

CREDITS

Project managed by Ray Bonds
Designed by Megra Mitchell
Picture research by TRH Pictures
Colour separation by Studio Technology Limited
Printed in Italy

THE AUTHOR

David Miller is a former British Army officer, who spent most of his service in the Far East, Central Europe, and the Falkland Islands. He subsequently worked as a freelance author and then spent three years as a journalist with Jane's Information Group, where he was a staffer on *International Defense Review*, before producing the first edition of *Jane's Major Surface Warships*. He is now a freelance author once again, writing on a wide variety of defense subjects. He has contributed to many international military journals and has had some 35 books published.

ADDITIONAL CAPTIONS

JACKET FRONT: US Army Ranger, a member of an elite unit trained to conduct a variety of missions in arctic, mountain, jungle, urban, and amphibious warfare.

JACKET BACK: Top, Land Rover Multi-Role Combat Vehicle, specially designed for rapid-reaction forces. Bottom left, a member of Spain's Grupo Especial de Operaciones (GEO) preparing to fire during abseiling. Bottom right, French special forces trooper armed with silenced sub-machine gun.

ENDPAPERS: Dutch Marines race ashore under realistic-looking fire during a training exercise. This elite unit is an important element of NATO's amphibious forces.

PAGE 1: Black-clad special forces with respirator masks typify the deliberately formidable appearance of such international units on a counter-terrorist training mission.

PAGES 2-3: Soldiers of the French Army 1er RPIMA (Regiment de Parachutistes d'Infanterie de Marine) storm a house during training for hostage rescue.
PAGES 4-5: Members of Canada's 300-strong Joint Task Force 2 counter-terrorist unit.

CONTENTS

FOREWORD

This is not the first book that has been written about the elite forces that exist in various countries throughout the world. However, this highly researched and authoritative volume is certainly one of the most definitive of its kind written to date, and most likely will remain so for the foreseeable future. The authors have compiled an extensive presentation of organizations that have often been exaggerated, misunderstood or misrepresented.

The establishment of elite forces has greatly increased since the end of World War II – a fact recognized and documented by this book, There are many reasons for this growth, among them:

- Improvements in the sophistication and lethality of weapons and the quantum jump in the complete spectrum of conducting conventional warfare, concomitant with the increased costs required to man and equip sizable modern forces.
- The recognition by many nations that a highly trained, truly professional force, committed in a timely and judicious manner, could possibly deter an aggressor. This has the added benefit of preventing the commitment of much larger conventional forces at a later time.
- Recognition that a requirement exists to have a highly trained organization that can rapidly respond to terrorist threats or acts.

Many nations recognize the requirement to form, organize, equip, train and support elite or special operations forces in peacetime so that they can operate, when directed to do so, in all phases of pre-conflict and conflict.

They must be prepared to conduct operations during this period of "violent peace," and they must also be ready to conduct their wartime missions without having to take the time for extensive training after conflict starts, as was the case during World War II.

Many of the requirements are discussed in this book which differentiate elite forces from conventional forces. This is as it should be since selection and training are so critically important to the successful performance of any elite unit. Personnel in these units are for the most part volunteers who undergo some form of selection process which greatly tests individual physical ability, stamina and the capability to plan and operate under great mental and physical strain,

In most organizations, this selection process serves as an assessment system which helps determine whether individuals measure up to the standards of the organization. In fact, it is during this initial selection process that those who aren't likely to meet those standards are separated from the unit.

Some organizations, when not selecting certain individuals within their ranks (for whatever reason) return them to their parent unit or to another organization, usually a support type, with high praise and as much good will as possible. This is done to ensure that non-acceptable volunteers do not poison the recruiting well throughout the regular formations.

Those who do go forward are language-trained, area-oriented forces capable of providing sustained assistance to individual countries. This is vital to any nation whose national policy it is to assist in obtaining or preserving freedom.

Many nations control their elite forces at the highest national levels, and, when committing them externally, they call upon them to perform strategic missions. Some forces are controlled and supported by operational commanders, while others may be committed independent of the conventional force chain of command.

Whatever the mode of commitment, there exists in all phases of special operations the need for extensive planning so that psychological and deception operations are an integral part of the overall operation whenever possible. I believe that some of the most important factors in planning and conducting these kinds of operations are the need for timely, accurate intelligence and good security.

The authors have done exceptional research on the various elite forces. While some information is readily available from open sources in the Western countries, the Communist nations have not been as open with information in this area. Despite this limitation, the authors have produced a work that should be indispensable for the practitioner and student of elite forces and special operations organizations,

I predict that anyone associated with special operations, terrorism or counterterrorism will welcome this book and use it as a reference many times.

by **Robert C. Kingston,**
General, US Army (Ret.)

Robert C. Kingston,
General, US Army (Ret.)

General Kingston enlisted in the US Army in 1948 and has commanded a platoon, a company. a battalion, two brigades and special operations forces in two conflicts. He wears 16 battle stars and also earned the Combat Infantry Badge (two awards); the Master Parachutist Badge (US); Ranger Tab; Gliderman Badge; Korean Parachutist Badge; Parachute Wing (UK); Cambodian Parachutist Badge; Vietnamese jumpmaster Badge; Vietnamese Ranger Badge; and 12 overseas bars.

His special operations experience includes a tour in Korea as commanding officer, Far East Command Special Mission Group. He was executive officer of the Ranger Mountain Camp, Dahlonega, Georgia (1954-55). In 1960-1961, he served as the exchange airborne officer with the 16th Independent Parachute Group, UK.

General Kingston was also senior advisor to the Vietnamese Ranger Command (1966) and commander of the 3rd Special Forces Group (Airborne), 1st Special Forces, Fort Bragg, North Carolina.

In January 1973, General Kingston assumed command of the joint Casualty Resolution Center, Nakhon Phanom, Thailand, In October 1975, he became

commander of the US Army John F. Kennedy Center for Military Assistance and the US Army Institute for Military Assistance at Fort Bragg, The general pinned on his fourth star and assumed command of the United States Central Command, MacDill Air Force Base, Florida, on 1 January, 1983. He retired from active duty on November 30, 1985.

INTRODUCTION

ABOVE: The traditional image of terrorist attacks is a hijacked airliner burning on a Middle East airfield. Constant vigilance and firm action by governments and airlines has reduced the prevalence of such attacks but the threat is ever-present.

THERE HAS ALWAYS BEEN A fascination with the exploits of uniformed warriors who dash deep into enemy territory, create utter havoc and, having successfully completed the mission, return to camp to prepare for yet another foray. It is the stuff from which legend springs.

Even so, these warriors—usually members of special or unconventional military formations—are viewed with skeptical ambivalence. When they are successful, a certain aura of glamor attaches to that success; when they are not—particularly when the failure is publicized—opprobrium comes all too swiftly.

Make no mistake about it: there is an inherent distrust of secret or "special" operations and those associated with them, particularly in open and democratic societies. It is a distrust that runs deep and which causes the fortunes of elite or special forces to wax and wane.

"Elite" and "special" are simply ways to describe unconventional or supreme and paramilitary formations. Other labels that have been applied, with various relevance, are commando, paratrooper, irregular, guerrilla, even "cowboy," or simply—and perhaps more embracing—special operations forces. Whatever the choice of designation, however, these forces have always had an important role to play in their nations' defense forces, and their historical legacy is particularly rich.

The Roman legions, for example, were denied success by irregular African forces using camels and arrows. They were also thwarted in Great Britain by the guerrilla tactics of a female warrior named Boedicia. In America the sharpshooting Minutemen played an undeniably significant role in the outcome of the Revolutionary War. General George Washington's famous crossing of the Delaware on Christmas Eve just prior to the Battle of Trenton was a special operation. And in Britain, what we now know as the Special Air Service (SAS) had its genesis in North Africa in 1941, where it performed daring raids behind German lines during World War II. That undeniably elite and special force performed just as spectacular feats toward the end of the 20th Century, notably alongside American Delta and other special forces in the Iraqi desert in 1991, and, undoubtedly, in the trouble-torn Balkans. Today it is influential in the training, actual and by example, of many elite units the world over.

The post-World War II era saw a decline in special forces; in fact, many were disbanded.

Without a war, the argument went, there was no mission. Marry to that the distrust of special forces, as well as the uneasy tolerance accorded them by the regular forces, and it's easy to see why elite forces seemed to be approaching their nadir.

But the mission for special forces can never truly go away for one very basic reason. They are and must be an integral part of any nation's defense forces and, as such, will always have a role in defending the sovereign. These forces are now stronger than they ever were, and the reasons for this are both practical and historical.

In the 1960s, a netherworld existed in which a state of neither "true peace" nor "true war" developed. It featured so-called "wars of national liberation" characterized by conflict in which the postwar process of decolonization played itself out. By the 1970s, these postwar spasms were over in Africa, East Asia, and the Middle East and hands previously at the tiller of revolutionary movements were now firmly on the reins of power.

But that did not mean that the use of upheaval and instability had been abandoned. Far from it. In fact, the distorted and grotesque outrages of terrorism, state-sponsored and otherwise, plagued the globe. As an instrument of national will, this highly dangerous situation represented a more deliberate type of conflict with severe consequences for the security of many nations, large and small.

In the past 30 years, conflict in one form or another has led to violent changes of government in many countries. During the Cold War there were many conflicts—some of them, like the Vietnam War, on a large scale—but the need to avoid global conflict resulted in a variety of pressures to localize their impact. With the ending of the Cold War, however, and, in particular, with the demise of the Soviet Union and the emergence of the United States as the only—and frequently reluctant—Superpower, such constraints have been lifted and conflicts of one sort or another continue unabated.

In the words of one observer, "World War III has already begun and...is comprised of brush-fire conflicts, assassinations, terrorist bombings, coups, revolutions, and civil strife." The prophetic views of George Orwell come pretty close to the mark. War may not be peace, he claimed, but the peace of our time has assumed some unmistakably warlike characteristics.

ABOVE LEFT: In the never-ending war against terrorists, the consequences of lapses of vigilance are severe and instantaneous, as the United States discovered when its Beirut Embassy was seriously damaged by a lorry-bomb in 1983.

ABOVE: Typically clad Beirut street fighters man a barricade, wearing US webbing but carrying Russian Kalashnikov assault rifles.

That is unlikely to change in the near future. Just as in the Gulf in 1991, and in Kosova in 1999, the early decades of the 21st Century seem certain to bear witness to an increasing number of situations requiring responses short of full mobilization to address. There is no clean and easy way to categorize these crises and the types of conflict they represent. However, it is clear that terrorism and what has been dubbed "low intensity conflict" (along with its 1940s-style disgraceful "ethnic cleansing" characteristics), and special operations need to be considered together. Nobody has devised a universally appropriate definition of "low intensity conflict," although an understanding of what it represents is critical to understanding special and elite forces and their roles.

One definition claims that low intensity conflict is a political-military confrontation bewteen contending states or groups below the level of conventional war and above the routine, peaceful competition among states. It involves protracted struggles of competing principles and ideologies and ranges from subversion to the use of armed force. It is waged by a combination of means employing political, economic, informational, and military instruments. Such conflicts are often local in nature, but contain regional and global security implications. Accepting this definition, imperfect though it may be, at least provides a working framework in which to put low intensity conflict.

The spectrum of potential conflict ranges from terrorism through mid- and high-intensity conflict, readily recognized since they involve the application of conventional military power, to strategic nuclear warfare. Terrorism, properly identified as a form of warfare, cuts across the entire spectrum. So, too, can elite and special forces be employed anywhere across the spectrum.

But even the most elite of special forces can deal with only a small portion of the threats posed by subversion, international criminality, and terrorism. This is why more of these forces have come into being; it is why nations are cooperating in framing strategies to deal with the problems of conflict; it is why there is increasing recognition that terrorism is a form of conflict that must be met by forces specially trained for the counter-terrorist mission.

There are literally hundreds of special and elite formations in existence—some with a handful of members, some with a cast of thousands. Many, despite the sensitive nature of

BELOW: Virtually every country now has its special operations forces. These are from Argentina's Halcon, formed in 1986. Like a number of such forces, it is a police unit, answering directly to the police chief in Buones Ayres. It is responsible for counter-terrorist duties and VIP protection.

their missions, are relatively easy to identify, explain, and describe in some detail. Most of these units operate in open societies—the French Foreign Legion, and the Special Air Service units in Britain, Australia, and New Zealand are examples.

In some cases, the mission of an elite force is strictly military in character—like the US Army Rangers, and their operation in Grenada in 1983. In other cases, the mission is strictly counter-terrorist, such as that of the German GSG 9 and the French GIGN. In yet other cases, however, the two missions are combined in one force, such as with the British SAS and American Delta.

Units such as Italy's COMSUBIN are charged with military responsibilities first and counter-terrorist activity second—unless that mission is reversed in the national interest.

It would be blatantly presumptuous to claim that one has come up with a comprehensive guide to elite and special forces. To begin with, there is no accepted definition of what an elite force truly is beyond the fact that—generally—it has a quite different mission from that of a conventional force. Moreover, these units are constantly being formed, disbanded, and realigned to meet individual circumstances. Bulking large in the overall equation is the security factor; for some time questions about America's premier counter-terrorist special force, Delta, received the standard reply, "Delta is an airline," and because what was probably the most famous British SAS operation, the Iranian Embassy Siege in 1980, was played out in front of the world's TV cameras, it is quite understandable that there has been a reluctance on the part of the authorities to provide information to the media lest future special operations become compromised.

This book is divided into three main sections, which describe, respectively, the special and elite forces, some of the major operations in which they have been involved, and a selection of their weapons. It must be appreciated that this coverage cannot, by definition, be comprehensive. Some elite units are so secret that even their very existence is totally unknown to the general public, while a number of operations, even by acknowledged units, remain highly classified. Similarly, some weapons and techniques are secret in order that an elite unit can achieve tactical surprise over its opponents.

Four major points emerge from this study. The first is that, as the Gulf War conclusively demonstrated, special forces have a firm place in conventional war. In such conflicts, their ability to operate clandestinely in the enemy's rear enables them to attack targets which

ABOVE: An Italian COMSUBIN trooper with the highly specialized H&K P11 underwater pistol. The 5-round weapon is electrically operated, with power provided by two 24-volt batteries. Out of water the weapon has a similar effect to a conventional 7.62mm pistol.

ABOVE: A defining moment in counter-terrorist warfare was the British SAS attack on the Iranian Embassy in London to rescue hostages; only one terrorist survived to tell the tale. This event was widely shown on TV, serving notice that terrorists would be treated with the same violence that they meted out to their victims.

cannot be reached by any other means, and to exert an influence out of all proportion to the actual numbers deployed.

Secondly, elite forces involved in the counter-terrorist mission face a unique challenge. Their successes dissuade their opponents from trying again, leading to long periods without action, making it harder to maintain the essential high degree of training and readiness. In addition, protracted periods of apparent inactivity result in government financiers starting to question the large expenditure necessary, sometimes even resulting in cutbacks. It is then that the terrorists strike again, often using some totally new technique.

Thirdly, there is a high degree of lateral cooperation between special forces, ranging from exchanging information, through conducting joint exercises and the exchange of personnel to taking part in each other's operations.

Finally, the great majority of special forces traditionally find their recruits from elsewhere in their country's armed forces. This ensures that their operators have experience of the armed forces as a whole and are a known quantity when they start the selection process. However, the rapid down-sizing of most military forces since the end of the Cold War means that the size of the pool from which such volunteers can be found is also diminishing.

As this book will show, elite units have a very important task in modern society, their value lying not just in their capability in conventional warfare, but also in the clandestine world of counter-terrorism, where they must be ready to meet any threat at any time. In addition, while most counter-terrorist forces are confined to their national homelands, some others, like those of the USA, UK, France, and Israel, may be committed anywhere in the world. It is a daunting challenge.

SPECIAL FORCES IN THE BALKAN WAR, 1999

Special Forces of the NATO Alliance countries were called into action in early 1999 as war erupted in the Balkans in Europe, when Serbian forces pursued a two-pronged campaign of forcing hundreds of thousands of ethnic Albanians from the neighboring province of Kosovo and engaging in a brutal offensive against the rebel Kosovo Liberation Army (KLA).

Serbia's hard-man President Slobodan Milosevic ignored NATO's repeated threats that it would use force if Serbia failed to comply with United Nations' requirements for internal self-government for the ethnic-Albanian province of Kosovo and to agree to the deployment of an international, NATO-provided monitoring force to supervize implementation. The Balkan War (NATO designation - Operation Allied Force) was launched during March, with NATO air forces and missiles striking Serbian air defense assets, including missile bases, radars, and command/control centers. NATO's political leaders·proclaimed that their intention was to conduct the campaign entirely from the air, and thrust thousands of fighter, ground attack, bomber, reconnaissance, and electronic warfare aircraft into the conflict. Cruise missiles were also launched from US aircraft and surface warships, and from British and US submarines.

The air strikes had considerable initial effect, but it rapidly became clear that air power alone would not suffice. The capabilities of the attack aircraft were limited by a number of factors. First, since aircrew safety was considered vital, there was a need to avoid shoulder-launched air defense missiles which the Serbs were known to possess, which meant that they had to bomb from over 10,000ft (3,000m). However, the Rules of Engagement (RoE) stipulated that pilots had to identify targets positively, a factor which assumed even greater importance when it was realized that a massive exodus of ethnic-Albanian refugees was under way. This problem was further complicated by the bad weather over the Balkans, especially clouds, which made target acquisition and actual attacks difficult or, at times, even impossible. Then, even when the weather was clear, the hilly terrain over large parts of Kosovo made target acquisition difficult.

So, as had happened in the Gulf War, it quickly became apparent that special operations forces were essential to the resolution of some of these problems and it was not long before it was publicly acknowledged that, although their activities had been shrouded in secrecy, special forces had actually deployed, some of them almost certainly inside Kosovo. Such forces were based in neighboring Albania and the Former Yugoslav Republic (FYR) of Macedonia, with further bases across the Adriatic in Italy.

Among the first special forces to be employed were personnel and aircraft of the US Air Force's 1st Special Operations Wing (1 SOW) which had deployed before the start of the operation and were able to swing into action when a USAF F-117A "stealth" fighter bomber was shot down by SAMs over Bosnia early in the campaign. Among those involved in the totally successful pilot rescue operation were HH-53H Pave Low III and MH-60K helicopters, both specifically designed for such missions.

Other special forces deployed included units of varying sizes and capabilities from France, Germany, Norway, and the UK, although there may well have been others. French special forces in the Balkans included elements of 13th Airborne Dragoon Regiment, Marine Infantry, and parachutists, while the British sent in elements of the SAS.

It was reported that British and American special forces were working under cover in Kosovo with the Kosovo Liberation Army to identify Serbian targets for NATO bombing raids. SAS soldiers fluent in Albanian and Serbian were said to have skirted minefields and Serbian patrols around the devastated villages along Kosovo's borders with Albania and Macedonia to enter the Kosovo province on surveillance missions. Their mission was said to be to locate and report on Serbian tanks, command posts, and patrols hidden in the villages. One unconfirmed report stated that 80 SAS soldiers had been sent deep into Kosovo to target Serbian "death squads."

Apart from observation, surveillance, and rescuing downed aircrew, a primary role of the special forces in the region was as forward air controllers (FAC) using the latest range of laser target markers, some of them specifically designed for use by special forces. One particular role (again, as in the Gulf War) was to locate and destroy Serb ground communications systems, particularly those using metal cables or fiber optics, which cannot be intercepted by signals intelligence means.

As this was being written, Milosevic had capitulated to NATO pressure and, after protracted negotiation, pulled his Serb forces out of Kosovo. NATO forces under K-FOR entered Kosovo to return the province to order and to safeguard the returning Kosovo Albanians. The role of the special forces remained crucial, and their mission could include:

• snatching war criminals, including Milosevic and the Bosnian-Serb "General" Radko Mlavic, who was identified in Kosovo in April 1999, and possibly also the villainous Zeljko Raznatovic (also known as "Arkan") who had formed a paramilitary unit called the "Tigers" which had reportedly been involved in the most murderous ethnic cleansing operations against the Muslims in Bosnia and Croatia in 1991/92, and who was said to be preparing to become involved in Kosovo in 1999;
• rescue of NATO personnel and any hostages taken by the Serbs;
• direct action, and advisory roles, by NATO special forces with the Kosovo Liberation Army.

As NATO forces were trying to keep the retreating Serbs and the KLA apart, attempting to disarm the latter, and systematically clearing the province of unexploded munitions, Serb-laid mines, and booby traps, there task will be difficult and their deployment, and that of the special forces, could last for decades.

Men of the US Army's Special Operations Forces undergo rigorous training to be ready for all-terrain, all-weather operations worldwide. It has been reported that US SOF, together with other NATO special forces, have operated in Serbia and Kosovo.

PART 1

SPECIAL FORCES

MOST COUNTRIES HAVE at least one "elite" unit in their armed forces, although there are various types of elite. Some are selected and trained for a special role, for which conventional troops do not have either the special weapons or training needed. Other elites are given a special designation earned by a particularly meritorious performance in battle and are then expected to set an example which other elements should follow; thus, for example, the designation "guards" used by the British and Russian armies, among others.

Other elites are formed on an ethnic or tribal basis, of which the best known are the Gurkhas. Two well-known elites are formed by units of foreigners: the French Foreign Legion and the Spanish Legion. However, it is worth noting that both contain a substantial proportion of Frenchmen and Spaniards, respectively.

The majority of special units are, however, associated with countering modern terrorism, and there have been two events of great significance in this area, both of which attracted huge publicity. First was the 1972 Munich Olympic Games when terrorists kidnapped some members of the Israeli team and then forced the German authorities to provide them with transport to a nearby airfield where a rescue attempt by the German police and troops resulted in considerable loss of· life. This gave the public the impression that terrorists would, one way or another, achieve their goal, but it also spurred governments, armed forces and police into seeking an answer to this increasingly powerful threat. This resulted in the setting up of a number of totally new elite forces (eg, the German GSG 9) or in the re-roling of existing units (eg, the British SAS). It should be noted, also, that some countries decided to place this role on their civilian forces, rather on their military forces.

The second significant event was the British assault by the SAS on the terrorists occupying the Iranian Embassy in London. This also took place in the full glare of publicity but, unlike many earlier operations, it was totally successful, thus not only demonstrating the value of special units but also giving governments and the public some hope that terrorists could be beaten.

Many special forces, particularly those with a counter-terrorist role, are shrouded in secrecy and little is known about some units except that they exist; indeed, there must be other units whose existence is totally unknown. This is for security reasons if no other, and to maintain their surprise and shock elements of their actions.

An assault team of the Brazilian Army's 1st Special Forces Battalion about to rush a building during a training exercise. In the absence of actual emergencies, it is a major task of all special forces to keep their units trained in operations and use of weapons so that they will be at the peak of their performance when they are needed for real.

ARGENTINA

BRIGADA ESPECIAL OPERATIVA HALCON

ARGENTINA'S PRINCIPAL ANTI-TERRORIST unit is the Brigada Especial Operativa Halcon (= Special Operations Brigade - Falcon), which was formed in 1986. It is a police unit answering directly to the commander of the police in the national capital, Buones Ayres. Apart from counter-terrorist duties, it is also responsible for VIP protection.

Brigada Halcon has a strength of 75 men, who are organized into five 15-man teams. The teams are identically organized, with 8 troopers and 7 specialists: communications - 1; explosives – 1; intelligence – 1; negotiator – 1; medical – 1; and snipers – 2.

The unit wears locally manufactured uniforms and protective gear. Weapons are mostly foreign and include Glock 17 and the Franchi SPAS 12 shotgun. The snipers use the Heckler & Koch HK G3 GS/1.

AUSTRALIA

SPECIAL AIR SERVICE REGIMENT

AUSTRALIAN TROOPS PLAYED a significant role in the Malayan Emergency, the fight against the Communist insurgents which lasted from 1949 to 1961. During that campaign the British re-formed their Special Air Service (it had been disbanded after World War II) for deep-jungle operations and the Australian Army used this as a model when it formed its first special forces unit, 1st Special Air Service Company, on July 1 1957. With the termination of the Malayan campaign, however, the SAS Company was absorbed into the regular infantry (Royal Australian Regiment [RAR]), but separated again in 1964 and expanded to become the Special Air Service Regiment (SASR) with three "Sabre" squadrons. Sub-units of the SASR took part in Indonesia's Konfrontasi (= confrontation) campaign in Borneo, Brunei, and Sarawak in the early 1960s, and then also took part, with other Australian troops, in the Vietnam War, between 1966 and 1971.

Following disengagement from Vietnam one squadron of the SASR was disbanded, but a terrorist bomb attack on the Sydney Hilton on February 13 1978 showed that Australia was not immune to such activities and on February 23 the SASR was formally designated the national counter-terrorist unit. To help meet the new tasks the third squadron was reformed in 1982 and since then, while other elements of the Australian Defense Forces have been cut back, the SASR has remained virtually untouched.

Recent operations have included the Gulf War when one SASR squadron (110 men) deployed to Kuwait in February-May 1991 where it joined with 23 men from the New Zealand SAS to form the ANZAC SAS Squadron, which was part of a joint force with British and US special forces. Another deployment was to Somalia, where a 10-man close-protection group from the SASR formed part of the 67-strong Australian Contingent.

As of 1999 Australian special forces comprised:
- SPECIAL AIR SERVICE REGIMENT (SASR), consisting of 1, 2, and 3 "Sabre" Squadrons, 152 (SASR) Signal Squadron.
- 1ST COMMANDO REGIMENT (1 CDO REGT), consisting of 1 and 2 Commandos and 126 (Commando) Signal Squadron. These are reserve units, consisting of mainly reservists with a small regular cadre.
- 4TH ROYAL AUSTRALIAN REGIMENT, COMMANDO (4RAR CDO) (four companies), including an air platoon.
- NAVY CLEARANCE DIVING BRANCH (two regular and one reserve clearance diver teams).

In addition, each state and the capital territory (Canberra) has a counter-terrorist force, known variously as "special operations groups" or "emergency response teams."

ORGANIZATION

SASR is approximately 550 strong, with its main base at Campbell Barracks, Swanbourne, Western Australia, and comprises a Regimental Headquarters (RHQ) and six squadrons. There are three "Sabre" squadrons, which operate a thee-year training/operational cycle, starting with a work-up year, during which volunteers are inducted and more experienced soldiers attend advanced courses. The second year sees the squadron training for overt commitments, including special operations in a conventional war, while in the third year it trains for clandestine tasks, and forms the counter-terrorist Tactical Assault Group (TAG) (see below). Base Squadron provides administrative and logistic support, while Operational Support Squadron is responsible for specialist training and trials of new techniques and equipment. The highly specialized communications needed by such a force are provided by 152 (SASR) Signals Squadron.

ABOVE: Australian SAS trooper coming in to land using a Ram-Air parachute which enables silent and extremely precise landings to be made. Note pack under his feet.

TASKS

In peace-time the SASR's main task is counter-terrorism, which is being given special emphasis in the run-up to and during the Olympic Games, being held in Sydney in the year 2000. Prime responsibility for counter-terrorism lies with the Tactical Assault Group (ie, the "Sabre" squadron in the third year of its operational cycle). The enemy could include assassins, bombers, hijackers, kidnappers, or snipers. Tasks to be performed against such targets could include the neutralization and/or capture of individuals or groups on the land or at sea; the neutralization of hostile aircraft or ships; the safe recovery of hostages; and evicting terrorists from buildings, installations, ships or aircraft which they may have captured. Such tasks could take place anywhere in continental Australia or overseas where an Australian interest is involved.

Counter-terrorism training includes Close Quarter Battle (CQB) tactics, explosive entry using frame or water charges, tubular assaults as in vehicles, buses, trains, aircraft and high rise structures, and room and building clearance operations. The Offshore Assault Team (OAT) is part of the TAG and is responsible for similar tasks, but at sea, where the terrorist incident could involve ships, or gas/oil platforms, of which there are appreciable numbers around the Australian coastline.

The SASR is trained in counter-insurgency operations which provides troopers with the skills necessary to recruit indigenous people in wartime such as the SASR did in Borneo to help them gather information about the enemy or to help them fight the enemy. The SASR is trained in Southeast Asian languages, customs and traditions and has many Southeast Asian experts in the regiment.

In conventional war, most of the SASR's tasks will be in the enemy's rear areas, and would include reconnaissance and surveillance, as well as ambushes, sabotage, raids on important targets (eg, HQs, airfields, communications centers), and target designation for air strikes.

The SASR works and trains in close liaison with US, British, and New Zealand special forces. Since 1992 there has also been considerable, and politically more controversial, contact with the Indonesian special forces, Kopassus, which has included annual special forces' exercises in the other's country.

UNIFORMS AND EQUIPMENT

SASR parade, working and field uniforms are the same as those of the Australian Army, but with a sand-colored beret, cap-badge and wings similar to those worn by the British SAS. Special uniforms (eg, black coveralls) are worn according to the tactical situation.

Equipment includes the whole range of normal Australian weapons and equipment, but with some specialist equipment according to the role. For example the normal rifle is either the M16A3 or the F88 Austeyr (locally manufactured version of the Steyr AUG), but could include Ta'as 7.62 Galil, H&K PSG1, Parker Hale 82, Finnish Tikka Finlander .223, Mauser SP 66, or SR98 Accuracy International AW-F sniper rifles, or Beretta or Remington shotguns.

For road transport specially modified Nissan Patrol 4-wheel drive vehicles are used, while most air insertions are done by helicopter, usually naval UH-60 Sea Hawks or CH-3 Seakings, or Army UH-60 Black Hawks or CH-47 Chinooks.

ABOVE: An SASR trooper adopts a nonchalant pose, as he pauses for a drink atop a pinnacle in the Australian Stirling Range; getting the laden pack up must have been quite a struggle. Note the 7.62mm Self-Loading Rifle (SLR).

TOP: All special forces' selection courses are rigorous, but few more so than for these aspiring members of Australia's tough Special Air Service Regiment (SASR)

AUSTRIA

ABOVE: GEK operator with Steyr SSG69 5.56mm rifle, an Austrian weapon proving very popular with special forces around the world.

GENDARMERIEEINSATZKOMMANDO COBRA

IN THE LATE 1960s and early 1970s there was a wave of terrorist incidents, particularly in Europe, with the small, neutral country of Austria being particularly badly affected. At that time Jewish refugees were being allowed to leave the Soviet Union but they were not permitted to travel direct to their ultimate destinations (usually, either Israel or the USA) and the great majority staged through Austria. This led to several Palestinian terrorist operations which resulted in the Austrian government ordering the formation in 1973 of Gendarmeriekommando Bad Voslau (Bad Voslau was the name of the unit's base). It was put on high alert during several crises, once when terrorists seized hostages but were allowed to leave, and on another occasion when the international terrorist, Carlos Sanchez, seized several OPEC oil ministers who were meeting in Vienna, but was paid a multi-million dollar ransom and given a passage out of the country.

The Israeli rescue mission at Entebbe and the German GSG 9 assault on the airliner at Mogadishu showed that determined action by well-trained and properly equipped men could overcome even the most fanatical terrorists. This led to a restructuring of Gendarmeriekommando Bad Voslau in 1978 and the new unit was redesignated Gendarmerieeinsatzkommando (GEK) (= police commando unit) "Cobra." The GEK's first commander, Oberst Pechter, established close ties with other counter-terrorist units, including, among others, the Israeli Sayeret Mat'kal and the (then) West German GSG 9.

BELGIUM

BELOW: Belgian ESI troopers storm a bus during a hostage-rescue exercise at an "anti-terrorist workshop" hosted by Italy's GIS (see p. 34). As the fire team (right) brings the bus under fire, the assault team (left) comes into action from a Range Rover, with ladders being extracted for use in entering the target vehicle.

ESCADRON SPECIAL D'INTERVENTION (ESI)

LIKE MANY OTHER European nations, Belgium was shocked by the terrorist attack on the 1972 Munich Olympic Games into forming its own counter-terrorist unit as part of the Gendarmerie Royale. At first this was given the cover-name "Diane" but although this was changed to Escadron Special d'Intervention (ESI) in 1974. The name "Diane" continues to be used unofficially.

ESI's primary mission is counter-terrorist operations, but it is also used to fight organized crime, particularly where the criminals are armed, and anti-narcotics work. Volunteers for the ESI must undergo a two-week selection process, following which they attend a three-month course. The ESI also has an amphibious capability.

Weapons used include the Heckler & Koch MP5 sub-machine gun, Remington 12-gauge shotguns and the Sako TRG-21 7.62mm sniper rifle.

PARA COMMANDO BRIGADE

THE BELGIAN ARMY'S elite military unit is the Para-Commando Brigade. Separate parachute and commando units were formed by the Belgian government-in-exile in Britain during World War II, and continued in existence after the war. In 1952 they were amalgamated into the Para-Commando Regiment, which continued in existence until 1991 when, in the reorganization and realignment following the end of the Cold War, new units were added, enabling the regiment to be upgraded to the Para-Commando Brigade. The brigade, which has a peacetime strength of about 3,000, comprises:

INFANTRY
1ST AND 3RD PARACHUTE Battalions and the 2nd Commando Battalion, each some 500 strong (despite the different titles all three are organized identically).

- RECONNAISSANCE: 3rd Lancers Parachutists Battalion
- ARTILLERY: Para-Commando Field Artillery Battery, 35th Para-Commando Anti-Aircraft Artillery Battery.
- SUPPORT: Engineer, Logistics and Medical Companies.

The Para-Commando Brigade is part of Belgium's contribution to NATO's Immediate and Rapid Reaction Forces, but also takes part in national and United Nations missions.

SELECTION AND TRAINING

All members of the brigade are volunteers and after a thorough medical examination they must attend a five-month commando course. On graduation they are entitled to wear the commando badge. They then proceed on a one-month parachute course, which involves seven jumps, which must include at least one balloon jump, one night jump, one from a C-130 aircraft and one with full equipment. To remain current every member of the brigade must carry out four jumps every year.

During World War II the Belgian Army raised an SAS Regiment, which was an integral part of the British SAS Brigade. The Belgian SAS was reduced to battalion size until the early 1950s, when it converted to a conventional parachute battalion. The present 1st Parachute Battalion is directly descended from this unit and wears the SAS Dagger as its cap-badge, but with the paratroopers' red beret.

THE BELGIAN NAVY

THE BELGIAN NAVY operates a small frogman section, which is believed to be about 30-men strong and similar in organization and training to the British SBS.

BRAZIL

LEFT: Special forces' troopers of Brazil's *I Batalhoo de Forcas Especials* undergoing training in fighting in built-up areas. One man is spraying chemical smoke into a man-hole, which provides access to an underground sewage system, in order to flush out terrorists sheltering there.

1ST SPECIAL FORCES BATTALION

THE FIRST BRAZILIAN counter-terrorist group was formed in 1953 but the present CT unit, 1st Special Forces Battalion, was raised in 1983. In common with many other such units in other armies, *I Batalhòo de Forcas Especials* (1st Special Forces Battalion) does not recruit civilians direct, but takes volunteers only from other units in the Army. The selection process is very severe and is followed by a 13-week training course.

Other Brazilian special forces units include:
Grupo de Mergulhadores de Combate (GRUMEC) (= combat divers group).
Comandos Anfybios (COMANFI) (= amphibious commandos).
Comandos de Reconhecimento Terrestre (RECONTER) (= land reconnaissance commandos).
Grupos de Operaces Especiais (GOE) (= special operations groups).
PARASAR (paratroops).

CANADA

JOINT TASK FORCE 2

THE PRESENT-DAY CANADIAN special operations force is "Joint Task Force 2" (JTF 2), which was formed in April 1993. For most of the past 50 years special operations were the prerogative of the "Special Service Force," with counter-terrorist operations being the responsibility of the Royal Canadian Mounted Police's (RCMP) Special Emergency Response Team (SERT).

During World War II there were two Canadian Army airborne units: 1st Canadian Parachute Battalion, raised at Camp Shiloh in the USA in 1942; and 2nd Parachute Battalion, formed later in Canada. Following the war the Canadian parachuting capability was reduced to cadre level until 1968, when it was expanded and the Canadian Airborne Regiment (CAR) was formed, which was intended to be a light, independent, all-arms unit for deployment in low-intensity operations in jungle, desert or arctic warfare conditions. The capability was later expanded yet again with the formation of the Special Service Force, whose "teeth" elements comprised an armored battalion, an infantry battalion, the CAR, plus artillery and engineer battalions, and communications and logistics support. It also included the Canadian SAS, which had been formed in 1946 as a company-sized unit, closely modeled on the British SAS.

The CAR was disbanded in the mid-1990s as a result of an enquiry into activities of some elements during its participation in the UN operation in Somalia, and its three component companies were dispersed to form airborne companies in three conventional infantry battalions.

Joint Task Force 2 (JTF 2) is a counter-terrorist unit on the lines of US Delta and British SAS, with whom it maintains close contact. Volunteers can come only from those already within the Canadian Forces (CF) and their tour length is normally 4-5 years, although it is believed that it may also include people from other Canadian government services – eg, Canadian Security Intelligence Service (CSIS). It is approximately 300 strong and is commanded by a lieutenant-colonel.

VOLUNTEER STANDARDS

Volunteer standards are not normally specified, but the Canadian Forces have made their requirements for JTF 2 public (CANFORGEN 078/97 Adm(per) 056 301330Z Jul 97) and these are summarized below:

- RANKS: Volunteers must be in the ranks of: officers - captain only; soldiers - warrant officer, sergeant, master-corporal, corporal, private.
- GENERAL QUALIFICATIONS: At least three years' service and re-engaged for a second three-year engagement; no known phobias (eg, fear of heights, water or enclosed spaces); a valid civilian driving license; and a demonstrated wish and ability to learn a second language.
- PHYSICAL REQUIREMENTS: A high standard of medical fitness and a demonstrated capability of: running 1.5 miles (2.5km) inside 11 minutes; 40 consecutive push-ups; five consecutive overhand grip, straight-arm pull-ups; 40 sit-ups in 60 seconds; 143lb (65kg) bench press.
- COMMANDING OFFICER'S RECOMMENDATION: A statement that the volunteer has achieved all the above requirements plus a general assessment of his suitability for special forces, in areas such as: maturity, stability lifestyle, and financial.
- PRELIMINARY SCREENING: by a qualified JTF recruiting team.
- PHASE 3: Those passing Phase 2 then participate in a three-week course in which their levels of physical fitness, weapons handling, and confidence are improved, following which they undergo a one week assessment of suitability for special forces. Officers have an additional four-day assessment of their planning and leadership skills.
- PHASE 4: five months of training.

BELOW: A stick of paratroopers descend from a Canadian Lockheed C-130, as a marker team awaits their arrival on the ground. The men belong to Joint Task Force 2, a new organization, which was raised in the mid-1990s as a successor to the Canadian Airborne Regiment (CAR), which had been disbanded.

OPERATIONS

It is not known for certain where and when JTF 2 may have been deployed, although press reports suggest that elements were sent to (but not used in) Bosnia, and that the unit was on stand-by for a possible operation in Peru during the Japanese Embassy hostage crisis

GRUPO DE OPERACIONES POLICIALES ESPECIALES

CHILE

GRUPO DE OPERACIONES POLICIALES ESPECIALES (GOPE)(= Group for Special Police Operations) was formed in 1980. Chilean personnel were originally trained by German and Israeli instructors and the unit is currently believed to be approximately 100 strong. Its principal task is to undertake military special forces/commando duties but it also has a commitment to support the UAT (see below) in counter-terrorist operations in government and diplomatic buildings.

Unidad Anti-Terroristes (UAT)(= anti-terrorist unit), also known as "Cobra," belongs to the National Police Force. It is approximately 120 strong and is divided into seven-man teams, each led by an officer. The unit is based just outside Santiago.

Military Special Forces comprise two groups:
* Buzos Tacticos del Ejercito (Army SF commandos).
* Buzos Tacticos de la Armada (Navy SF commandos).

JAEGERKORPTSET

DENMARK

LEFT: An observation post (OP) manned by men of the Danish Jaegerkorptset (Ranger Corps).

FACED WITH A GROWING THREAT of international terrorism in the late 1950s, the Danish Army sent a number of officers to the US Ranger School and on attachment to the British Special Air Service in 1960/61. These officers were then used to raise a new body, the Jaegerkorptset (= Ranger Corps), which was trained for counter-terrorist duties in support of the Danish police's Aktions-Styrken (Action Force) and for long-range patrol and sabotage duties in conventional war.

The Jaegerkorptset is based at Aalborg in North Jutland, and works and trains closely with other special forces, particularly the British SAS. It also receives helicopter support from the British Royal Air Force and German Army, since the largest helicopter available from Danish sources is the Hughes MD-500

Weapons known to be used include: pistols - SIG P-210 7.65mm "Neuhausen;" SMC - H&K MP5, H&K MP53; rifles – H&K G41; sniper rifle - H&K PSG-1 7.62 sniper rifle.

FROEMANDSKORPSET (FROGMAN CORPS)

THE ROYAL DANISH NAVY'S Froemandskorpset was created in 1957 as part of the naval diving school, but it was taken away and made directly subordinate to naval headquarters in 1970. The unit's tasks include: beach reconnaissance; boarding suspect ships; diving; underwater demolition; and ship underwater security. The unit was deployed during the Gulf War aboard ships of the Royal Danish Navy

EGYPT

TASK FORCE 777

FACED WITH CREDIBLE THREATS from extremists such as the Abu Nidal Organization (which had split from the PLO in 1974), Egypt established Task Force 777 in 1977, with an initial strength of three officers, four NCOs, and 40 soldiers. They received an early baptism of fire in 1978 when Arab terrorists, claiming to represent the PLO, killed an Egyptian newspaper editor in Nicosia, Cyprus, on February 19 1978, and then seized 30 hostages. Task Force 777 went into action and killed the terrorists but then, due to misunderstandings on the spot in which the Cypriots thought the Egyptians were actually reinforcements for the terrorists, an attack by Cypriot National Guard and police resulted in the deaths of 15 members of TF 777. The incident resulted in a major row between the governments, with the Egyptians accusing the Cypriots of a lack of cooperation and killing their troops, while the Cypriots accused the Egyptians of failing to inform them of the arrival of Task Force 777 and of blatantly disregarding their national sovereignty.

Unfortunately, even worse was to follow in a second operation in October 1985 in the aftermath of the *Achille Lauro* hijacking when Palestinians hijacked an Egyptair Boeing 737 airliner, Flight 648, and forced the pilot to land at Luqa in Malta. Egypt promptly ordered the despatch of Task Force 777 and this time ensured that the Maltese authorities knew that it was on its way. The operation was botched, however, probably due to pressure on the commander of TF 777 to effect a very rapid solution. Although TF 777 did not have a plan of the internal layout of the Boeing 737, even though it belonged to Egypt's own national airline, it was decided to create a diversion by blowing a hole in the roof which would distract the terrorists' attention, thus enabling the main attack to go in through the doors. The explosives team got on to the roof without being detected by the terrorists. Unfortunately, they then added extra explosive to ensure success with the result that the blast was so violent that some 20 passengers in the rows immediately beneath were killed. At this, the main attack commenced but the TF 777 men used high-explosive grenades and fired indiscriminately into the interior of the cabin, while some of the passengers who did actually get out of the aircraft were then mistaken for fleeing terrorists by TF 777 snipers outside the aircraft and several were shot. The result of all these errors was that 57 hostages were killed, making it one of the most costly rescue operations ever undertaken.

Despite the failure of these two missions, however, it was clear that the Egyptian authorities were determined to take immediate and forceful action against terrorists and it should be noted that there has been no major airliner hijacking incident since. Nevertheless, Task Force 777 has been kept busy by Egypt's internal war against the "Brotherhood" in which they have undertaken numerous actions and lost several men.

BELOW: The aftermath of a rescue attempt that went wrong. This Egyptair Boeing 737 was hijacked to Malta, where it was assaulted by Egypt's TF 777. Scorch marks show where the engineers blew a hole in the roof, but they added so much extra explosive as insurance that some 20 passengers in the rear cabin were killed. A further 37 passengers were killed in the main assault.

WEAPONS AND EQUIPMENT

Like all such units, Task Force 777 maintains a "rapid reaction force" at very short notice to move, with further elements at longer notice. The unit is supported by a number of dedicated Westland Commando troop-carrying helicopters at similar degrees of notice.

Task Force 777 is known to have received training from US special operations forces (Delta and SEALs) as well as from European forces, including the British SAS, French GIGN, and the German GSG 9.

FRANCE

FRANCE HAS TRADITIONALLY created elite groups within its armed forces and over the past 50 years the two leading groups have been the *Legion Etrangere* (Foreign Legion) and *les paras* (the "paratroops"). There are also a number of "marine" units, which despite their name are not amphibious troops as understood in American and British usage, but are elite units which in the 19th Century were raised specifically for overseas land service. One example is *6er Regiment de Parachutistes d'Infanterie de Marine* (6th Parachute Regiment of the Marine Infantry). The French Armed Forces are being reduced in size and reorganized according to Plan 2002. While this will have some effect on the size of the Foreign Legion and the Paras, they will be affected less than other parts of the army.

The French police counter-terrorist unit is the *Groupe d'Intervention de la Gendarmerie Nationale* (GIGN), whose most recent success was the rescue of hostages from a hijacked airliner at Marseille-Marignane airport in December 1994.

French military special forces are under the command of *Commandement des Operations Speciales* (COS) (= Special Operations Command), which was formed after the 1991 Gulf War, and comprises units from Army, Navy, and Air Force. It is answerable direct to the Chief of the Joint Staff.

The primary Army special force is the *Premier Regiment de Parachutistes d'Infanterie de Marine* (1er RPIMa), which is similar in most respects to the British SAS. This is not surprising, since their traditions stem from the French SAS units raised in England during World War II. Missions include counter-terrorist operations in conjunction with GIGN and RAID (see below) and special operations in conventional war, similar to those conducted by the US SOFD-Delta and the British SAS.

Naval special forces are designated *Groupement des Fusiliers-Marins Commandos* (GROUFUMACO)(= Naval Commando Group) which is composed of four assault commandos (= teams or companies), plus a special commando of *nageurs de combat* (= underwater swimmers). Their missions and tactical methodology are similar to those used by US SEALs and British SBS, with whom they have frequent exchanges.

The *Gendarmerie Nationale* is a national paramilitary police force administered by the Ministry of Defense. This organization includes its own special forces, *Groupement Speciale d'Intervention de la Gendarmerie Nationale* (GSIGN) (Special Action Group of the National Gendarmerie), which has three company-sized components:

Groupe d'Intervention de la Gendarmerie Nationale (GIGN). With a strength of 87, the GIGN is commanded by a commandant (major).

Groupe de Securite du President de la Republique (GSPR) which is responsible for the personal safety of the president.

Escadron Parachutiste d'Intervention de la Gendarmerie Nationale (EPIGN).

ABOVE: Members of the French GIGN attack a simulated target in a specially adapted training house. A grenade has been thrown into an understair cupboard by the man in the center, while his two colleagues cover the doorway, ready to arrest or shoot anyone emerging. GIGN, part of France's Gendarmerie Nationale, is one of the most professional of all counter-terrorist units, its most recent known success being the rescue of hostages from a French airliner at Marseille in 1994.

ABOVE: Marines of the French naval special forces GROUFUMACO (Groupement de Fusiliers-Marins Commandos) coming ashore in an inflatable dinghy. These men have similar roles to the US SEALs and British SBS, with which they conduct frequent training.

RAID

RAID is a highly secretive group, formed in 1985, and appears to counter the general practice among elite counter-terrorist forces by recruiting direct from the public, rather than from already-trained soldiers or police. The unit has a strength of 60: headquarters and support - 10; special task group (negotiators, explosives disposal, etc) - 10; four assault teams - 10 each. The normal operational uniform is a black coverall and mask (hence their nickname "Black Panthers") and the operators are permitted to make personal selections of weaponry, either foreign or French. The selection tests are very severe and are followed by a nine-month training course.

LEGION ETRANGERE

THE LEGION ETRANGERE (= Foreign Legion) forms a solid core of highly professional soldiers at the center of the French Army. In March 1988 the French government announced the outcome of a thorough review of the nation's defense requirements, as a result of which the Army is being reduced from 200,000 to 136,000 (-47 percent). Of this, however, the Legion's share of the cut is only from 8,300 to 7,500 (-10 percent), although Legion units will withdraw from many overseas bases. The Legion continues to attract recruits, and according to current statistics the national origins of its manpower can be roughly divided into: Eastern Europe – one-third; France itself – one-third; and the rest of the world (103 nations) – one-third.

TRAINING THE LEGION

The Legion is responsible for its own administration, including recruiting, recruit training, specialist training (eg, radio operators), NCO training, career management, and discharges. To achieve this, there are two regiments:

1er Regiment Etranger (1RE) (1st Foreign Legion Regiment). Located at Caserne Vienot in Aubagne, 1RE is responsible for the administration of the whole Legion. It also runs the band and the museum, and administers the large training camp. Of even greater importance, 1RE is the senior regiment of the Legion and the custodian of the Legion's traditions and keeper of its relics. For the individual legionnaire, his service begins and ends at Aubagne.

4er Regiment Etranger (4th Foreign Legion Regiment [4RE]). 4RE is based at Castelnaudary, where it is responsible for recruit and NCO training.

THE COMBAT UNITS

There are five major combat units:

2er Regiment Etranger d'Infanterie (2REI) (2nd Foreign Legion Infantry Regiment). Stationed at Nimes, in France, 2REI has had a very busy time. It was raised in 1841 and has served in virtually every one of France's colonial campaigns since then.

3er Regiment Etranger d'Infanterie (3REI) (3rd Foreign Legion Infantry Regiment) is stationed at Kourou in French Guyana. It specializes in jungle warfare and consists of four companies, although it is normally reinforced by a fifth company from another Legion unit. 3REI is composed of two infantry companies, whose basic responsibility is that of the security of the French missile launching site, plus an air defense company and an administrative company.

1er Regiment Etranger de Cavalerie (1REC) (1st Foreign Legion Cavalry Regiment) is one of the two armored regiments in 6eme Division Legere Blindee (6th Light Armored Division) and

BELOW: Foreign Legionnaires at range practice with their 5.56mm FA MAS assault rifles. The MAS is unusual in that it is normally fired using the built-in bipod, which compels the firer to adopt a rather higher firing position than with other rifles. Note the flash suppressor at the end of the barrel and the long carrying handle/sight protector, with the prominent cocking handle beneath.

LEFT: Combat frogmen of the *Detachment d'Intervention Operationelle Subaquatique*, a special forces unit manned by engineers from the Legion's 6th Engineer Regiment. One frogman is checking their direction with his compass, while the other stands guard, carrying a standard FA MAS 5.56mm assault rifle.

is stationed at Orange, France. It consists of three armored car squadrons and an APC-borne infantry company. It is one of the spearhead units for the French rapid deployment force.

2er Régiment Etranger de Parachutistes (2REP) (2nd Foreign Legion Parachute Regiment) is a rapid deployment airborne-commando regiment, stationed at Calvi on the island of Corsica. The regiment is divided into specialized companies, each of which is specially trained in a particular form of combat, although there is regular cross-training between companies. There are six companies: 1 Company - night combat, anti-tank, urban combat; 2 Company - mountain and arctic warfare; 3 Company - amphibious warfare, combat swimmers; 4 Company - demolition, sabotage, sniping, unconventional warfare; HQ Company - administration, communications, medical, maintenance, and supply; and reconnaissance and support company.

5er Regiment Etranger (5RE) (5th Foreign Legion Regiment). The Legion's 5th Regiment served with distinction in Indochina, but now performs security and labor duties on French islands in the Pacific, including Mururoa Atoll where French nuclear weapons tests were carried out.

6eme Regiment Etranger de Genie (6REG) (6th Legion Engineer Regiment) is the most junior unit in the Legion, having been raised as recently as 1984, although it is the bearer of the traditions of the former *6eme Regiment Etranger d'Infanterie*. 6REG was based at Nimes, France, until recently when it moved to the camp on the Plain d'Albion, which was formerly the base for the French IRBM missiles. 6REG maintains engineer detachments overseas and includes *Detachement d'Intervention Operationnelle Subaquatique* which is responsible for combat swimmer operations and underwater explosive ordnance disposal. It is the engineer regiment for 6th DLB (= 6th Light Division). It consists of five companies: three field engineer companies; a bridging company; and command/support company.

13eme Demi-Brigade Legion Etrangere (13DBLE) (13th Half-Brigade of the Foreign Legion) is stationed in the Republic of Djibouti on the "Horn of Africa," a location of major strategic importance. 13 DBLE consists of an armored car squadron; an infantry company; and a headquarters and support company, armed with mortars and anti-tank missiles (Milan), and a medical section.

Detachement de Legion Etrangere a Mayotte (DLEM) (Foreign Legion Detachment - Mayotte). The DLEM is responsible for the security of the Indian Ocean island of Mayotte, in the Comoros group of islands, an important staging post on the route to the Pacific.

BELOW: Like other special forces, the Foreign Legion is ready to operate in a wide variety of terrains. In this rock-strewn desert, the legionnaire in front carries an FA MAS assault rifle, but the second man is a sniper and is armed with a French 7.62mm sniping rifle.

SELECTION AND TRAINING

Legionnaires come from any country except, in theory, France itself. However, the Legion has always contained a large proportion of Frenchmen, who circumvent the regulations by claiming to be Belgians, Swiss or French Canadians. On enlisting the new recruit is immediately given an alias, whose use is mandatory for three years. If he survives the first three weeks of training - and he may either leave or be expelled in that period - he is then a legionnaire for the remaining five years of his contract. Training is extremely thorough and lasts for one year, being conducted by 4RE at a camp at Bonifacio, on the southern tip of the island of Corsica. Great importance is placed on obedience and physical condition; nobody, it is claimed, goes through Legion training without soaking his socks in his own blood at least once. Forced marches are frequent and a high standard of marksmanship is required, with live firing taking place two days a week for 13 weeks.

SPECIALIST AND ADVANCED TRAINING

Once the basic training has been completed selected legionnaires proceed to advanced training (for example, as a communicator or as an engineer) at one of the special schools in or near Castelnaudary. Potential non-commissioned officers must attend the Corporal's course, which lasts for eight weeks and is considered to be one of the physically most demanding courses in any army. The successful corporal would then expect to attend a 14-week course prior to promotion to sergeant.

UNIFORM

The Legion wears standard French Army uniform, but with several special items, the most famous of which are the greatly prized *kepi blanc* (= white hat), which is worn on parade, and the green beret used for daily and operational wear and by the Legion's paratroops, who do not wear a red beret. The *kepi blanc* is actually a standard blue *kepi*, with a red top and gold badge, but with a white cloth cover, which is permanently removed on promotion to *sous-officer*. Special items of parade dress are the *kepi blanc*, green shoulder-boards with red tassels, a green tie, white belt over a blue sash, and white gauntlets. Officers also wear a green waistcoat. Members of the assault pioneer platoon also wear a white, hide apron, carry a ceremonial axe with a chromed blade, and are permitted to grow a beard.

BELOW: French paratroops deploying from a Puma helicopter. Apart from conducting more operational parachute drops than any other army, the French paras also pioneered the tactical use of helicopters in ground wars during their campaign against the Algerian FLN in the late 1950s.

PARATROOPS

THE FRENCH PARATROOPS have probably carried out more operational jumps than any other parachute corps in the world in their campaigns in Indochina, Suez (1956) and Algeria, with others since (eg, Kolwezi). They have also at times become heavily politicized, to their detriment.

They were among the units in the French campaign in Indochina and carried out some 156 operational drops, but were defeated in the battle of Dien Bien Phu in 1954-55.

Following the Indochina ceasefire and the French withdrawal in 1955, the paratroop units went to Algeria, arriving just as the war there started.

LEFT: French special forces on patrol, passing a running civilian. Note the black helmets with the built-in radio, giving communications to every man in the unit. The black uniforms, covered faces, and aggressive attitude are intended to present a daunting impression.

In January 1957 10th Parachute Division took over the city of Algiers which was virtually in the hands of the FLN, and inside two months restored control. Their methods were seriously questioned, however, and there were many allegations of torture. To this day, an element of distrust of *les paras* remains; for example, the number of years an officer may serve with paratroop units is now limited.

After the Algerian war the paratroops returned to France, but the French have maintained a strong parachute capability, and have regularly used these excellent troops overseas in pursuit of French diplomatic policies. Units of what is now 11th Parachute Division have served in Zaire, Mauretania, Chad, and Lebanon, among other locations.

ORGANIZATION
The approximately 14,000-man 11th Parachute Division is based at Tarbes. At least one-third of the Division is abroad, either on training missions of one kind or another, or maintaining a visible presence in Africa or the Indian Ocean. It is part of the French rapid-intervention force, together with 9th Marine Light Infantry Division, 27th Alpine Division, 6th Light Armored Division, and 4th Airmobile Division. 11th Parachute Division comprises two brigades, with seven battalion-sized parachute units, one of which (1^{er}RPIMa) is under divisional control and has a para-commando/special forces role.

The other six units are: 3, 6 and 8 RPIMa (equivalent to the former "colonial" paratroop units); 1 and 9 RCP (*chasseurs* or light infantry); and 2 REP (the Legion parachute unit).

SELECTION AND TRAINING
All French paratroops are volunteers and undergo the same sort of selection and training as other parachute forces. The standard of training is high and certain volunteers can go on to join one of the para-commando units (eg, 1^{er}RPIMa).

WEAPONS AND EQUIPMENT
For many years the French Army was using the MAS 49/56 7.5mm rifle, but they have now re-equipped with the revolutionary short, light but effective 5.56mm FA MAS "bullpup" assault rifle, with the parachute units being among the first to receive it.

UNIFORMS
French paratroops wear standard French Army uniforms. Their parachute status is indicated by their red beret (except for Foreign Legion paras who wear a green beret). Para wings are large and in silver, and are worn on the right breast.

BELOW: Close-up of a French special forces trooper. Note his face-mask, personal radio, and the large silencer on his sub-machine gun.

GERMANY

GSG 9

AN APPROPRIATE CHARACTERIZATION of the special operations forces in Germany would be "defensive," both with respect to its military elements, Fernspähkompanie (long-range reconnaissance company), and its paramilitary national border police arm, the Grenzschutzgruppe 9 (GSG 9).

The Fernspähkompanie, said to be about 140-150 personnel, is assigned to each German Army corps. It is oriented toward stay-behind operations against forces that have passed beyond them, or insertions behind enemy lines. Apart from performing long-range reconnaissance, they can also carry out sabotage missions if required. In fact, their operational concepts closely parallel those of the missions of the US Special Operations Forces. Basic training is conducted at the parachute and ranger course in Schongau. Further training is conducted at the Long Range Reconnaissance Training Center at Neuhausen ob Eck.

Following the Black September terrorist attack at the 1972 Munich Olympics, the West Germans created a totally new counter-terrorist group, but as part of the Bundesgrenzschutz (the Federal Border Police), and designated it Grenzschutzgruppe 9 (GSG 9). This unit proved itself in October 1977 at Mogadishu in Somalia when a team of 27 men took part in a six-minute assault on a hijacked Lufthansa airliner and released all 87 hostages. Since then there have been no overt GSG 9 operations, although there have been rumors of clandestine successes.

BELOW: GSG 9 troopers descend from a balcony using an Ikar descender during a training exercise. The men are all wearing "flak jackets" and carry MP5 sub-machine guns. The men in GSG 9 are required to be physically very tough, but also receive intense academic training in subjects as diverse as law and terrorist theory and practice.

ORGANIZATION

The unit was 180 strong at the time of Mogadishu and as a result of that operation it was decided to increase it to 300, but recruiting difficulties kept the strength at about 160 to 200 for some time. GSG 9 is in the process of increasing the unit strengths of its four combat units to 42 each. Overall, GSG 9 consists of a headquarters unit; a communications and documentation unit; an engineer unit; a training unit that can be used as another combat unit; a helicopter flight of three helicopters and 11 pilots and mechanics; and a supply unit. GSG 9 has three operational sub-units: GSG 9/1, the counter-terrorist assault group; GSG 9/2 specializes in maritime operations; GSG 9/3 specializes in airborne missions. Total strength is about 250.

SELECTION AND TRAINING

All members of GSG 9 must be volunteers from the ranks of the Police or Border Police. Thus, any soldier who wishes to join must first leave the Army and join the Border Police. The training course is 22 weeks long and is directed at mind and body. The first 13 weeks are devoted to police duties, legal matters, weapons skills, and karate.

Training takes place in a variety of locations as befits a unit which does not necessarily know in advance where it will be committed. The second part of the course comprises a detailed examination of terrorist movements combined with a final development of individual skills, including new developments in the optics and communications industries. The students become acquainted with sharpshooter tools such as night vision devices, observation glasses and the like. Evasive driving techniques are also taught.

Failure rate on the course is about 80 percent. There is a stronger emphasis on academic work than in most such counter-terrorist units.

WEAPONS AND EQUIPMENT

A wide variety of weapons are used, but the basic weapon is the standard police sub-machine gun - the Heckler and Koch MP59mm - but when used by GSG 9 it is fitted with a silencer. The H&K PSG-1, Mauser SP-86, and Mauser SP-66, all 7.62mm caliber, are used for sniper missions. The men are allowed to select their own model pistol, a rare degree of choice in such units. Most unusual of the weapons is the H&K P9P 9mm P7 pistol which features a unique cocking device operated by gripping the gunframe - release it and the gun is totally safe!

UNIFORMS

GSG 9 members wear standard Bundesgrenzschutz uniform - a green battledress with a dark green beret. On operations the standard German paratrooper helmet is worn, together with a flak jacket where necessary. No special unit identification is worn, although the wearing of a parachute qualification badge by a policeman may be an indication of his role.

KOMMANDO SPEZIALKRÄFTE

K OMMANDO SPEZIALKRÄFTE (KSK) (= special commando unit) was formed in 1994 and became operational in 1997, although it will not reach its full, trained strength until the year 2000. Unlike GSG 9, this is a military unit, which serves two functions. The first is the wartime military function of long-range patroling, with surveillance, sabotage, and disruption missions against command-and-control and logistics targets deep in hostile territory. The second, however, is the peacetime mission of protecting or rescuing German citizens in conflict zones overseas, with special emphasis on rescuing hostages or downed aircrews.

The KSK was formed by removing the commando companies from the three airborne brigades and two of the three independent long-range reconnaissance and patrol (LRRP) companies, one of which had been allocated to each corps (the third was disbanded). The KSK, commanded by a brigadier-general, will comprise four commando companies, a long-range reconnaissance company, a headquarters/communications company, a logistic company, and a training center. Within the commando and LRRP companies the organization will be based on four-man teams.

The KSK will be the German equivalent of the US Delta and British SAS, with similar organization, and selection and training procedures. The unit will probably use the black operational outfit pioneered by the British SAS and will be armed with predominantly standard German weapons, although the sniper rifle will be a German adaptation of the Accuracy International AW (known in Germany as the G22 Sniper Weapon System).

The difficulty with GSG 9 has been that it is a unit of the German Bundesgrenzschutz (Border Security Police) and thus, by a strict interpretation of the German Law, ineligible for overseas missions (even though it undertook the Mogadishu operation). Being a military unit, however, KSK overcomes this legal nicety. It will also, of course, enable the German government and military to deploy a direct national equivalent of Delta and the SAS.

BELOW: GSG 9 trooper in a fire position at the corner of a building. His weapon is a silenced Heckler & Koch MP5, one of the most widely used special forces' weapons (see pages 116-117).

BOTTOM: Unusual ball-mounting in the armored-glass windscreen of a Mercedes-Benz field-car, enabling an MP5 sub-machine gun to be fired straight ahead of the vehicle (the distance between the mounting plates shows how thick the glass is). This mounting would be of great value when deliberately driving into a terrorist position.

GERMANY

HUNGARY

POLICE SPECIAL FORCE

THE POLICE SPECIAL FORCE (PSF) was formed in 1991 with two roles: first, to counter any terrorist activities, and, second, to aid conventional police in their fight against organized crime. The PSF is recruited only from police officers who have given three years unblemished service, who are physically and mentally fit, and, as is usual in all such forces, pass stringent security checks.

The PSF looked to Israel for help in forming and training the unit, which, as a result, now uses much Israeli equipment.

INDIA

AS IS TO BE EXPECTED in such a large and populous country, the armed forces of India are also large, with 1,100,000 in the Army, 55,000 in the Navy and 110,000 in the Air Force, and every one of them a volunteer. Since Independence in 1947 the Indian Army has seen a great deal of active service and aggressive confrontation, particularly against its traditional enemies, Pakistan and China. There are also numerous internal problems, ranging from the long-running dispute in Kashmir to numerous internal anti-guerrilla campaigns, many of them involving terrorist tactics. Finally, there has been a variety of other military commitments, including operations in Sri Lanka and the Maldives. It is not surprising, therefore, that the Indian armed forces should have given birth to a large number of special forces.

PARA COMMANDOS

THERE ARE THREE Parachute/Commando battalions, the first to be raised being the 9th Para Cdo Bn in 1966, followed by 10th Para Cdo Bn in 1967; the third, 1st Para Cdo Bn, was converted from 1st Parachute Battalion in the mid-1970s. Some years after being formed 9th Para Cdo Bn specialized in desert warfare and 10th Bn in mountain warfare, but 1 Para Cdo Bn has not specialized and remains as a strategic reserve.

The primary mission of the Para Commandos battalions in wartime is to conduct covert operations in the enemy's rear areas in order to disrupt his operations and to attack enemy command-and-control and logistic facilities. In peacetime their mission is to serve as a highly capable and flexible, rapid-reaction force.

All the para commandos saw active service in the 1971 Indo-Pakistan war. 9th and 10th Para Commandos deployed to Sri Lanka in 1987-88 as part of the Indian government's aid to the beleaguered government in Colombo, where they conducted several heliborne assaults, albeit with varying degrees of success. 10 Para Cdo Bn also took part in the peace-keeping operation in the Maldive islands in November 1988. The para commandos have also taken part in numerous internal security operations including the 1984 attack on the Sikh Golden Temple, although they lost 17 killed and many wounded.

BELOW: Special forces of India's National Security Guard (NSG) on deployment outside the Sikhs' Golden Temple at Amritsar in May 1988. As in many such operations they are awaiting the call to action, which sometimes can be a long time coming and, without good leadership, can result in a loss of morale and efficiency.

NATIONAL SECURITY GUARDS

The National Security Guards (NSG) were raised in 1985 and form one of the largest special forces groups in the world, with a current strength of some 7,000. It also unusual in that, whereas other countries have units which are either all military or all police, India's NSG is a mixture of the two. In overall terms it is divided into two elements: the Special Action Group (SAG); and the Special Rangers Group (SRG). The SAG, which is slightly the larger of the two and composed entirely of soldiers, is responsible for offensive action, while the SRG, whose task is to support the SAG, particularly by cordoning off the area of the intended action, is entirely composed of policemen. Men serve with the NSG for 3-5 years and are then rotated back to their parent unit. Like many other modern units they wear an all-black operational uniform, which has earned them the nickname of the "Black Cats."

The main tasks of the NSG include: counter-terrorist action, resolving hijacking operations in the air or the ground, rescuing hostages, explosive ordnance disposal (EOD), VIP protection, and anti-sabotage checks prior to VIP visits. The scale of SAG commitment to an incident depends upon the site, the number of terrorists, the surrounding situation, and so on. The SAG is committed in "hit teams," each of which is composed of five men: two two-man pairs, and a technical support specialist. Four "hit teams" make an "action team" which is commanded by a captain. The NSG can, however, deploy in much larger units and on at least one occasion has fielded an entire battalion.

Three occasions when the NSG is known to have deployed were twice against the Sikh Golden Temple in Amritsar in 1986 and 1988 when they deployed in considerable strength, and once in an aircraft hijacking incident at Amritsar in 1994 where a lone hijacker was successfully overcome.

Like most special forces, the NSG maintains close links with similar organizations in other countries and some are known to have visited Israel for additional training.

BELOW: Indian Army paratroopers await to emplane for the flight to the Maldives, following the attempted coup in October 1988. Indian armed forces have been involved in many operations since Independence in 1947, with the special forces being kept particularly active.

MARINE COMMANDO FORCE

THE INDIAN NAVY'S Marine Commando Force (MCF) was raised in 1987 as an elite force for special operations in a maritime environment, with tasks which include reconnaissance, raids, and counter-terrorist operations in coastal, beach, and riverine environments.

Volunteers for the MCF undergo arduous physical tests over a period of a month following which they start on a nine-month training course. This is followed by posting to an operational unit on probation where they undergo further training, which, if they pass, ends with them being declared fully qualified some two years after starting.

Strength of the MCF is believed to be well over 1,000 and these are divided into three groups, one with each naval command: West (Bombay); South (Cochin), and East (Vizag). Each group includes a small platoon-sized Quick Reaction Section (QRS), responsible for the counter-terrorism commitment.

One of the unusual roles undertaken by elements of the MCF is harbor attack and ship sabotage, for which they are equipped with 11 two-man submarines capable of carrying explosive charges or magnetic anti-ship mines, and being delivered to the operational area by conventional, diesel-electric submarines. The MCF can also deploy using the Indian Navy's small force of landing-ships, landing-craft, and air-cushioned vehicles, as well as helicopters.

SPECIAL PROTECTION GROUP

THE SPECIAL PROTECTION GROUP (SPG) is responsible for guarding VIPs, a task not without its difficulties in a country which has lost two prime ministers by assassination: Indira Gandhi in 1984 and Rajiv Gandhi in 1991. The SPG numbers approximately 3,000, who are believed to come principally from the police.

INDONESIA

KOMANDO PASUKAN KHUSUS

THE 6000 STRONG KOMANDO PASUKAN KHUSUS (KOPASSUS) (= special forces command) has been at the center of Indonesian counter-terrorist activities, recent operations including those in the disputed territory of Irian Jaya. In January 1996 the Free Papua Movement (FPM) kidnapped a number of Indonesian citizens and foreigners and after four months of negotiations special forces attacked the terrorist hideout. This was successful although the terrorists killed two of the Indonesian hostages.

REPUBLIC OF IRELAND

ARMY RANGERS WING

THE IRISH DEFENCE FORCES started to send a small number of men from all branches of the Army, Army Air Corps, and Navy to the US Army Ranger School in the early 1970s. Some of these were used to establish the Sciathán Fianóglach an Airm (= Army Rangers Wing [ARW]), which became fully operational in March 1980, The ARW's roles can be divided into conventional warfare and counter-terrorist missions, Missions in a conventional war comprise offensive operations in hostile territory, such as raids, ambushes, sabotage, and the capture of key personnel, as well as long-range patrols, surveillance, and intelligence gathering. In the counter-terrorist role ARW's tasks could include: VIP protection; anti-hijack operations in ships, aircraft, buses or trains; hostage rescue; search

ABOVE: Men of the Irish special forces, the Army Rangers Wing, on exercise in the Irish Republic.

operations; pursuit operations; and the recapture of terrorist-held objectives such as offshore gas/oil rigs or buildings. The ARW is in regular contact and trains with similar units in other countries, including GIGN (France), GSG 9 (Germany), and Royal Dutch Marines (Netherlands), although political sensitivities probably exclude contacts with the British SAS.

The ARW uses the same weapons as the Irish Army, in particular the Austrian-manufactured 5.56mm Steyr Aug A1 assault rifle, which came into service in 1988. The sniper rifle is the latest Accuracy International .308-caliber A196, which is an improved version of the L92A1.

ISRAEL

ZAHAL

AS A RESULT OF its experiences, Israel has devised an organization in which its counter-terrorist units are placed into one of three functional categories:

"First-on-scene" units are those with a secondary counter-terrorist function, but which, because of their geographical spread, are likely to arrive first at a terrorist incident. Their task is to exert immediate control in the general area, to cordon off the scene, and, wherever possible, to stabilize the situation pending the arrival of an "assault" unit. A "first-on-scene" unit is, however, allowed to take direct action if the terrorists actually start killing hostages before the arrival of an "assault" unit. There are nine "first-on-scene" units, three in each of Zahal (Israel Defense Forces [IDF]) territorial commands. "Assault" units are those with counter-terrorism as their principal task and they will normally carry out the direct action. There are three known units in this category:

- Sayeret Matkal, which is also known as "Unit 262," is under the direct control of the IDF chief-of-staff, and is given the most important, highly classified, and difficult missions. Included within its ranks is a specialist counter-terrorist and hostage-rescue team with the cover name "Unit 269."
- Shayetet 13 is the Israeli Navy elite unit. It is also known as the Naval Commandos and the qualifying course is reputed to be even more exacting than that for land-based units. As with Sayeret Matkal, there is an integral hostage-rescue and counter-terrorist team.
- Yamam, a civilian-manned group under police command.

The basic division of responsibilities is that the civilian Yamam group undertakes operations inside Israeli borders; Sayeret Matkal external land operations; and Shayetet 13 external maritime incidents.

"Support" units provide direct on-scene support to the "first-on-scene" and "assault" units. Not surprisingly, these units are highly classified, although several have been identified. Sayeret Yael is an engineer corps special unit which provides "hot entry," demolition, and explosive ordnance disposal support to the IDF's "assault" units, Sayeret Matkal and Shayetet 13. There is a similar, but separate, police-manned unit which supports Yamam. Other specialist units provide intelligence, communications, and electronic warfare.

OTHER ELITE UNITS

TODAY, THE IDF MAINTAINS three regular paratroop brigades (202nd, 890th and 50th Na'ha'l) as well as three reserve brigades. It is within these formations and the infantry branch that the proliferation of elite units has taken place. Most of these are designated sayeret (reconnaissance) units, were originally formed for border defense, and were an outgrowth of regular paratroop units. They are set up according to their roles in special operations under the command of the brigade. Sayeret Orev is the reconnaissance anti-tank unit of the paratroops. Sayeret Tzanhim is the unit employed in the capacity of "shock troops"; and the Sayeret Shaldag handles infiltration and demolition.

There are numerous other paratroop-trained units that are not connected to the paratroop brigades, one of which is Sayeret Hadruzim, which is manned by Druze Muslims and serves as a reconnaissance unit in sensitive border areas under the IDF Northern Command.

SELECTION AND TRAINING

There is a six-month basic training course for all regular paratroops and the training for those in the sayeret units is similar. The first phase of the training is geared towards physical fitness and personal weapons proficiency. In the two months of the second phase, the soldier is assigned his role within the unit (machinegunner, ammunition carrier, or whatever), becomes proficient in that task, and learns to apply it. APC and helicopter training are introduced – with heavy emphasis on night fighting and urban area combat. The last phase of training is at the Tel Nof Jump School. After five static line jumps the soldier earns wings and becomes a full-fledged paratrooper. Advanced training is carried out with the units and it is at this stage that the relationship between the soldier and commanding officer relaxes. Officers are addressed by their first names.

For the Naval Commandos, training is given in Scuba diving, infiltration, demolitions, sabotage, intelligence gathering, parachuting and HALO techniques. Medical techniques and driving skills are also taught at an intense pace.

AIR FORCE SPECIAL OPERATIONS UNITS

The Israeli Air Force maintains at least four special operations units. One is Unit 5101, whose primary mission is laser designation of targets for air attack, with a secondary, counter-terrorist capability. This unit is believed to have been responsible for marking the targets during the Israeli attack on an Iraqi nuclear reactor in 1981. Another is Unit 669, which is responsible for rescuing pilots downed in hostile territory.

BELOW LEFT: Weary Israeli paratroops in Sidon passing in front of a Centurion tank and an armored personnel carrier. They are heavily armed with a variety of weapons, including (third trooper from front) the Israeli-built Galil assault rifle.

BELOW: Naval commandos of Shayetet 13 are among the most highly trained of all Israeli special forces. All are armed with the Russian AK-47 assault rifle. Special forces use a wide variety of weapons, partly to obtain the best weapons, but also to avoid leaving a "signature."

ITALY

ABOVE: Italian GIS troopers carry out a simulated building assault in a training area, using specially adapted Range Rovers with ladders to climb the wall. Note the helmets and army combat uniforms. Some are armed with Beretta SC90 assault rifles, others with MP5 sub-machine guns.

GRUPPO D'INTERVENTO SPEZIALE

ITALY'S PRIMARY COUNTER-TERRORIST team, the 100-strong Gruppo d'Intervento Speziale (GIS) (= Special Operations Group) was raised in 1978 and is found from volunteers from the paramilitary police force, the Carabinieri. It is one of the most experienced groups in any country, having been involved in numerous operations against the Red Brigade, the Mafia and, more recently, northern separatists. The most recent known event took place in May 1997 when a group of separatists occupied the belltower in St. Mark's Square in Venice.

SELECTION

The selection process is rigorous and, as with any elite organization, starts with an exhaustive security check, which is followed by a stringent medical examination and an interview with a panel of GIS officers. More unusually, it also includes an interview with a psychiatrist. Successful candidates then undergo a two-week selection board and the relatively few who pass that hurdle then attend a 10-month training course.

WEAPONS

GIS operators have a large choice of weapons for their counter-terrorist operations, including the widely used Heckler & Koch MP5 sub-machine gun family. The group also uses Italian weapons such as the Beretta SC70/90 5.56mm assault rifle and the Beretta Model 92 SB 9mm automatic pistol. Some operators prefer revolvers, using such types as the Smith & Wesson .38 caliber and .357 magnum. Sniper rifles include the Heckler & Koch PSG-1, Mauser SP86 7.62 rifle and the Barret M82 .50in (12.7mm) caliber.

COMSUBIN

THE USE OF SWIMMERS in combat is anything but new — it has been a part of warfare since ancient times. But the Italian Naval Assault Divisions of World War I and World War II can rightfully be considered among the pioneers of modern warfare of this type. Their record at Trieste, Pola, Suda Bay, Gibraltar, and Malta only serves to under-score the point. Heirs to this legacy are the Italian Navy's current special operations force, known formally as Commando Raggruppamento Subacqui ed Incursori (COMSUBIN), or the Navy Frogmen and Raiders Group.

RIGHT: COMSUBIN trooper immediately after landing from an Italian Navy Agusta-Sikorsky AS-61 Sea King. COMSUBIN is descended from the Italian Navy's 10th MAS, known as "Decimo," one of the most successful special forces unit in World War II, which had many spectacular raids against British targets to its credit.

LEFT: A major development in the sniping business is this command station, using Sinco and Elbit equipment, which takes video feeds from individual sniperscopes to enable the commander to control and coordinate his men's shooting. It is being used by GIS; note their black balaclava helmets, black uniforms, and the distinctive GIS unit shoulder badge.

As a special operations force, its missions include clearing mines, explosives and underwater obstacles from Italian waters; landings on friendly or foreign territory for reconnaissance purposes; clearing beaches of obstacles prior to amphibious landings; and commando raids to destroy ships, dry-docks, and fuel storage areas.

Rumors of a counter-terrorist role for COMSUBIN first came to the surface in 1978 and were substantiated the following year, when the unit was called out when a hijacked airliner from Beirut was brought to Rome. Involvement in this role continues: for example, COMSUBIN elements were deployed on Italian vessels near Lebanon during the *Achille Lauro* incident.

Elements of COMSUBIN have taken part in recent operations in Albania, the Lebanon, Persian Gulf, Ruanda, Somalia, and former Yugoslavia.

ORGANIZATION

The 200-man strong COMSUBIN reports to the Navy Chief of Staff and is headquartered just outside La Spezia. From an organizational standpoint, the Raider Operations Group has responsibility for offensive operations, while the Frogman Group provides Italian coastline support. Personnel for both units are drawn primarily from the crack San Marco naval infantry battalion - the 1,000-man Italian "marine corps." San Marco battalion personnel receive general commando training from the COMSUBIN - but they must leave the battalion when they volunteer for service with it. The Raider Operations Group (Gruppo Operativo Subacqui) support is provided by a schools group, research and study group, and a special naval group.

ABOVE: COMSUBIN troops on a training range, armed with the ubiquitous Heckler & Koch 5.56mm MP5 sub-machine gun. Most COMSUBIN personnel come from the San Marco marine battalion, some from elsewhere in the navy, but all are volunteers and all must pass the very demanding entry tests and training course.

SELECTION AND TRAINING

Currently, the all-volunteer Incursori (mostly from the San Marco battalion) are required to complete a 10-month training course. Rigorous physical tests are a part of it and, in fact, are required every three months for everyone in the unit for as long as they remain in the unit. The program includes ranger, parachute, hand-to-hand combat, demolitions, and weapons training, of course. These are in addition to Scuba and other swimming skills.

Those who go on to be part of the Raiders Group get an additional 42 weeks of specialized training with emphasis on parachuting, mountain climbing and vigorous physical endurance tests. This is capped off with a six-week command course. The COMSUBIN unit, not surprisingly, is rated quite highly by those who have observed it.

The Incursori use the same weapons as other Italian units in the main, with the Beretta 9mm Model 12 sub-machne gun a particular favorite because of its compactness.

NORTH KOREA

ABOVE: A North Korean special forces' submarine is kept afloat by flotation bags. The hatches were sealed from inside and the South Koreans eventually gained access through the torpedo tubes to find a gruesome scene with all occupants dead; most had been killed by their colleagues, while the final few committed suicide.

BELOW: South Koreans struggle to keep the captured Sang-O class submarine afloat in September 1996. These small submarines were developed from "reverse engineered" Yugoslav prototypes and carry six combat swimmers.

THE PARANOID NATURE of the Communists ruling North Korea is reflected by the large number of special forces, estimates of whose size vary from 50,000 to 100,000, the width of the bracket reflecting the lack of knowledge about this most secretive regime. Within the Ministry of Defense there are two bodies involved in special forces operations: the Reconnaissance Bureau and the Light Infantry Training Guidance Bureau.

The Reconnaissance Bureau is responsible for collecting strategic intelligence, which involves despatching and controling both individual agents and small teams. The bureau also controls four self-contained reconnaissance brigades, consisting of some 10 battalions each (normally divided into 2-10 men teams) and supporting units.

The General Staff Directorate controls the efforts of 14 "sniper brigades," six of which are airborne, two amphibious and six conventional. These brigades could, in theory, fight as an entity, but it appears much more likely that they would disperse their 5-10 battalions for independent operations. The airborne and conventional brigades are approximately 3,500 strong, but the two amphibious brigades are somewhat stronger - approximately 5,000 men each - with one brigade on each coast.

Corps: At the operational and tactical levels the "special purpose" units are roughly equivalent to the "Spetsnaz" units of the former Soviet Army. Each forward corps would be supported by a "special purpose" brigade, with, in addition, one "special purpose" battalion allocated to each infantry division. These "special purpose" troops would be responsible in war for infiltrating enemy positions, and attacks on enemy command-control-and-communications and logistics facilities.

Navy: There are a number of naval special forces units, including those which operate submarines in support of Reconnaissance Bureau operations.

SELECTION AND TRAINING

The North Korean soldier is a highly disciplined and well trained fighter. Indoctrinated against South Korea since childhood, he is likely to be conscripted between the ages of 17 and 21, and will remain in service until the age of 27. Annual training is between March and August and consists of a month-long basic training program. Once assigned to his unit, the trainee goes through further basic unit, small unit and large-scale unit training exercises.

Soldiers in the special warfare units get special emphasis on infiltration, Intelligence gathering, sabotage, underwater demolition, hand-to-hand combat, night operations, surprise attack and political education. Specific indoctrination and information sessions on all aspects of communist ideology are carried out on a daily basis.

WEAPONS AND EQUIPMENT

Equipment is flexible and varies considerably. Common to all are a dagger and/or bayonet; pistols, including the silenced versions of the 9mm Browning automatic and the Soviet Tokarev 7.62mm automatic; the AK-47 or M16 rifle; hand grenades and demolitions; rocket launchers, either the RPG-7 or the AT-3 Sagger; and 60mm mortars.

UNIFORMS

The light infantry, during training, are provided with the same standard uniforms as the infantry of the North Korean People's Army. However, during combat operations they can be attired in civilian clothing, South Korean Army uniforms (usually with incorrect ranks for the personnel wearing them), mottled camouflaged uniforms in summer, and an all-white over garment in winter.

REPUBLIC OF KOREA

707TH SPECIAL MISSIONS BATTALION

THE ROK ARMY first raised "special warfare" units in 1958, but the dedicated counter-terrorist unit, 707th Special Missions Battalion, was not formed until hostage-taking at the Munich Olympic Games showed the need for such a unit. The unit was on stand-by throughout the Seoul Olympics in 1988, but was not used. The unit is about 200 strong and comprises a headquarters, support and specialist staff, and two companies, each consisting of four 14-man teams.

Volunteers for the unit must come from elsewhere in the "Special Warfare" organization and undergo a rigorous selection and training procedure. Once in the unit, training is particularly tough and all men are trained as underwater swimmers.

707th Special Missions Battalion uses Korean weapons wherever possible, including the Daewoo 9mm pistol and Daewoo K1 and K2 assault rifles. However, foreign weapons, such as the Heckler & Koch MP5 sub-machinegun, are also used.

NATIONAL POLICE UNIT 868

IN THE LEAD-UP TO THE 1988 Seoul Olympics ROK National Police Force formed a special counter-terrorist squad, designated Unit 868, intended for counter-terrorist and hostage rescue missions. Strength is about 100, with the bulk organized into 12 seven-man teams.

ABOVE: S. Korean special forces, having come ashore from canoes, ascend a cliff face. Lead soldier is armed with Uzi SMG, designed for police and special forces use.

SPECIAL WARFARE BRIGADES

THE ROK HAS SEVEN special warfare brigades organized on the same lines as US special forces groups, with whom there is a close working relationship. The battalions of these brigades are often used in the ranger role for the destruction of tactical targets. These ROK special forces units are capable of using either continuous guerrilla operations from bases within enemy territory, or carrying out single operations from bases within friendly territory. The usual allocation of the special forces is one battalion to each Army corps.

SELECTION AND TRAINING
Following the usual physical and psychological tests, the volunteers undergo a hard training course which includes weapon handling skills to a very high standard and parachute training. All ROK special forces troops must also reach black belt standard in Tae-Kwon-Do or a similar martial art, and when not on operations some four to five hours a day are spent in

BELOW: All members of the South Korean special forces must reach "black belt" standard in the traditional Korean Tae-Kwon-Do or similar martial art. They are required to practise for several hours every day.

practise of such arts. They are also trained in tough, realistic exercises for dangerous missions along the DMZ, such as clearing North Korean tunnels. They have also been used as pursuit units when North Korean raiders have infiltrated the South.

UNIFORM
Normal uniform is a camouflage combat suit. The Special Forces distinguishing mark is a black beret with the SF badge in silver. Weapons and personal equipment are all of US origin. Pocket patches are sometimes worn for each brigade: a lion on the special warfare patch; an eagle on the 3rd Brigade's; a dragon on the 5th's; a Pegasus on the 7th's; a winged cat on a parachute on the 9th's; a bat over a lightning bolt on the 11th's; and a panther on the 13th's.

MEXICO

FORCE F

FORCE F IS AN ALL-VOLUNTEER unit of the Mexico City Police and was formed in the early 1980s as a specialist unit to counter drug-related crime and armed gangsters, but has since also been tasked with counter-terrorist and hostage rescue missions. It is quite large, between 300-400 strong, and is divided into three special-to-task elements, responsible for explosive disposal, snipers and assault missions. The unit has the nickname "The Zorros."

NETHERLANDS

RIGHT: The Royal Dutch Marines are one of the most efficient marine troops in NATO and, together with the British Royal Marines, form the Anglo-Dutch Amphibious Warfare Group. Here they assault over dunes on the North Sea coast, watched by observers in a Dutch Navy Westland WG.13 Lynx.

BIJZONDERE BIJSTANDS EENHEID

THE MAIN DUTCH COUNTER-TERRORIST group is the Bijzondere Bijstands Eenheid (BBE) (= Special Support Unit) which is part of the Royal Dutch Marines' 1st Amphibious Combat Group. The unit has three 30-man platoons, organized into a small headquarters and five 5-man teams. The unit includes the usual complement of specialists, such as snipers and explosives experts, but is also known to include psychologists, trained in communicating with terrorists, particularly in hostage-taking situations. The BBE is composed of volunteers from the Royal Dutch Marines who must complete the usual selection process, followed by a 48-week course.

The BBE uses a variety of weapons, although it has a publicly declared policy of seeking to solve terrorist situations by non-violent means, wherever possible. Weapons used include the Colt Lawman .357 revolver or SIG-Sauer P-226 pistol, and the almost inevitable Heckler & Koch MP5 sub-machinegun. Snipers use either the Heckler & Koch G3 MSG or Steyr SSG.

The BBE has seen action on a number of occasions. In 1974 it regained control of Scheveringen prison from armed Palestine terrorist prisoners, using only stun-grenades and hand-to-hand combat. Then, on June 11 1977, they rescued hostages who had been seized by South Moluccan terrorists. Six terrorists and two hostages were killed, but over 200 hostages were released. Small elements of the BBE were deployed aboard Royal Dutch Navy ships to the Adriatic in the early 1990s.

AMFIBISCH VERKENNINGS PELOTON

THE ROYAL DUTCH MARINES have a long tradition of working closely with the British Royal Marines, and the Amfibisch Verkennings Peloton (amphibious reconnaissance platoon) is similar in mission and structure to the British Special Boat Service (SBS). The Dutch unit is 25 strong and is divided into mission-oriented teams for boat-handling; underwater operations; and counter-terrorist operations. As with the British SBS, the Dutch unit is responsible for the security of Dutch passenger-carrying vessels and oil rigs in peacetime, and for intelligence gathering and sabotage missions in war. A variety of weapons is used, including Glock and Browning pistols, Uzi and Heckler & Koch MP5 sub-machine guns, and the Steyr SSG sniping rifle.

LEFT: Dutch marines storm ashore under simulated artillery fire. The landing craft is an LCA Mk2, which can carry either 25 troops or one vehicle (Land-Rover or BV-202 tracked over-snow transporter) and a lesser number of men. Alongside the LCA are two inflatable two-man canoes.

BELOW: A New Zealand SAS trooper at the moment his drogue parachute deploys. This unit has carried out many overseas deployments, for example, to Malaya during the Emergency, to Thailand and South Vietnam during the Indochina War, and to Saudi Arabia during the Gulf War. Many exchanges also take place (eg, with the British SAS).

SPECIAL AIR SERVICE

NEW ZEALAND

THE NEW ZEALAND Special Air Service Squadron was formed in 1954 to join the British and Rhodesian SAS in Malaya. As in Rhodesia, the initial volunteers were taken straight from civilian life and 138 were accepted from a list of some 800. With 40 regular officers and NCOs, they were trained in New Zealand from June until November 1955 when the survivors were sent to Singapore to complete their parachute and jungle training. They soon deployed onto operations and spent 17 months out of the next two years in the jungle, killing 26 terrorists for the loss of just one of their own soldiers.

The squadron returned to New Zealand in November 1957 to be disbanded, but was resuscitated in August 1958. A troop of 30 men was sent to Korat in Thailand from May to September 1962 in support of SEATO. In 1963 the unit was redesignated 1st Ranger Squadron, New Zealand Special Air Service, and shortly afterwards the unit deployed to Borneo where it served, once again, along-side the British SAS. It also operated from time to time with Britain's SBS. 4 Troop NZSAS served in Vietnam from November 1968 to February 1971, where it served with the Australian SAS Squadron.

The unit is now stationed near Auckland, New Zealand. It has five troops, a headquarters, and a separate small training establishment. Its task is to support New Zealand defense forces in their operations and, like the SAS in the United Kingdom, has a major commitment to counter-terrorist missions. The uniform is standard New Zealand Army, but badges are similar to those of the British Special Air Service.

NORWAY

ARMY

FORSVARETS SPESIAL KOMMANDO (FSK) (= Armed Forces' Special Commando) is the Army's counter-terrorist team, and is manned mainly by former members of the Fallskjermjeger Kommando (parachute-hunter commando) and the Marinejeger Kommando (naval hunter commando). The FSK has close links with the British SAS. Its roles include hostage rescue and the protection of North Sea oil rigs.

NAVY

MARINE JEGERE (= NAVAL HUNTERS) are equivalent in function and organization to the British SBS and US Navy SEALs, with both of whom they regularly train. Their main missions are deep penetration reconnaissance and sabotage on enemy naval installations and during the Cold War their main targets would have been Soviet Northern Fleet bases on and around the Kola Peninsula. They can be delivered to their targets by parachute, submarine or canoes.

POLICE

THERE IS A SPECIAL UNIT of the National Police Force which specializes in counter-terrorist and hostage-rescue missions. It is designated the Beredskaptrop.

PAKISTAN

SPECIAL SERVICES GROUP

SINCE THE ACRIMONIOUS SPLIT when the two countries obtained their independence in 1947, India and Pakistan have maintained a state of armed confrontation, which has sometimes spilled over into actual warfare. This has dominated Pakistani defense thinking for the past 50 years, but problems on its northern and western borders have also begun to merit greater attention, and the Soviet invasion of Afghanistan made Pakistan a country of paramount geostrategic importance. Pakistan has developed its special forces in this context, although the long periods of military rule have also affected the way in which such forces have developed.

There is one Special Forces Group of three battalions and an independent counter-terrorist company. The tasking of these units is the responsibility of three top-level bodies: the Army's Directorate for Inter-Services Intelligence (ISI), Military Intelligence [MI], and the Intelligence Bureau [IB]. Ever since their inception there has been a large degree of overlap between them. A further complication has been that they have tended to become involved in political matters, particularly during the periods of military rule.

POLAND

GROM

Right: Polish paratrooper with flak jacket and AK-74 assault rifle. Poland joined NATO in March 1999 and its military equipment is becoming Western-oriented as rapidly as finance will permit. GROM's international reputation was strengthened when it provided VIP protection during the US-led Operation Restore Democracy in Haiti in 1994.

GROM, THE POLISH ARMED FORCES' counter-terrorist unit was formed in 1991 and consists of volunteers from 1 Pulk Komandosow Specalnego Przeznaczenia (1 PSK) (1st Commando Regiment) and combat swimmers from 7th Lujcyka Naval Assault Division. The unit is estimated to have some 300 members, including women, the great majority of whom work in four-person teams. The operators are trained in counter-terrorist techniques, including hostage rescue and VIP protection. A number are trained as combat swimmers.

Despite their relatively recent appearance on the counter-terrorist scene, GROM participated in the USA's Operation Restore Democracy in Haiti in 1994, where one of their main roles was in

VIP protection. It is also believed that approximately 50 members of GROM accompanied the Polish battalion to Bosnia.

Weapons include Heckler & Koch MP5 sub-machine guns and the Polish-designed Tantal 5.45mm assault rifle. Sniper rifles are usually either the Mauser 86 or Heckler & Koch PSG-1.

PORTUGAL

GRUPO DE OPERACOES ESPECIALS

PORTUGAL TOOK SEVERAL YEARS to absorb the lessons of the 1972 Munich Olympic Games disaster and did not start to form its Grupo De Operacoes Especiais (GOE) (= Special Operations Group) until 1979, with the unit becoming fully operational in 1983. The careful groundwork, most of it in close liaison with the British Special Air Service (SAS), did pay off, however, and the unit has established a fine reputation during its relatively short existence. It is believed that close ties with Israeli special forces have also been established.

Personnel are all volunteers and after the usual rigorous vetting and selection process they undergo an intensive eight-month training course. This covers hostage-rescue techniques against targets such as aircraft, buildings, buses, and trains, as well as maritime assault and VIP protection.

Weapons used include Heckler & Koch MP5 sub-machine guns and the same company's PSG-1 sniper rifle, although some Israeli weapons, such as the sniper version of the 7.62mm Galil, may also be used.

The only known GOE operation was a hostage rescue attempt against a group of terrorists holed-up in the Turkish Embassy in Lisbon. This ended unsuccessfully because the terrorists blew themselves up, apparently by accident.

Above: Four RIBs (rubberized inflatable boats) of the Portuguese Marine Battalion. Following the end of their colonial wars, Portuguese forces and special forces (Grupo de Operacoes Especiais) are now totally committed to national and NATO missions.

RUSSIAN FEDERATION

RIGHT: Russian Spetsnaz troops deplane from a Mil Mi-8 "Hip" armed helicopter in mountainous country. The (then) Soviet Army brought such operations to a high degree of efficiency during the war in Afghanistan, even though they lost the overall campaign.

BELOW: Spetsnaz troops undergoing urban warfare training. These troops established a fearsome reputation during the latter years of the Cold War and would have been a major threat to NATO, particularly to HQs and nuclear units, had conflict broken out.

SPETSNAZ

DURING THE 1970s, when the Cold War was at its height, the West became aware of the existence of Soviet Spetsnaz troops, which were grouped into what were known as "diversionary brigades." Today, although the Cold War is long since ended, Spetsnaz units are still part of the Russian order-of-battle, although their missions have changed.

Spetsnaz (Spetsialnoye nazranie = troops of special purpose) were raised as the troops of the Glavnoe razvedyvatel'noe upravlenie (GRU) (= main intelligence directorate [of the General Staff]) and in the 1980s numbered some 30,000. These were deployed: one Spetsnaz company per Army; one Spetsnaz regiment in each of the three "theaters of operations"; one Spetsnaz brigade in each of the four Soviet Fleets; and an independent Spetsnaz brigade in most military districts of the USSR. There were also special Spetsnaz intelligence units, one to each Front and Fleet: total 20.

A Spetsnaz company was 135 strong, normally operating in 15 independent teams, although they could also combine for specific missions. A Spetsnaz brigade was 1,000-1,300 strong and consisted of a headquarters, three or four parachute battalions, a communications company, and supporting troops. It also included an anti-VIP company, composed of some 70-80 regular troops (ie, not conscripts) whose mission was to seek out, identify and kill enemy political and military leaders. A naval Spetsnaz brigade had a headquarters, two to three battalions of combat swimmers, a parachute battalion, supporting units, and an anti-VIP company. It also had a group of midget submarines, designed to deliver combat swimmers to distant targets.

The existence of Spetsnaz was a closely guarded secret within the Warsaw Pact and individual troops were not allowed to admit membership, to the extent that army Spetsnaz wore standard airborne uniforms and insignia, while naval Spetsnaz wore naval infantry uniforms and insignia.

SPETSNAZ IN 1999

Some of the republics which broke away from the old Soviet Union took over the Spetsnaz units within their borders or have converted parachute units to the Spetsnaz role. Within the Russian Federation Spetsnaz units are less well trained and equipped, at a lower strength, and at a lesser degree of readiness than during the 1970s and 1980s. Despite that, they continue to exist, although their numbers are not known for certain.

Naval Spetsnaz also continue to serve in the Northern, Baltic, Black Sea, and Pacific fleets. Most of these are subordinate to the Fleet commanders, but some are under the direct control of the Naval Commander-in-Chief in Moscow. Again, their manning levels are not known and it may be that, like other areas in the Russian armed forces, they are seriously under strength.

MISSIONS

Although Spetsnaz units may be used for other purposes during peacetime, their primary role is to carry out strategic missions during the final days prior to war breaking out and in war itself. These wartime tasks would include: deep reconnaissance of strategic targets; the destruction of strategically important command-control-and-communications (C3) facilities; the destruction of strategic weapons' delivery systems; demolition of important bridges and transportation routes; and the kidnapping or assassination of important military and political leaders. Many of these missions would be carried out before the enemy could react and some even before war had actually broken out.

UNIFORMS

The Russian Federation now acknowledges the existence of Spetsnaz units and, as a result, special badges are now worn, identifying such troops.

WEAPONS

On operations the majority of Spetsnaz soldiers would carry a 5.45mm AKS-74 rifle and a 5.45mm PRI automatic pistol. All would also carry combat knives, which are specially designed for Spetsnaz troops. One such design is the NR-2, an ingenious device which in addition to the blade incorporates a short 7.62mm caliber barrel in the handle and is fired by clipping the scabbard and knife together to give some control. Quite when such a weapon would be used instead of a knife or a pistol is open to question. Spetsnaz troops are also trained in all types of foreign weapons.

TRAINING

Those joining Spetsnaz with no previous military experience must be given the normal recruit's basic training in discipline, marching, fieldcraft, weapon handling and range work. Once the recruit moves on to proper Spetsnaz training, however, the pressure intensifies:

- weapon handling, including the use of foreign weapons and marksmanship;
- physical fitness, with an emphasis on endurance and strength;
- tracking, patroling, camouflage, and surveillance techniques, including survival in a variety of harsh environments;
- hand-to-hand combat, both unarmed and with knives (both hand-held and throwing), and assassination of designated targets;
- sabotage and demolitions;
- language training and prisoner interrogation;
- infiltration by air, including parachuting for fixed-wing aircraft, and exit from helicopters by parachute or ropes.

Naval Spetsnaz must, in addition, learn combat swimmer techniques, the use of underwater weapons, canoeing, arrival and exit over beaches, exit and entry to submerged submarines.

BELOW: Russian airborne troops (note the blue beret) conduct unarmed combat training. Despite the post-Cold War rundown the Russian Federation maintains several parachute divisions, together with the massive air transport to deliver them.

OTHER SPETSNAZ TROOPS

During the 1970s and 1980s special operations troops became increasingly the vogue in various ministries of the (then) Soviet Union. Further, such was the large and disorganized nature and wastefulness of the Soviet system that similar bodies with similar missions were set up by different parts of the same ministry, particularly within the Committee for State Security (KGB) and the Ministry of Internal Affairs (MVD). These special troops went under the generic title of Spetsgruppe and were paramilitary forces which received special training and indoctrination for a variety of missions. Many of these units served in a variety of roles in the war in Afghanistan but for most of them a defining moment seems to have been reached during the 1991 coup, when they were forced to take sides, or at least to refuse to take action. After the coup had been defeated President Yeltsin transferred most of them to his personal control but they have since been transferred yet again back to various ministries. Many of the groups have been involved in the recent conflicts in the Russian Federation, including Chech'nya.

Spetsgruppa "Al'fa" (= special group A) was set up by the KGB's Seventh Directorate in 1974 and appears to have been inspired by the British SAS and US SFOD-D (Delta) as a counter-terrorist and hostage-rescue group. Al'fa is generally credited with being the unit that attacked the Presidential palace in Kabul, Afghanistan, on December 28 1980 and murdered President Hafizullah Amin and his family. Al'fa is now controlled by the FSB (Federal'naia sluzhba bezopasnosti = Federal Security Service) in general terms, equivalent to the USA's FBI. Current strength is estimated to be about 300, with the main group in Moscow and three smaller groups elsewhere in the federation.

Also raised by the KGB, but this time the First Chief Administration, was Spetsgruppa Vympel whose mission was to fullfil the KGB's wartime role of assassinations and kidnapping. After the collapse of the Soviet Union it was transferred to the MVD but is now with the FSB with a primary responsibility for a hostage rescue.

The Ministry of Internal Affairs also has at least two groups of special troops known as the Omsn (= black berets), which were originally raised to provide additional security and (if necessary) hostage rescue at the 1980 Moscow Olympics. Since then they have been used for counter-terrorist activities and defeating armed criminals, and are currently involved in campaigns against drug cultivation.

Symbolizing the disorganized nature of contemporary Russia is the GROM Security Company, which is a quasi-private organization working under exclusive contract to the Federal Government. GROM (the Russian word for "thunder" and with no relationship to the Polish group of the same name) is manned by former troops of the various KGB special forces and provides security for selected government personnel and buildings, as well as for trains and aircraft.

BELOW: During the Soviet era, the Naval Infantry — morskaya pekhota — was a large and well-organized force, with superb equipment, including the Aist-class air-cushion vehicle and PT-76 amphibious tank shown here, some of which remain in service. All naval Spetsnaz are found from volunteers serving in units of the naval infantry.

NAVAL INFANTRY

R USSIA'S NAVAL INFANTRY, "morskaya pekhota," it is graded as a "Guards" unit, and great emphasis is placed on the elite status this confers, a status reflected in special uniform and accoutrements. Like many elite forces the Russian Naval Infantry has its own battlecry: "Polundra," which roughly means, "Watch out below."

ORGANIZATION
The basic amphibious assault unit is the battalion group, and its likely composition was described in a Russian military journal as, "A motorized infantry battalion detailed to operate as advanced detachment was reinforced with an artillery battery, an ATGM battery, AA, frogman and engineer platoons. It also included reconnaissance and obstacle-clearing parties, road-building teams, communications facilities, transport vehicles, and landing craft to perform transportation missions. The advanced detachment was to be supported by aviation, tactical airborne troops, support ships and minesweepers."

SELECTION AND TRAINING
While some members of the Naval Infantry may be volunteers, most are conscripts, although, as befits its elite status as a "Guards" unit, it is allocated high quality men. Units and individuals are highly trained in amphibious operations and land warfare, and, like all marines, must also know something about life on board ship as well.

Physical training for the Black Beret is emphasized during routine unit training. Forty percent of the training program is devoted to wrestling, drill with the bayonet, and the techniques of knife attack. The training is identical for both officer and enlisted man. Marines are also required to undergo training in the Military Sports Complex and master the set of skills offered there, such as horizontal bar work; sprint in uniform; a cross country rush; a swim in uniform with assault rifle; and a longer version of the cross country rush.

WEAPONS AND EQUIPMENT
In the platoon the officer, NCOs and most marines are armed with the AKM assault rifle, while the APC driver has the AKMS folding-stock version. Each squad also has an RPK machine gun and an anti-tank rocket launcher. Sniper teams are armed with the highly effective SVD 7.72mm Dragunov sniper rifle.

LEFT: Frogmen from a Naval Infantry unit. Such men would be the first ashore in an amphibious operation, being responsible for beach reconnaissance; the location, identification and demolition of beach obstacles; destruction of enemy positions likely to interfere with a landing; and setting up beacons to guide the first waves of the assault onto the correct beaches.

UNIFORMS

The uniform of the Naval Infantry is a combination of Army and Navy items, with a few unique embellishments of their own. Combat dress consists of black fatigues, with a "bush" type blouse and calf-length black leather boots. A black leather belt is also worn, with the appropriate fleet badge on the buckle. A horizontally striped blue and white T-shirt is standard with all forms of dress. The usual range of metal award brooches is worn, with all officers and men wearing the "Guards" badge. A round cloth badge with an embroidered anchor is worn on the left sleeve just above the elbow.

Various items of headgear are worn. In assault operations a black steel helmet is worn with a large five-pointed red star on the front, and a stenciled anchor inside a broken anchor on the left. On other occasions a soft black beret is worn with a small anchor badge above the left ear; the main badge is a large enameled naval badge for officers and a small red star for NCOs and marines.

AMPHIBIOUS SHIPPING

The Naval Infantry would be of limited value without special-role shipping, and a whole range of purpose-built craft has been developed. Largest of these is the Ivan Rogov class of 14,000-ton Landing Platform Dock (LPD), of which one is now in service and two are in reserve, capable of carrying a complete battalion group with all its vehicles and supporting arms. There are also some Ropucha class and Alligator class Landing Ship Tanks (LST), both of some 4,500 tons displacement, and a number of smaller vessels. Particular investment has been made in the area of air-cushion landing craft

ABOVE: Confident and alert, these men wear the typical Naval Infantry uniform of black coverall, black calf-length leather boots, blue and white striped T-shirt, "guards" badge, and black beret.

LEFT: Naval Infantry trainees emerge from a tunnel complex wearing camouflage pattern coveralls, rather than the considerably more menacing black. Training standards among Russian units has dropped since the end of the Cold War and the dissolution of the Soviet Union, but elite units like the Naval Infantry are still forces to be reckoned with.

SPAIN

OR MANY YEARS following its Civil War Spain held itself apart from the rest of Western Europe, but following the accession of King Juan Carlos and the restoration of democracy it has become increasingly integrated. Its primary defense commitment is to NATO, but it also has to deal with internal strife involving the long-running Basque separatist movement, which has frequently employed terrorists tactics, and also has a national commitment to the defense of its last two remaining enclaves on the North African coast at Ceuta and Melilla.

The Spanish armed forces and police maintain a number of special forces. Some of these are either earmarked or assigned to the *Fuerza de Accion Rapide* (FAR) (= rapid action force), which is part of NATO's Allied Rapid Reaction Corps (ARRC). Such special operation forces include the army's *Brigada Paracaidista* (BRIPAC)(= parachute brigade) and the Navy's *Unidad Especial de Buceadores de Combate* (UEBC) (= SEALs), but here two specific organizations will be covered: the Spanish Legion and the Garda Civil's *Unidad Especial de Intervencion* (UEI).

ABOVE: A Spanish legionnaire crawls through an assault course under live fire from instructors. The men are carefully selected and highly trained and the Spanish Legion has its own, somewhat idiosyncratic, military ethos. Although a number of foreigners are admitted to its ranks, some 90 percent of its men are of Spanish nationality.

SPANISH LEGION

IN CONTRAST TO THE better-known French Foreign Legion, the Spanish Legion consists almost entirely (90 percent) of native Spaniards. Following the Moroccan War (1920-27), the Legion continued to guard Spain's remaining African possessions. These included two small enclaves – Melilla and Ceuta – in northern Morocco, where Spanish Legion units are still based today. Ultimately, the decolonization process played itself out, armed conflict erupted with the Algerian-backed Polisario Front, and by 1981 the last of the Legion's monuments commemorating African battles was dismantled.

ORGANIZATION

The Spanish Legion is approximately 7,000 strong and is made up of *tercios* (regiments), each of which is named after a person famous in Spanish history. These are made up of four *banderas* (battalions), each of a number of companies, depending on the unit's role. In addition, Legion headquarters, stationed at Almeria, is responsible for the selection, training and administration of the Legion, but also provides the operational staff for *Brigada de la Legion Alfonso* XIII, which is committed to the FAR. This brigade would comprise VII, VIII and X Banderas, supported by artillery, logistics, and communications elements. The permanent elements of the Legion are:

1st Tercio Gran Capitan is stationed in the Spanish enclave of Melilla on the north African coast and consists of I *Bandera Legionaria Mecanizada* (1st Legion Mechanized Battalion), II *Bandera Legionaria Motorizada* (2nd Legion Motorized Battalion), each of three rifle companies, a headquarters company and a service support company. There is also an anti-tank company armed with MILAN missiles. Its primary mission is the defense of Melilla.

2nd Tercio Duque de Alba is stationed at the second Spanish enclave of Ceuta. It is organized the same as 1st tercio, with one mechanized battalion *(V Bandera)* and one motorized battalion and an anti-tank company.

3rd Tercio Juan de Austria is stationed at Fuerteventura in the distant Canary Islands. It consists of VII and VIII *Banderas* and is earmarked for the FAR, although it would obviously take some time for it to return to the mainland prior to an operational redeployment.

4th Tercio Alejandro Farnesio, which is assigned to the FAR, is stationed at Ronda, Malaga, and is composed of two *banderas*, one of which, *X Bandera*, is a parachute-assault unit. The second unit, *XIX Bandera*, has the additional title of *Bandera de Operaciones Especiales* (BOEL) (= special operations battalion) and has amphibious, mountain, parachute and long-range patrolling capabilities.

BELOW: Legionnaires man a Spanish-manufactured version of the German 7.62mm MG3 light machine gun, which, in this setting, is mounted on a tripod and has the butt removed for use in the sustained-fire role, in which it has an effective range of 2,400yd (2,200m). This highly effective weapon is a direct development of the World War II 7.92mm MG42.

WEAPONS AND EQUIPMENT

The Spanish Legion uses basic infantry weapons, which include the 7.62 CETME Model 68 rifle, the 9mm Star Z-70B sub-machine gun, and the 60.7mm ECIA mortar. The Legion also has M41 and AMX-13 light tanks, and AML-90 light armored cars, as well as a number of American eight-ton trucks, British Land Rovers, and Nissan 4x4 field cars.

SELECTION AND TRAINING

Enlisting in the Legion is an easy and relatively straightforward process. A passport will work, or the applicant need only certify to the information he gives. To enroll, he need only go to a military or government building, police station or civil guard station at any port, airport or city within Spanish national territory or its islands. After a thorough briefing, the candidate is given the option to quit; however, after passing a medical examination and upon being accepted, he incurs a minimum obligation of three years – a term he can expand to four or five years if desired. Training is short, intensive and strict. The Legion's objective is to instill basic military skills in as short a time as possible – the usual training period is three months. It takes place at Ronda and includes drill, physical courses and familiarization with the traditions and disciplines of the Legion. Discipline is harsh and based on fear. Offenders are liable to find themselves in prison (not a desirable thing since prisoners sleep on concrete slabs and can be beaten at whim by the guards), or the recipient of a rain of blows to the head for poor shooting at a standard target. All things being relative, however, this punishment is mild compared to earlier times when, under some circumstances and for certain offenses, the legionnaire could be shot.

Much time is devoted in the field to the route march. Long distances are covered over rough terrain - either in light order or with heavy pack, depending upon the individual commander.

The typical legionnaire, however, is heavily dependent upon his officers for such basic things as navigation, tactics and first aid in the field. His training in advanced weaponry and modern forms of warfare is negligible, something that may change with the anticipated modernization of the Army.

To become an officer, it is first necessary to become a Spanish citizen. The highest rank to which one can be promoted as a legionnaire is that of major.

UNIFORM

Green is the traditional color of the Legion's uniform. The caps are specially designed and have a small red tassle. Short sleeve blouses are worn, which are open at the collar. Breeches are like jodhpurs, and legionnaires wear gauntleted gloves and white-lined capes with a fur collar and hood for cold nights. Webbing straps and belts are used instead of the leather versions found in the rest of the Spanish Army.

UNIDAD ESPECIAL DE INTERVENCION (UEI)

THE UNIDAD ESPECIAL DE INTERVENCION (UEI) (Special Intervention Unit) is the elite unit of the Guarda Civil any is the country's premier counter-terrorist unit. It is responsible for countering any foreign terrorists who may commit crimes on Spanish territory, but also has a major domestic commitment in the continuing war against the Basque separatist movement, ETA. Although its strength is secret it is believed to be in the region of 50 men, all volunteers from the Guarda Civil who have passed stringent selection tests.

The unit was officially formed in February 1982 and troops wear normal Guarda Civil uniforms, except when on operations, when they will usually wear the black Nomex coveralls adopted by most counter-terrorist squads. Weapons are the usual mixture of Uzis, plus Heckler & Koch and Mauser sniper rifles.

ABOVE: A very smart and confident member of the Spanish Legion stands in front of the barrack gate. Behind him the arch carries the Legion's uncompromising motto: "Todo Por La Patria" (death for the motherland). His cap is the hallmark of the Legion, with a red tassel and chinstrap.

BELOW: Spanish special forces in their camouflage suits, helmets, face masks, and body armor. The soldier on the left is armed with a Heckler & Koch 9mm MP5 SD4 silenced SMG with night-sight, while the man on the right is carrying a Mossberg 12-gauge, automatic shotgun.

SWEDEN

Below: Sweden has a very long coastline, for whose defense special troops are trained and special equipment procured. These soldiers are coming ashore from a Stridsbat (combat boat) 90H, which is capable of carrying 20 fully equipped troops over a 240 mile (385 km) range at a speed of 30 knots and then discharging them onto a beach over the bow ramp, as shown here.

ONI

THE ONI (= NATIONAL RESCUE UNIT) is part of the Stockholm City Police Force and is estimated to be 50-strong, divided into five teams: a command-and-control team; an intelligence-and-negotiating team; a sniper team; and two assault teams.

The Stockholm Police Force has overall responsibility for the day-to-day running of the unit, but on deployment on a counter-terrorist mission it comes under the direct orders of the Prime Minister, although discussions are under way to change this. Even if changes are made, however, the Prime Minister will remain the sole authority for the use of weapons, unless the lives of the hostages are perceived to be in immediate danger, when a local decision could be taken.

Weapons include SIG P226 automatics, the inevitable Heckler & Koch MP5 sub-machine guns, and Heckler & Koch sniper rifles.

TURKEY

Right: Turkish amphibious troops come ashore in a rubber dinghy. Turkey has a very long coastline facing the Black, Aegean, and Mediterranean Seas, the latter two being areas of potential conflict.

TURKEY HAS LARGE ARMED FORCES to face up to a number of major threats. These include: shared borders with Armenia, Azerbajan, Georgia, Iran, Syria, and Greece; the continuing problems with Kurdish separatists in the east; and confrontation with Greece on the island

of Cyprus as well as in the Mediterranean and Aegean seas. The total armed forces number well over 500,000 and it is not surprising that these should include a large number of special forces.

ARMY

THE TURKISH ARMY has at least one counter-terrorist special forces battalion, some 150 strong. It may be assumed to have similar characteristics and capabilities to British SAS and US Delta. There are also three commando brigades:

1st Commando Brigade, whose mission is described as Su Alti Savunma (SAS) (= underwater defense). This unit is based in Kayseri, but has recently operated in Southeast Anatolia against separatist terrorists.

2nd Commando Brigade, whose mission is described as Su Alti Taaruz (SAT) (= underwater attack) is based at Bolu.

3rd Commando Brigade is responsible for conventional amphibious operations, including infiltration from the sea, intelligence gathering, and sabotage. It is based at Foca and Izmir and its wartime missions could include operations against island targets - eg, in the Aegean and Mediterranean.

AIR FORCE

A NUMBER OF TURKISH air force helicopters, including UH-60 Blackhawks and AS-90 Cougars, have been fitted for CSAR (Combat Search And Rescue) missions and are also used for covert insertion and extraction.

ABOVE: A Turkish soldier crossing a single rope bridge. Turkish troops are tough, loyal and very well trained, and would make formidable opponents.

UNITED KINGDOM

GURKHAS

THE BONDS WHICH LINK the legendary Gurkhas from the hills of Nepal with the British Army are slightly difficult to understand, but their strength is self-evident. The British in India fought two short wars against the Gurkhas in 1813 and 1816, which resulted in a very hard-won British victory and considerable mutual respect for each other's martial qualities. As a result three battalions of Gurkhas were immediately raised (1815) and Gurkhas have served the British Crown ever since.

ORGANIZATION
The original three battalions expanded and changed titles over the years, but basically there have been 10 regiments (of varying numbers of battalions) for most of the Gurkhas' history. In 1947 when the British left India, the 1st, 4th, 5th, 8th and 9th Gurkha Rifles went to the Indian Army, and the balance - 2nd, 6th, 7th, and 10th Gurkha Rifles - to the British Army. Still serving in the British Army are the 1st Royal Gurkha Rifles (1RGR) stationed in Brunei (and paid for by the Sultan) and 2RGR in Shornecliffe, England. Individual battalions are on the standard British Army organization, with some very minor amendments to comply with Regimental custom.

The infantry battalions have very few British officers, the great majority being Queen's Gurkha Officers who have worked their way up through the ranks to Warrant Officer before being commissioned. The most senior is the Gurkha Major, a figure of immense prestige, who is the Commanding Officer's adviser on all Gurkha matters.

In addition there are five Gurkha infantry companies, one each attached to 2nd Battalion Parachute Regiment, 1st Battalion Royal Scots, and 1st Battalion Prince of Wales's Royal Regiment, plus Demonstration Companies at the Royal Military Academy Sandhurst and the Infantry Training Center at Brecon in Wales. There are also Gurkha-manned engineer, signals, and transport regiments.

SELECTION AND TRAINING
Gurkhas are recruited from the hill tribesmen in the Himalayan kingdom of Nepal. They are signed up at the age of 17 by itinerant gallah-wallahs (ex-Gurkhas who get a bounty for each successful sign-up) and serve a minimum commitment of 15 years.

Instead of being called by name, Gurkhas are referred to by serial numbers - the last two

Above: British Gurkha troops rapelling from a US Army UH-1 during training at Fort Lewis in Washington state. These soldiers have a reputation second to none.

RIGHT: A British Gurkha infantry company headquarters on patrol in the Brunei jungle. The company commander is on the right (note his M16 rifle), while the operator sends a message over the company radio net. Although they come from a mountainous country, Gurkhas have proved especially adept as jungle fighters.

digits of this number becoming "nicknames." Gurkha tribal names are left behind for the new life. A concept called kaida, which translates into a system of order, ritual, and loyalty to officers and each other that is unquestioned, is the secret of their training and fortitude. As might be expected, boot camp is rigorous and transforms the Gurkha recruit in nine months from an often illiterate and barefoot mountain tribesman into a solid member of one of the world's most unusual - and ferocious - fighting forces. Recruits arrive in the UK in January of every year to begin training.

UNIFORM AND WEAPONS

Gurkhas wear their own variations of British Army uniform. Combat kit is standard camouflage pattern smock and trousers, with green canvas webbing, except, of course, for the addition of the famous kukri weapon. Parade uniform is rifle-green in temperate climates and white in the tropics, with black, patent-leather waist belts for soldiers and cross-belts for officers. Buttons and badges are black. Soldiers wear a black pill-box hat on parade or the Gurkha slouch-hat, and a green beret in other forms of dress.

The kukri is the subject of many myths. The knives come in various sizes, but the dog-legged shape is constant. The rear edge is thick and blunt, making the knife quite heavy, but the cutting-edge is razor sharp. The kukri is in no way a throwing knife, but it is quite excellent for hand-to-hand fighting and is the Gurkhas' preferred close-combat weapon. It is therefore always carried in war and there are many stories of its use against Germans, Japanese, and Malayan Communists, to mention but a few of the Gurkhas' more recent enemies.

THE GURKHAS' FUTURE

It would be a very sad day were the ties between these legendary soldiers and the British Crown they have served so well to be severed. Nowhere is the depth of this unique relationship more clearly described than in (of all places) the introduction to a Nepali language dictionary compiled by Sir Ralph Turner some 70 years ago: "As I write these last words, my thoughts return to you who were my comrades, the stubborn and indomitable peasants of Nepal. Once more I hear the laughter with which you greeted every hardship. Once more I see you in your bivouacs or about your fires, on forced march or in the trenches, now shivering with wet and cold, now scorched by a pitiless and burning sun. Uncomplaining, you endure hunger and thirst and wounds, and at last your unwavering lines disappear into the smoke and wrath of battle. Bravest of the brave, most generous of the generous, never had a country more faithful friends than you."

Or, in the words of a Gurkha commander, "They are just bloody good soldiers."

THE PARACHUTE REGIMENT

THE VERY NAME OF The Parachute Regiment (the "Paras") has come to signify both a type of soldiering and a certain "style" - dramatic, forceful and with panache, Paratroops would, it seems, always need to be fighting against heavy odds and either succeed brilliantly or suffer glorious defeats: the one performance that is never allowed is an indifferent one.

It was Winston Churchill who demanded that a slightly reluctant War Office establish a corps of parachutists on the German model, and after a somewhat hesitant start the first unit was formed in late 1940.

There was a major reduction in parachute troops in the immediate post-war years, and again in the 1960s and 1970s. 16th Parachute Brigade existed in Aldershot from 1949 to 1977 when it was redesignated 6th Field Force in one of the British Army's endless series of reorganizations, and only one battalion of The Parachute Regiment was left in the parachute role. On January 1 1982 6th Field Force became 5 Infantry Brigade and included among its units 2nd and 3rd Battalions The Parachute Regiment.

With the South Atlantic War in 1982, these two battalions were hived off to 3 Commando Brigade and sent south with the Marines. In the Falklands these two units performed very well, and at Goose Green 550 men of 2 Para took on 1,400 Argentines and defeated them utterly, even though their commanding officer, Lt. Col. "H" Jones, died in the battle. In the finest Para tradition he died at the head of his men, personally leading an attack against a machine gun position that was holding up the entire attack. He was posthumously awarded the Victoria Cross.

In December 1982 the British Secretary of State for Defence, Michael Heseltine, went to Aldershot to announce in person that 5 Infantry Brigade was to be redesignated 5 Airborne Brigade forthwith. The long-awaited British Strategic Defence Review was published in July 1998 and, as expected, The Parachute Regiment featured, although the effects of the Review on it were much less significant than had been feared in some quarters. The Review stated that "we can no longer identify circumstances in which Britain would need to undertake parachute operataions at greater than battalion-group level. Maintaining a smaller battalion-level capability, which confers important operataional flexibility, and modernizing the role of the remainder of The Parachute Regiment to take advantage of their unique skills and ethos, has been central to the Review."

As a result, a new 24 Airmobile Brigade is being created, which will consist of three attack helicopter regiments, equipped with Apache AH-64 attack helicopters and two battalions of The Parachute Regiment, which, together with parachute-capable support units, will enable the new brigade to undertake a single battalion-group parachute assault. A third battalion of The Parachute Regiment will also be retained, but will be employed elsewhere in the Army as a normal infantry battalion, although it will take its turn to serve in 24 Airmobile Brigade.

ORGANIZATION

There are currently three battalions of The Parachute Regiment in the British Regular Army (1, 2 and 3 Para), and a further three battalions in the Territorial Army (4, 10 and 15 Para). Two of the three regular battalions are part of 24 Airmobile Brigade.

A parachute battalion is organized similarly to a standard infantry battalion, with three rifle companies and a support company. However, it has a far lighter scale of transport. Because the battalion depends on the physical fitness and fighting efficiency of the men, more emphasis is placed upon selection and effective training.

BELOW: British paratroops reaffirmed their high reputation during the 1982 Falklands War. These men of 2 Para are on guard in typical Falklands foggy conditions; the soldier on the right is armed with a 7.62mm general-purpose machine gun (GPMG), while the man on the left carries a 9mm Sterling, a sub-machine gun with notoriously poor stopping and penetrating power except at very close quarters.

SELECTION AND TRAINING

All officers and men must volunteer for The Parachute Regiment. Prospective recruits undergo thorough mental, educational, and psychometric tests - and then only the most educationally and mentally alert are selected as candidates for the Regiment.

RIGHT: British paratroopers on patrol. Despite the tactical setting, they wear their red berets, the symbol of their prowess, high standard of training, and excellent morale.

BELOW: Soldiers of 1st Battalion, Parachute Regiment (1 Para) on exercise (note the para wings on their right shoulders). The tripod-mounted weapon is a US M2HB 0.50-cal heavy machine gun with a blank-firing attachment (BFA), which enables the weapon to be used semi-realistically during field training.

The extremely arduous training course of 23 weeks is similar in many ways to that for Royal Marine Commandos. The first eight weeks follow the lines of what is laid down for recruits for the Army: drill, weapons training, everything on the double, plenty of exercise, and map reading. The 12th week is the dreaded "P Company" week, in which members are selected for further training. About 80 percent of the recruits who have gone this far will pass.

Following completion of training, the men, who pride themselves on being the "Spearhead of the Army" and on their ability to fight in any terrain and climate, will join their battalions. Only 35 percent of those who started the course will have gained their "wings."

WEAPONS AND EQUIPMENT

When there was an independent parachute force (16 Parachute Brigade) there was sufficient demand for it to be economical to produce special equipment for paratroop units. When the commitment was reduced in the past few years to just two battalions in the parachute role, with virtually no back-up from parachute-trained and -equipped supporting arms and services, such special equipment virtually disappeared. Thus, UK parachute units currently use standard British Army weapons and equipment, such as the 5.56mm L70A1 Individual Weapon, an excellent weapon using the "bull-pup" design. This rifle is neat, compact and well-balanced and has proved very popular in service. Obviously, The Parachute Regiment is also able to take full advantage of advanced weaponry and equipment as it enters service with the British Army.

UNIFORMS

The British paratroops' red beret has been adopted around the world and has given rise to their nicknames of "The Red Devils" and "The Red Berets." (History has it that Major-General Browning and another general were arguing over the color of a beret for the paratroops and, unable to agree, they turned to the nearest soldier to ask his views. "Red, sir," came the instant answer.) The red beret can be worn only by members of The Parachute Regiment (throughout their service) and by members of other corps who are parachute-qualified, but only when on service with a parachute unit. The sleeve badge is a winged Pegasus.

ROYAL MARINE SPECIAL BOAT SERVICE

TO A LARGE EXTENT, the whole of the 7, 000 Royal Marines is an elite force in itself; every Marine would certainly claim it so. However, within the Royal Marines there are a number of smaller and more select groups of which the best known and most highly trained is the Special Boat Service (SBS), the Royal Marines' equivalent to the British Special Air Service (SAS). It has its roots in the special units raised in World War II for raiding and reconnaissance on the shores of the European mainland. The techniques evolved so painfully in war were, fortunately, preserved in peace, despite many cutbacks and amalgamations. The Amphibious School of the Royal Marines at Eastney (now at Poole in Dorset) included a "Small Raids Wing," which was later redesignated the "Special Boat Company" then the "Special Boat Squadron," but it is known as the "Special Boat Service."

The SBS is the headquarters for the Special Boat Sections which are deployed under the operational command of Commando units, but can also act autonomously on special tasks. Its activities and organization are always secret. The mission of the SBS can roughly be equated with that of the Spetsnaz in the Russian Federation and the SEALs in the US Navy. They are responsible for coastal sabotage operations and ground, surface, or underwater reconnaissance of potential landing beaches and enemy coastal facilities. They also have particular responsibility for security of Britain's off-shore oil and gas rigs. The unit is about 100 strong and it is now located at Whale Island in Portsmouth.

LEFT: Men of the British Royal Marines' Special Boat Service (SBS) emerge from the hatch of a submarine before deploying onto a hostile shore, a task in which they have much experience.

BELOW: SBS canoeists in a Klepper canoe. This lightweight, collapsible canoe has a wooden frame over which is fitted a tough rubber and polyester skin, which is tightened when the internal buoyancy bags are inflated. The canoe is designed for maximum stability and ease of handling, both afloat and ashore.

The SBS has seen action in Oman, Borneo, and during the Falkland Islands War. In the latter, the SBS were early ashore on South Georgia, having flown from the UK in a C-130 and then parachuted to a submarine in the South Atlantic. The submarine took them close inshore and they then completed their long journey in inflatable Gemini boats. The SBS is also rumored to have put patrols ashore on the Argentine mainland, landing from the conventional submarine, HMS *Onyx*, although this has never been confirmed. The SBS and SAS operated on the Falkland Islands 12 days before the amphibious landings, and the SBS reconnoitred the actual landing sites at San Carlos Bay. They welcomed the first landing-craft to reach the shore, and also silenced the Argentinian outpost on Fanning Head, overlooking the landings.

The way in which the SBS fits in with the much larger SAS organization is a matter for speculation, particularly as the SAS is known to have a Boat Troop, with similar equipment and capabilities to the SBS. Nevertheless, there is no known friction between the two units, and it must therefore be assumed that the responsibilities are not a problem in practice.

SELECTION AND TRAINING

Recruitment to the SBS is from volunteers who have already had two years' service in the Royal Marine Commandos. All such officer and Marine volunteers undergo the usual physical and psychological tests, followed by a three-week selection test. Successful candidates then go on a 15-week training course in reconnaissance, demolitions, diving, and use of the Klepper canoe or Gemini craft. They then complete a four-week parachute course, following which they join an operational Special Boat Section.

SBS officers and Marines are not compelled to leave the SBS after a set period, but like some other special forces they are usually forced to leave if they wish to obtain promotion past a certain point.

UNIFORMS

The SBS wear standard Royal Marine uniform and the Commando green beret. The only indication in parade and barrack dress that a man belongs to the SBS is the wearing of Royal Marine parachuting wings on the right shoulder and of the "Swimmer Canoeist" badge on

the right forearm. The latter has a crown above the letters "SC," flanked by laurel leaves. In parade dress both badges are embroidered in gold on a black backing. Officers of the SBS wear the wings, but not the "SC" badge (even though they are qualified to wear it by having passed the course).

WEAPONS AND EQUIPMENT

The SBS four-man half section patrols are usually armed with the US MI6A2 Armalite rifle and M203 grenade launchers, although a special silenced version of the Heckler & Koch MP5 is also used. Included in the patrol's equipment are plastic explosives, laser designators, and burst-transmission radios.

SBS reconnaissance patrols travel light and have three-layered kits (escape and evasion, belt, and pack). Very little is known about the escape and evasion kit, which presumably has survival devices and equipment hidden in clothing and other equipment, A handgun, knife, fishing line, water bottles, snares, and a food pouch are in the belt kit. The pack kit contains some extra food, dry clothing and a waterproof poncho.

Boats used by the SBS include paddle-boards (akin to surfboards), specially produced Klepper Mark 13 collapsible boats, and the somewhat larger Gemini boats powered by 40bhp outboard motors. The SBS can also be transported by "Rigid Raider" boats, a militarized version of the glassfiber "Dory" fishing-boat, powered by outboards of up to 140bhp, operated by the specialists of the Royal Marines' Rigid Raider Squadron, with the capacity to carry 10 personnel. There is also the "Kestrel," a three-man collapsible, which is small enough to be attached to the leg of a parachutist. Powered by a 9.5hp motor, which is dropped separately, the Kestrel is inflated by carbon dioxide.

Above: Royal Marine SBS use these Avon Rubber dry diving suits and dry sacs. The sacs are invaluable for protecting weapons, explosives, ammunition, and provisions, thus enabling the marines to arrive ashore "ready to fight." This marine is carrying a US model M16 rifle, commonly used by the British SAS and SBS.

SPECIAL AIR SERVICE

THE SAS WAS FORMED early in World War II with the appropriate motto "Who Dares Wins" at a time when many "special" units were being raised. Known originally as "L Detachment," the unit grew to 390 men in 1942 and was redesignated 1st Special Air Service Regiment (1 SAS). After various reorganizations and a period of further growth, an SAS Brigade was formed in Scotland in January 1944, consisting of two British regiments (1 and 2 SAS), two French regiments (3 and 4 SAS), a Belgian squadron (later 5 SAS), and a signal squadron.

At the end of the war in Europe the British Army divested itself of "private armies" (SAS among them), and it appeared the British Army had washed its hands of the "SAS idea" forever. It takes more than that to keep a good idea down, however, and within months it was decided that there would be a future role for SAS-type activities. This led to the conversion of a Territorial Army (TA) unit, "The Artists' Rifles," into 21st Special Air Service Regiment (21 SAS) (Artists) - (Volunteers), the number 21 being obtained by combining and reversing the numbers of the two British wartime SAS regiments (1 and 2 SAS).

During the Malayan "Emergency" (1948-60) the "Malayan Scouts (Special Air Service)" quickly built up to regimental size. In 1952, the Malayan Scouts was formed and were redesignated 22nd Special Air Service Regiment (22 SAS), thus marking the official return of the SAS to the regular Army's order of battle.

The SAS carried out successful operations following which they moved to the UK where, after a short period in Malvern, they settled down in their now-famous home base at Bradbury Lines, Hereford. But by now they had been reduced to an HQ and two "sabre" squadrons.

The Far East soon beckoned again. however, with the "Confrontation Campaign" in Borneo, and a squadron of SAS arrived there in January 1963. Their success led to more demands for the SAS and the third squadron was re-formed in mid-1963. All three were involved in campaigns in Borneo and Aden during 1964-66 in a period known in the regiment as the "happy time." By 1967, these two wars were over and the SAS had a short period of consolidation and retraining.

In 1969 the situation in Northern Ireland exploded and the SAS began a long acquaintanceship with the Province. Simultaneously, renewed problems in Malaya and the Oman led to a return there. The SAS remained in the Oman for many years and in August 1983 it was disclosed that the SAS was training a similar unit for the Sultan of Oman's "Special Force."

The anti-guerrilla campaigns of the 1950s, 1960s, and early 1970s were succeeded by a new role in which the SAS quickly built up an unrivaled expertise - counter-terrorist actions.

Spurred on by operations in Northern Ireland against the Irish Republican Army (IRA) and Irish National Liberation Army (INLA), the SAS has developed techniques which are copied throughout the Western world. This has led to the SAS not only being consulted by overseas governments and special forces, but also in being directly involved in some "foreign" operations. Thus, in October 1977, two SAS men were with the West German GSG 9 unit at the attack to recapture a hijacked German airliner at Mogadishu, and SAS members were also involved in the earlier Dutch operation against the Moluccan terrorists who had taken over a trainload of hostages.

ABOVE: SAS soldier during the Borneo campaign in the 1960s. In this "small war" the SAS operated deep inside Indonesian territory, causing considerable disruption to the lines-of-communication. They also rallied the local people, such as Ibans and Dyaks, thus ensuring that they remained loyal to the government of the newly formed Federation of Malaysia.

Most famous of all UK episodes was the London Iranian Embassy siege of May 1980 when the SAS had perforce to conduct the operation in front of the world's TV cameras. In strict compliance with English law, the Metropolitan Police conducted the operation until the terrorists murdered one of the hostages and threw his body out on the street. The police then requested the SAS to take over, and the troops stormed in, using special weapons and tactics. The hostages were rescued, four of five terrorists killed, and not a single SAS man was lost. This spectacular success, while a godsend for the hero-hungry world media, gave the SAS far more publicity than it liked.

By 1982 the SAS seemed to be settled in a counter-terrorist role when the Falklands War broke out with Argentina. 22 SAS was immediately involved, being given the opportunity to remind the world that they are first and foremost professional soldiers, trained for war. They spearheaded the return to South Georgia island, although the first reconnaissance landing in helicopters had to be aborted in truly appalling weather. The second landing was by inflatable boats and most men got ashore. One boat, however, broke down and the soldiers refused to compromise the operation by calling for help on the radio and were blown rapidly eastwards and were later rescued by helicopter. Meanwhile, at Grytviken, the squadron headquarters and one troop of D Squadron took advantage of the crippling of the Argentine submarine *Santa Fe* to rush in and overwhelm the garrison, and South Georgia was quickly back under British control.

The first SAS soldiers were ashore on East Falklands by May 1 and remained there, close to the enemy and in foul weather, for some 30 days. They provided vital intelligence on troop movements and deployments, and also targeted enemy aircraft and naval gunfire support. On May 14 the SAS raided Pebble Island and blew up 11 Argentine aircraft; they also reportedly operated on the mainland of Argentina itself, although this has never been confirmed officially.

Their final role in the Falklands was to carry out a noisy and valuable diversionary attack on the eastern end of Wireless Ridge on the day before the Argentine surrender.

LEFT: SAS troops on the roof of the Iranian Embassy in London moments before they launched their successful operation to free the hostages and kill or arrest the terrorists holding them. This was the first time the operational gear of black coveralls, hood, and respirator had been seen in public and its use spread rapidly.

RIGHT: SAS soldiers scramble out of a British Army Westland Scout helicopter at Bluff Cove, during the Falklands War. The battles against the Argentine Army showed that the SAS was as capable in conventional war as it was against terrorists, and that it could exercise an influence on the campaign out of all proportion to the numbers it deployed.

SAS teams were also inserted into Iraq during the Gulf War of 1991, their primary missions being to seek out and destroy Scud missile launchers, to report on Iraqi military movements from road watch patrols behind enemy lines, and to locate, report on, and destroy Iraqi communications systems.

Also during the 1990s, it is reported that SAS teams operated behind Serb lines in Bosnia, providing intelligence reports and calling down air strikes on Serb armor, artillery, and anti-aircraft positions.

As these examples make clear, the principal SAS mission is one of special operations - sabotage, raids, intelligence gathering, etc. - in denied areas. Contrary to popular belief, the counter-terrorist mission in the UK is not the sole province of the SAS; it provides assault and rescue forces when facilities have been seized in the UK proper and operates covertly against the Irish Republican Army (IRA).

A secondary SAS mission is to organize and train friendly resistance forces, as well as to provide specialized security assistance training to friendly nations.

ORGANIZATION

The present organization includes three regiments of approximately 600 to 700 men each. One regiment (22 SAS) is all-regular, while the other two (21 SAS (Artists Rifles) and 23 SAS) belong to the Territorial Army. There is a regular signal squadron with 22 SAS and another (63 (SAS) Signal Squadron) with the TA. These units are controled by Director Special Forces (DSF), a brigadier whose headquarters are in London.

Each SAS regiment is composed of four squadrons, each having around four 16-man troops that work, operationally, in patrols of four. Some variations in size exist, of course, to accommodate special requirements for elements such as the Mountain Troop and Boat Troop.

There is a very close relationship between 22 SAS and the Territorial regiments. 21 SAS (Artists) is based in London, with four outstations, and 23 SAS is based in Birmingham, with outstations in Manchester, Leeds, Newcastle, Dundee, and Glasgow. Both Territorial regiments have a strong cadre of regulars, who ensure that professional standards are maintained, and who pass on the benefits of recent operational experience.

22 SAS has been based at Hereford for 40 years, but it is moving to a new base at Credenhill, a former RAF station, which is only a short distance away.

SELECTION AND TRAINING

No officer or soldier enlists directly into the regular regiment (22 SAS). Instead, volunteers come from the other regiments and corps of the British Army, which sometimes leads to the accusation that the regiment is "poaching" some of the best and most enterprising young officers and soldiers. All volunteers for the SAS must first pass the selection course, which is based on the regimental depot at Hereford. The tests take place in the Brecon area of Wales and consist of a series of tasks designed to find out whether the individual has the qualities of mental resilience, physical stamina, self-discipline, initiative, independence, and spiritual toughness which the Regiment has found necessary for its missions.

The process starts with 10 days of fitness and map-reading training in groups of 20 to bring everyone up to the same basic standards. Typical of such training: SAS members are not allowed to write down map references or to fold maps in a way that will reveal the area they are concerned with. This is followed by 10 days of solitary cross-country marching, culminating in a 40-mile (64km) march in 20 hours carrying a 55lb (25kg) Bergen rucksack. They must also demonstrate an aptitude for languages, since they will be expected to know at least two. Those who have not either voluntarily or compulsorily withdrawn now undertake 14 weeks' continuation training which includes a parachute course and combat survival training. At the end of this phase the survivors are presented with their beret and badge, and are at long last members of the SAS, although the training continues with specialist courses in signaling, languages, field medicine, demolition, shooting, free-fall parachuting, and other military skills. Even after a soldier becomes a fully fledged member of the Regiment, there can be periods of high-intensity training for roles such as counter-revolutionary warfare commandos.

Unlike the earlier years ot the SAS the emphasis today is on pulling and encouraging men to get through the tests and course, but without relaxing the high standards, Nevertheless, the pass-rate is only about 20 percent, although it must be appreciated that only rarely is there any reason for any of the other 80 percent to feel ashamed; the fact is that the SAS are, of necessity, looking for a very special combination of talents which is possessed by or can be developed in only a few people.

Once fully in the Regiment, the normal tour of duty of several years is followed by return to the parent regiment or corps. This ensures that the Regiment does not become too introspective and also serves to spread around the rest of the Army that curious blend of ideas and training which constitute the SAS.

WEAPONS AND EQUIPMENT

In the past the SAS used standard British Army small arms but now it regularly uses a wide variety of weapons, foreign as well as British. In addition, the SAS specialize in training and using virtually any type of foreign weapon, either to take advantage of some particular attribute, or to blend in with some bit of local "scenery." Special "stun" grenades have been developed for SAS use in which the blast effect has been maximized at the expense of damage potential.

Since 1984 the SAS have used two Italian-built Agusta 109 helicopters captured from the Argentinians during the Falklands War. The aircraft, operated by the Army Air Corps, carry up to seven troops and are equipped for many roles.

The SAS have incorporated "high-tech" into their arsenal of tricks: thermal imagers to verify the presence of personnel in buildings, satellite communications systems, infrared night equipment, and a host of surveillance, target acquisition, and sensory devices.

UNIFORMS

The SAS wear standard British Army uniforms on operations, though they do not wear insignia of rank, with only the customary "regimental" items permitted under British practice. The three basic distinguishing marks of the SAS are the sand-colored beret, the capbadge (a winged dagger with the motto "Who Dares Wins") and SAS-wings worn on the right shoulder. In parade dress (No. 2 Dress) buttons, officers' Sam Browne belt, gloves, and shoes are all black. Combat dress is standard British Army pattern with either the sand-colored beret or the peaked camouflage hat with no badge. With this latter hat on there is nothing about a soldier's uniform to show that he is a member of the SAS. One small idiosyncracy of SAS uniform is that in "pullover order" (the popular dress worn in barracks) the rank chevrons of NCO are worn on the shoulder straps, not on the right sleeve.

A unique combat uniform is available for use on anti-terrorist operations. This is an all-black outfit, with a black flak-vest, belt, and boots. The standard issue respirator (made of black rubber) and gray anti-flash hood complete the outfit. Every item of this dress is worn for strictly practical reasons, but the effect is awe-inspiring.

BELOW: British SAS troopers in the desert during the 1992 Gulf War, with their faces blanked out for security reasons. The mission of "SCUD-busting" in the Arabian desert harked back to the function for which they were originally formed, destroying Axis aircraft on the ground in the Sahara.

UNITED STATES OF AMERICA

ABOVE: Lead scout of a Special Forces patrol group, armed with a 5.56mm Colt Commando assault rifle. Special Forces soldiers are also trained in the use of foreign weapons, enabling them to use such weapons if their own are damaged or, even worse, lost.

BELOW: Special Forces trooper blends into the background on a jungle operation. Originally raised in order to use guerrilla tactics against conventional forces, Special Forces are now trained to fight in all types of war, in all terrains, and against all types of enemy.

THE UNITED STATES has a long and rich history of military special operations which predate the Revolutionary War. However, the first truly integrated modern special operations organization in the United States Army did not begin until April 10 1952, when the Psychological Warfare Center was established at Fort Bragg, NC. Notably, psychological warfare in the. Army at the time also consisted of unconventional warfare - a legacy of the special operations of the Office of Strategic Services (OSS) headed by Gen. "Wild Bill" Donovan during World War II.

The Special Forces were resuscitated in the early 1950s, with 10th Special Forces Group being activated at Fort Bragg on June 20 1952, followed by 77th Special Forces Group on September 25 1953. (The numbering appears to have been entirely at random.) These were followed by 1st Special Forces Group, which was raised on June 24 1957 in Okinawa. This group sent a small team to train 58 men of the South Vietnamese Army at Nha Trang during that year, beginning a long association between the Special Forces and the Republic of Vietnam. Next, 5th Special Forces Group was raised on September 21 1961, initially at Fort Bragg, but later it moved to Vietnam and became responsible for all Special Forces activities in that country.

President John F. Kennedy was fascinated with the Special Forces and visited Fort Bragg, where he authorized the wearing of the distinctive and symbolic headress - the green beret - in 1961. Also a result of the Kennedy visit: the first troops of the Special Forces deployed to South Vietnam in November 1961.

The original idea was that the Special Forces would wage guerrilla operations against regular enemy troops in a conventional war. It soon became clear, however, that in Vietnam the enemy himself was a guerrilla, forcing the Special Forces to revise their basic concepts. One of the principal programs was the raising and training of Civilian Irregular Defense Groups (CIDG), with more than 80 CIDG camps being set up in the years 1961-65.

The Special Forces eventually operated throughout South Vietnam in a variety of roles, some of which have yet to be revealed. They had more extensive dealings with the ARVN (South Vietnamese Army) - and particularly with the Montagnard, or mountain people - than any other element of the US forces. They received awards for heroism and for dedication to duty far out of proportion to their numbers. Despite this, their relationship with some elements of the US chain-of-command was not always easy, with mistrust and suspicion sometimes interfering with their operations, an all too frequent problem for any elite force. The last soldier of the Special Forces left South Vietnam in March 1971.

The Special Forces have always operated throughout the US areas of responsibility. An early deployment was to Bad Tölz in Bavaria, Germany. Other groups operated in the Panama Canal Zone. Special Forces have also long been involved in "advising" friendly armies in Asia, Africa, Central and South America, as well as in other parts of the world. They have thus tended to be always just on the edge of the limelight. They are now very firmly a part of the US Army's order of battle and are likely to remain so.

ORGANIZATION

There are currently five known Special Forces Groups (Airborne) - 1st Special Forces Group (Airborne) (SFGA), Ft. Lewis, Wash, with 1Bn/1 forward-deployed to Torii Station, Okinawa; 3rd SFGA, Fort Bragg; 5th SFGA, Fort Campbell, Kentucky; 7th SFGA, Fort Bragg; and 10th SFGA, Fort Carson, Colorado. There are also two Army National Guard groups. Command is exercised by US Army Special Forces Command (Airborne).

The traditional organization pattern of the Special Forces has been based on the Operations Detachment A, more popularly known as the "A Team." While the individual elements that make up the profile of a typical special group may change from time to time, the group profile itself does not. Ideally, five A Teams are commanded by a B team, commanded by a major, with a further five officers and 18 soldiers.

SELECTION AND TRAINING

All officers and soldiers in the Special Forces must be airborne qualified, and many are also trained in free-fall parachuting and/or for swimming roles. All enlisted personnel must also have at least two specializations, eg, engineering, intelligence, weapons, communications, demolitions, in addition to the primary or military occupational specialty. Many must also be trained in foreign languages.

Training for the Special Forces is both thorough and tough. To some extent, the normally rigorous training standards declined following the Vietnam War - for a variety of reasons, including political. With the increasing emphasis of recent years that has been placed on special forces, this decline is in the process of being reversed and training attrition rates (now in the 60 percent plus range) are about what would be anticipated for a special force.

Further, like many Western special troops, US Army Special Forces troops frequently attend courses with other armies; other armies also train with them.

Their training is designed to fit them for six missions: Foreign Internal Defense (FID); Special Reconnaissance; Direct Action; Unconventional Warfare; Counter-Terrorism (CT); and Coalition Warfare. Particular emphasis is placed on the ability to operate with foreign troops.

WEAPONS AND EQUIPMENT

The US Special Forces are tasked to be the repository of knowledge on the world's small arms, and they are therefore trained on virtually every weapon likely to be found on operations anywhere in the world. Their own personal weapon, however, is the famed M16A2 rifle (the "Armalite"). Other, more esoteric small arms are on the drawing boards, but will not see service until after the year 2000.

UNIFORM

The basic hallmark of the Special Forces is the green beret, which was approved by President Kennedy, and has given rise to the "Green Berets" monicker. The Special Forces crest, which is worn on the flash in a beret, combines crossed arrows with a dagger. The motto in the scroll surrounding the dagger is "De Oppresso Liber" ("Freedom from Oppression") which reflects their mission. This crest is normally set on a patch whose colors vary with the groups. Officers show their rank in the flash itself.

BELOW: Green Berets "A-Team" speeding towards their objective on board a River Patrol Boat (PBR). These waterjet-powered craft have a maximum speed of 24 knots and some 500 were built, principally for use in the Vietnam War, although many remain in service. All the men are armed with M16s except for the man with a helmet who has an M60 machine gun with a large night sight attached.

As with other special forces the basic uniforms are those of the US Army, although particular items may be added to fit in with a role. The Special Forces are fairly high-visibility troops and tend not to act or dress covertly, leaving that to other and more recently formed units.

1ST SPECIAL FORCES OPERATIONAL DETACHMENT (DELTA)

1ST SPECIAL FORCES Operational Detachment – Delta (1SFOD-Delta), more familiarly known as "Delta," was the brainchild of Colonel Charles (Charlie) A Beckwith, US Army, who, as a major, served on an exchange posting with the British SAS in 1962-63. On his return to the United States he sought to form a new unit with the same organization, ideals and functions as the SAS, and eventually overcame the resistance of a very conservative chain-of-command, with Delta being officially formed on November 19 1977. Its credo, as laid down by Charlie Beckwith, was "surprise, speed, success."

The title of this unit sometimes causes misunderstandings. 1SFOD-D was a totally new unit and had nothing to do with the "Delta Project (Detachment B-52)" set up by the US Army Special Forces in Vietnam in the mid-1960s (and was, at one time, commanded by Beckwith), which was a totally different organization and concept. The reason for the name of the new unit was, in fact, quite simple. At that time, according to Beckwith, there were already three Special Forces Detachments, designated Alpha (commanded by a captain), Bravo (by a major), and Charlie (by a lieutenant-colonel). It was, suggested Beckwith, a natural progression in titles and ranks to call the new detachment "Delta" and for it to be commanded by a colonel.

Delta was always intended for use overseas, although even then it could only be deployed at the invitation of the host government, which, as will be seen, has not always been forthcoming. The main mission is counter-terrorism, and its priority tasks are hostage rescue, wanted-man "snatches," covert reconnaissance, and explosive ordnance disposal.

ORGANIZATION

Delta is based at Fort Bragg, in a large and well-protected area known as "The Stockade." Not surprisingly, the organization of Delta reflects the ideas brought back to the United States by Colonel Beckwith. Thus, the unit is composed of a headquarters and three operational squadrons, each of which is composed of two or more troops, each of four 4-man squads. There are also a support squadron, a communications squadron, and a covert troop using special equipment and techniques. The main aviation support for Delta comes from 160th Special Operations Aviation Regiment (160 SOAR) but Delta also has its own aviation troop which uses helicopters with civilian color schemes and registration in a similar manner to the British 22 SAS with its two Agusta A 109s.

SELECTION AND TRAINING

Delta is manned by volunteers who can come from anywhere within the US Army, although, in practice, the majority come from the Green Berets and Rangers. Under Colonel Beckwith's command, Delta's selection and training processes were essentially similar to those used by the British SAS, although it is reasonable to assume that these have been refined and adapted over the intervening 20 years to meet the demands of a larger army and changed conditions.

ABOVE: Unarmed combat is an essential skill for most special forces. Delta volunteers also have to be highly proficient in many other skills, such as signals, medical, engineering, weapons handling, resisting interrogation, and escape/evasion, to name but a few.

LEFT: Modern operational scenarios seldom permit a lengthy acclimatization period, so US Special Forces must be able to go into battle almost as soon as they arrive in a new theater. So, regular training in conditions such as these swamps is essential.

DEPLOYMENTS

Delta has undertaken a host of operational deployments, some of which have appeared in the press and some of which have been learnt about through other means; there have also doubtless been deployments which remain totally classified to this day. Some of the operations have been unsuccessful, but in most the aim has been achieved. Among the known deployments have been:

BELOW: The US Special Operations memorial wall tells its own story of deployments and deaths, as does the space which has been carefully left for future casualties.

Operation Eagle Claw (24-25 April 1980. The attempted rescue of the US hostages in the Embassy compound in Teheran.

Air Garuda Boeing 737 (March 1981). A single 4-man team killed four hijackers at Bangkok airport, successfully releasing the hostages.

Brigadier-General Dozier rescue (January 1982). Dozier was taken hostage by Red Brigade terrorists. A Delta team deployed to Italy, but the Italians carried out the rescue, which was successful.

Operation Urgent Fury (October 25 1983). Delta and Seal Team 6 took part in the US invasion of Grenada.

Olympic Games, Los Angeles (1984). Delta played a major role in the security arrangements for the Los Angeles Games, for which Colonel Beckwith, by then retired, was the security consultant.

TWA Flight 847 hijack (June 1985). Having been hijacked the aircraft was flown to Algiers, where two US passengers were murdered. Delta was deployed to Europe but the Algerian government refused permission for them to take action.

Achille Lauro Incident (October 1985).

Atlanta City prison riots (1987). Delta forces were deployed to help quell the riot, but prisoners surrendered before they arrived.

Operation Just Cause (1989). Delta and Seal Team 6 took part in the invasion of Panama, where their prime task was to apprehend President Noriega.

Operation Desert Storm (1990-1). Delta deployed to Iraq, where they worked alongside British, Australian, and New Zealand SAS units in seeking out and destroying "Scud" missile launchers.

"Branch Dravidian" siege (1993). Delta teams were sent to Waco, Texas, to join the FBI and other agencies in breaking the siege of the religious sect's headquarters. Delta was not used, possibly due to disagreements with the FBI.

Operation Restore Hope (1993). Delta was deployed to Somalia where it became embroiled in the attempts to arrest "General" Aidid.

Operation Uphold Democracy (1994). Delta took part in the peacekeeping operation in Haiti.

Atlanta Olympic Games 1996. Delta was again on stand-by to deal with terrorist incidents at the Games.

Bosnia (1996-1999). It is believed that Delta teams (possibly accompanied by SEAL Team Six) have deployed to Bosnia on several occasions. One possible mission was to arrest the war criminal Radovan Karadzic, although, in the event, this has never happened. It is likely that Delta was involved in the rescue of the pilot of the F-117 shot down over Belgrade.

US ARMY RANGERS (AIRBORNE)

GENERAL CREIGHTON ABRAMS, former US Army Chief of Staff defined the Ranger mission as follows: "The Ranger battalion is to be an elite, light and the most proficient infantry battalion in the world, a battalion that can do things with its hands and weapons better than anyone. Wherever the Ranger battalion goes, it is apparent that it is the best."

The US Army Rangers are the spiritual descendants of the old Indian fighters led by Major Robert Rogers, a woodsman from New Hampshire, in the pre-Revolutionary colonial army,

a tradition which was revived in World War II by Merrill's Marauders in Burma, and by Darby's Rangers in Europe. The latter comprised six battalions raised and trained in the United States and which fought with distinction in Sicily and Italy. Ranger units remained in the US Army's order of battle until the end of the Korean War, when they were quietly disbanded and most of their tasks were picked up by the special forces.

In the post-Vietnam trauma, the special forces were reduced drastically and devoted most of their energies to simply fighting for existence. The Ranger School had been operating for many years to maintain a high standard of leadership in the Army and in 1975 it was decided that two Ranger battalions should be reformed, to perform a number of unique missions.

The Rangers were prepared to take part in the Iranian hostages rescue mission and were about to

ABOVE: Medals are important to all soldiers, such as these men of 2/75th Rangers receiving their awards immediately following their return from Operation Urgent Fury in Grenada in November 1983.

RIGHT: Men of 1/75th Rangers board a USAF C-141 at Hunter Army Airfield in Georgia. They are deploying to take part in Operation Just Cause in Panama in December 1989.

LEFT: US Army Rangers. The trooper in front is armed with a 5.56mm Colt Commando (note the large cylindrical flash suppressor). The soldier behind wears the full sniper outfit which will enable him to blend into the background awaiting the chance to fire.

fly into Iran when the mission was canceled due to the disaster at Desert One. Their first operational opportunity did not, therefore, arise until Grenada in 1982, when they spearheaded the landing on Port Salines airfield. Since then they have deployed in a wide variety of missions including the US operation in Panama and the United Nations operation in Somalia.

Ranger tasks are quick strike and shock action deep in enemy territory. These include ambushes, raids, interdiction, and temporary seizure of priority targets. A less common mission for Rangers is the recovery of captured personnel and equipment.

ORGANIZATION

Today there are approximately 2,500 Rangers in one Ranger regiment, consisting of three battalions, with a further three training units. Headquarters 75th Ranger Regiment is at Fort Benning, Georgia, with 1st Battalion (1/75) at Hunter Army Field, Georgia, 2/75 at Fort Lewis, Washington, and 3/75 also with the regimental headquarters at Fort Benning. Each of these three battalions has a battalion headquarters and three combat companies, each with three rifle platoons and a weapons platoon. All men in these units are volunteers from elsewhere in the Army, have passed the Ranger course and remain with the Rangers for a standard two-year tour, which can be extended by six months, subject to recommendation by the commanding officer.

SELECTION AND TRAINING

The US Army Ranger School is an unusual institution which has existed for many years and has continued to function even at times when there were no full-time Ranger units in the Army. This is because the course serves two functions, the first of which is to train soldiers for Ranger units. The second, however, is to spread the "Ranger code" and training excellence, and to improve the standard of self-confidence and leadership not only within the US Army and within the other three US services, which send a small number to Ranger School, but also of friendly foreign armies, whose students take up some 20 percent of the places on each course.

To achieve this the course covers the whole gamut of Ranger skills, including land navigation, patrolling, weapons handling, hand-to-hand combat, survival, and mountaineering. During the course the trainees do not wear the rank badges they are normally entitled to and all take it in turns to serve in various leadership positions. According to unofficial figures the overall pass rate is about 35 percent.

The selection and training process starts at the 4th Ranger Training Battalion at Fort Benning. Having qualified there the trainees move to 5th Ranger Training Battalion in Dahlonega, Georgia, where they receive training in mountain warfare and finally to 6th Ranger Training Battalion at Eglin Air Force Base in Florida for training in jungle and swamp warfare. Training exercises are conducted all over the United States, and abroad wherever possible, with the aim of training in different climates and environments.

At the end of the course many return to their units, but a small number of carefully selected go to join the Ranger battalions for a two-year tour, which can be extended by six months if the commanding officer agrees.

BELOW: Special forces' instructors around the world take intense pleasure in devising ever more challenging obstacles for their trainees to cross. This huge ladder is at the Rangers base at Fort Bragg.

LEFT: Using the "buddy" system, US Rangers paratroops at Fort Bragg pair-up to help each other with the final preparations before a parachute jump. It is essential in such highly specialized units that soldiers work as a team - there is no place for a "loner."

UNIFORM

During their time at Ranger School trainees wear jungle fatigues and patrol cap. Then, all soldiers, regardless of unit, who pass Ranger School are entitled to wear the highly prized "Ranger" flash on their right sleeve for the remainder of their military service. Within the Ranger units the soldiers wear normal Army uniform and accoutrements and the "Ranger" flash, the only other outward sign that they are full-time Rangers being the black beret with a Ranger capbadge.

CURRENT MISSIONS

Today's Rangers have to prepared to conduct a wide variety of missions and must train constantly to maintain their standards in arctic, mountain, urban, and amphibious warfare. 75th Ranger Regiment is an Army unit, but operationally it comes under the Joint Special Operations Command (JSOC) and each of the three battalions takes it in turn to be the "Ranger Ready Force" for a month at a time, which requires it to be ready to deploy anywhere in the world within 18 hours. On deployment, the Ranger units can be required to operate on their own or as part of a larger force made up of different units, as, for example, on the ill-fated Teheran Embassy rescue mission.

BELOW: A competition between teams representing the Rangers and 82nd Airborne Division. Such competitions are essential to improve skills and to foster a healthy spirit of friendly rivalry, especially when there are no operations under way.

SEA, AIR LAND (SEAL) TEAMS

ABOVE: Members of an unidentified SEAL team return to an amphibious ship after a recent exercise. The aircraft is a Boeing-Vertol CH-46, a type which entered service in the 1960s, and this actual aircraft is almost certainly somewhat older than the young men it is transporting.

THE STORY OF SPECIAL OPERATIONS units in the US Navy started in 1943 during the "island-hopping" operations in the Pacific campaign, where Naval Combat Demolition Units were formed to reconnoitre and clear beaches prior to an amphibious landing. In the late 1940s these evolved into Underwater Demolition Teams (UDT) which were employed during the Korean War in the same role – for example, in clearing beaches prior to the Inchon landings.

Faced with the problems of the Vietnam War coupled with the increasing intensity of the Cold War, US forces sought some of the answers in "special operations forces" to which one of the navy's major contributions was the SEa Air Land (SEAL) teams. The first of these were formed in January 1962: SEAL Team 1 in the Pacific and SEAL Team 2 in the Atlantic. SEAL units became deeply embroiled in the Vietnam War, where they performed vigorously and successfully in riverine and other areas. Their missions included intelligence gathering, sabotage, ambushes, and other counter-insurgency activities. They helped to organize and train South Vietnamese special forces, and then frequently worked with them. In 1967, the Naval Operations Support Groups were renamed Naval Special Warfare Groups (NSWGs) as involvement increased in limited conflicts and special operations. In 1983 the hydrographic reconnaissance and underwater demolition became SEAL missions, as a result of which the remaining UDTs were absorbed into the SEAL organization.

Naval control over the SEALs is exercised by Naval Special Warfare Command (NAVSPECWARCOM), which is co-located with the Naval Special Warfare Center at the Naval Amphibious Base, Coronado, California. NAVSPECWARCOM's mission is to prepare Naval special warfare forces to carry out their assigned missions and to develop special operations strategy, doctrine, and tactics. There are two Naval Special Warfare Groups: NAVSPECWARGRU 1 with the Pacific Fleet and NAVSPECWARGRU 2 with the Atlantic Fleet. There are currently seven SEAL teams, of which SEAL Team 6 is in a special category and is dealt with separately (see below).

A SEAL team is typically made up of 10-12 platoons, each consisting of a number of squads. There are also three Special Boat Units and two SEAL Delivery Vehicle teams. Delivery to the operational area can be by air, parachute or surface warship, but the most effective is by submarine; these take the team to the destination and then lie offshore, where the team is taken ashore by Swimmer Delivery Vehicles (SDVs).

Left: Members of a US Navy SEAL team, who have just roped down from a helicopter, start to inspect a deck cargo of ISO containers on a merchant ship in the Adriatic in September 1995. Such inspections form an essential part of blockade operations.

SELECTION AND TRAINING

Volunteers for the SEALs must come from elsewhere in the Navy; there is no direct recruitment. Having been accepted for training they then undergo a gruelling 15-week course, most of which is conducted at the Naval Special Warfare Center at Coronado, and involves indoctrination, mental and physical toughening and extensive instruction. Officers and enlisted men undergo identical training, the only distinction being that officers bear the added responsibility of class leadership. As with most special warfare training courses, the attrition rate is high, varying between 55 and 70 percent.

SEALs receive extensive training in combat swimmer techniques, advanced demolitions, field communications, and weapons handling and must also qualify as parachute jumpers. This expertise, combined with the basic skills, ranging from gunner's mate to signalman, which they bring from their previous "regular naval service," molds the Navy SEAL into a combination of frogman, paratrooper, and commando.

Right: During Operation Desert Storm in the Gulf War in 1991, members of a SEAL team make final preparations prior to deploying. Note the unusual helmet, worn only by SEAL teams.

NAVAL SPECIAL WARFARE DEVELOPMENT GROUP

OPERATION EAGLE CLAW was a true turning point in US special operations and, following the debacle, all services reviewed their counter-terrorist organizations, capabilities, and training. Within the US Navy this led to the creation of SEAL Team 6 in October 1980 as a specialist maritime counter-terrorist unit, and it became operational in April 1981. At this point an earlier counter-terrorist unit, designated Mobility Team 6 (known as "Mob 6"), was disbanded. Mob 6 was an offshoot of SEAL Team 2 and had been developing counter-terrorist techniques before Eagle Claw, but for a variety of reasons it proved more practicable to disband it rather than to develop it into the new unit. SEAL Team 6's title was subsequently changed to the cover name Naval Special Warfare Development Group (NAVSPECWARDEVGRU), although it is quite clear that, while it may have a developmental role, it is basically an operational unit.

ORGANIZATION

NAVSPECWARDEVGRU is located on the east coast, at Little Creek, Virginia, where it comes under the command of Naval Special Warfare Command (NAVSPECWARCOM) although operationally it comes under Headquarters Joint Special Operations Command (JSOC) which is located at Pope Air Force Base, North Carolina. The strength of the unit has never been published, but a reasonable guess would be about 2-300, organized into troops which specialize in the unit's different roles. The unit will also need its own support (headquarters, logistics, medical, supplies, etc) which probably accounts for another 2-300.

OPERATIONS

It seems reasonable to assume that SEAL Team 6/DEVGRU has been involved in covert operations, particularly involving submarines, which have never been publicly acknowledged.

BELOW: The pilot's compartment of a submerged SEAL Delivery Vehicle (SDV), with the pilot at the controls and a SEAL returning from a mission. The US Navy has about 15 SDVs, which are carried in special Dry Deck Shelters on a number of SSNs and converted SSBNs. Latest version is SDV Mk VIII Mod 1, which carries a maximum of eight SEALs, each wearing a self-contained underwater breathing apparatus (SCUBA).

However, it is known that it has been involved in operations targeted at extracting specific individuals, some of which have been successful, including rescues of deposed, legal rulers - Scoones of Grenada (1985) and Aristide of Haiti (1991) - and the capture of Panamanian ruler, General Noriega (1989). The unit is also reported to have been involved in attempts to capture alleged war criminals in the former Yugoslavia, although, as far as is known, none of these has as yet been successful. SEAL Team 6/DEVGRU has also deployed several times for operations which never took place, including the Achille Lauro incident (1985). NAVSPECWARDEVGRU is known to cooperate closely with units of other nations with a similar role, including the British Special Boat Service (SBS) and Italy's COMSUBIN.

160TH SPECIAL OPERATIONS AVIATION REGIMENT (AIRBORNE)

One of the major lessons of Operation Eagle Claw was that it was inviting trouble to assemble a force for a specific operation. Instead, the units and individuals needed to have operated and trained with each other regularly, so that they understood their respective modes of operation, capabilities, strengths, and weaknesses. This particularly applied to the helicopters and in the aftermath of the Teheran rescue debacle the US Army formed a new aviation unit to provide just this type of support. It formally came into existence on October 16 1981, designated 160th Aviation Battalion, but in May 1990 it was reorganized, expanded and redesignated 160th Special Operations Aviation Regiment (Airborne) and assigned to the US Army Special Operations Command (SOCOM). Aircraft of 160th SOAR have taken part in US operations in Grenada, the Persian Gulf, Just Cause, Desert Shield/Desert Storm, and recent actions in Somalia.

ORGANIZATION AND AIRCRAFT

160th SOAR comprises three aviation battalions, with 1/160 and 2/160 at Fort Campbell, Kentucky, and 3/160 at Hunter Army Airfield, Georgia. Special operations helicopters are also operated by 1st Battalion, 245th Aviation Regiment of the Oklahoma Army National Guard.

The smallest helicopter in use with 160th SOAR is the McDonnell Douglas MH-6J "Little Bird," the latest in a long line of OH-6 developments for special operations use. The MH-6J is known to serve with 2/160 and, considering its small size, it is a highly capable aircraft. It can be fitted with FLIR and a laser designator, and can be armed with 7.62mm Miniguns or 0.50-cal Brownings; in addition, the MH-6J is so stable in the hover that it can be used as a platform for a sniper using a 0.50-cal rifle. The tail can be folded for transportation in a fixed-wing aircraft, while the MH-6J itself can carry a crew of two and six special forces operators on each side externally. 160th SOAR also provides MH-6s in support of NAVSPEC-WARDEVGRU for maritime operations such as assaults on oil rigs.

The Sikorsky MH-60K is the definitive special operations version of the UH-60 for the US Army, with deliveries to 1/160th starting in late 1992. The aircraft is comprehensively

ABOVE: A SEAL team member, with camouflage cream liberally applied, comes ashore, ready for anything. He is armed with a Colt Commando, the shortened, lighter, carbine version of the M16 assault rifle. The US Navy's SEALs have proved to be among the most efficient and most highly respected of the US Special Operations Forces community.

equipped for night/low level operations with AN/APQ-714 terrain-following radar and AAQ-16B FLIR, a night-vision imaging system, and a moving map display. Weapons can include Stinger and Hellfire missiles and two pintle-mounted M2HB 0.50-cal Browning machineguns.

Largest helicopter is the Boeing MH-47E (SOA) (= special operations aircraft) which has terrain-following radar, FLIR, and an extensive array of early-warning devices. Defensive armament consists of pintle-mounted M2HB Brownings and Stinger air-to-air missiles. The helicopter is also fitted with an in-flight refueling probe and a typical deep penetration mission could have a radius of 350 miles (570km) and an endurance of some 6 hours. MH-47Es serve with 2/160 and 3/160.

While aircraft are allocated to and operated by specific units, it should be noted that 160th SOAR's procedures enable mixes of types and numbers to be assembled to suit almost any operational requirement.

QUALIFICATIONS
The Officer Qualification Course for 160th SOAR lasts 14 weeks, while the Enlisted Men's Qualification Course lasts for three weeks. Two other qualification levels exist: Fully Mission Qualified, which is attained after 12-18 months in the unit, and Flight Leader, which only comes after 3-4 years.

BELOW: US Marine Corps Force Recon troopers help each other up a cliff face in sandy terrain. The Marine Corps, which is undoubtedly an elite force, has taken part in every US war since it was formed in 1775 and today its ground force is larger and better equipped than all but a few national armies, while Marine Corps Aviation dwarfs the majority of national air forces.

US MARINE CORPS

THE US DEPARTMENT of Defense does not formally list the Marine Corps as a part of its Special Operations Forces. In some respects, however, it is one - and it is certainly en "elite" force - and it would therefore be inappropriate not to include them in reviewing such capabilities. More specifically, Reconnaissance Marines (and Force Reconnaissance in particular) have similar training and missions as special operations forces - with training in parachute and other airborne operations, as well as in Scuba and other underwater operations.

The Marine Corps is the world's largest elite force; indeed, it is even bigger than the total armed forces of most countries. Since it was raised by order of Congress on November 10 1775, the USMC has taken part in every major war fought by the USA, as well as in numerous "police" actions and armed interventions all over the world. These fine traditions have merged to produce an amphibious assault force whose maintenance is the raison d'être for today's Corps. Further, the evolution of Marine aviation units has provided the Corps with its own air force. This overall capability enables the USMC to claim to be a unique, combined-arms, ground-air force with a special competence in amphibious warfare.

The missions assigned to the USMC fall into three broad categories. The principal mission is to maintain an amphibious capability for use in conjunction with fleet operations, including the seizure and defense of advanced naval bases and the conduct of land operations essential to the successful execution of a maritime campaign. In addition, the Corps is required to provide security detachments for naval bases and the Navy's principal warships. Finally, the Corps carries out any additional duties placed upon it by the President.

A major feature of the USMC's position in the US defense establishment is unique in that it is the only service to have its basic corps structure defined by statutory law. The amended National Security Act of 1947 tasks the Marine Corps with maintaining a regular Fleet Marine Force of no fewer than three divisions and three aircraft wings, with the additional support units necessary.

LEFT: With its world-wide mission, it is essential that the USMC is capable of deploying into any type of terrain, with only the most minimal notice. Jungle training, once carried out in Panama, is now practised using facilities made available by friendly countries.

ABOVE: Marine Corps arctic training is carried out at home in California, and overseas in Japan and Norway. During the Cold War the Marines had a major commitment to support Norway in the event of Soviet aggression, where they would have fought alongside the British, Dutch, Norwegian, and other NATO troops.

ORGANIZATION

The Marine Corps strength – 174,000 active duty personnel, including 9,300 women, and 40,000 reserves - is organized into four divisions and four aircraft wings (three regular and one reserve of each), but both organizations are larger than their counterparts in the other services. This is particularly apparent in a Marine division which, with a strength of 17,000, is some 20 percent larger than a US Army division.

The basic structure of the Marine division is essentially the traditional "triangular" model, with three infantry regiments, each of three battalions. The new infantry battalion, however, is smaller than before, with a headquarters company, weapons company, and three rifle companies, each of the latter being 20 percent smaller than its predecessors. Manpower and financial constraints prevented a fourth rifle company from being formed. Each Marine division has an artillery regiment, a tank battalion, an armored amphibian battalion, a light armored assault battalion (equipped with the new LAV), and other supporting units.

The standard Marine aircraft wing (MAW) has 18 to 21 squadrons with a total of 286 to 315 aircraft, ranging from fighter/attack (F/A-18), through medium attack (AV-8) and a tanker/transport squadron (KC- 130), to helicopter squadrons (AH-1, CH-53, CH-46, UH-1) plus supporting squadrons of electronic warfare, observation, and reconnaissance aircraft.

RIGHT: A US Marine practises the art of jungle survival in the former United States' training area at Subic Bay in the Philippines. He is cutting a bamboo, which can provide food, water, serve as a container, or be used to erect a shelter. Special forces must become expert at "living off the land," especially in hostile environments, since they may have to operate behind enemy lines for lengthy periods.

BELOW: Despite the vast technological and industrial resources of the United States, its most valuable military assets in war are its people, such as this member of the Marines' Force Recon.

WEAPONS AND EQUIPMENT

The single dominant characteristic of Marine tactical doctrine is the emphasis on the principle of offensive action, which applies to all aspects of the Corps' activities. This ethos has a major effect on the way the USMC is equipped. Improved M16 rifles are being issued as the basic infantry weapon, while each squad, 13 strong, has the new 5.56mm Squad Automatic Weapon (SAW) (M249) in each fire team. The battalion weapons company has a heavy machine gun platoon with eight firing teams, each of which mans a vehicle equipped with a 0.5in HMG and the Mkl9 40mm "machine gun" (actually, an automatic grenade launcher in all but name). An improved version of the 81 mm mortar is also in service.

SELECTION AND TRAINING

All members of the US armed forces are volunteers, and those for the USMC enlist directly into the Corps. Recruits go to one of two training depots, at San Diego, Ca, and Parris Island, SC, where they undergo the famous 11-week "boot camp."

Despite its size, the USMC does not have its own officer academy, although some are accepted from the Navy academy at Annapolis. The main source of officers is through the Naval ROTC, Officers Candidate School (OCS) or the Platoon Leaders Class. All officer candidates (including those from Annapolis) must undergo a rigorous selection and training course at Quantico, Va, before being accepted for a commission.

FLEET ANTI-TERRORISM SECURITY TEAM (FAST)

THE FLEET ANTI-TERRORISM Security Team (FAST) companies are one of a number of elites within the US Marine Corps. These units were formed in 1987 in response to the world-wide increase in threats to US armed forces and government facilities, their prime mission being to provide additional, highly trained protection over short periods, when the threat is beyond the capabilities of the usual security forces. Following the principle that "prevention is better than cure," however, FAST companies are also responsible for carrying out threat assessments, for helping security officers to prepare proper security plans, and for improving individual standards in a security force (eg, of surveillance, marksmanship).

The FAST companies are some 300-strong and can be deployed very rapidly when the need arises. Following the bombing of US troops in Saudi Arabia on June 25 1996, in which 19 people were killed and 500 injured, FAST Marines from Norfolk, Va, were actually on-site within 10 hours of the explosions. They then not only provided additional security by deploying their own Marines, but also carried out security assessments, which, in many cases, found the existing arrangements to be wanting.

FAST units hace deployed with US forces on numerous operations, including: the Gulf War; Liberia (Operation Sharp Ede); Panama (Operations Just Cause and Promote Liberty); Haiti (Safe Return); Cuban refugee evacuation (Operation Safe Passage); and the United Nations withdrawal from Somalia.

ABOVE: "Mission accomplished" as US Marines stand outside the re-captured US Embassy in Kuwait City in February 1991. The marine on the left is particularly well equipped. He carries an M16 fitted with an M203 pump-action grenade launcher below the weapon and a night sight to its left. He wears pouches carrying spare ammunition and grenades on his chest, and a bayonet is on his left shoulder, ready for instant use.

LEFT: Operation Just Cause in December 1989 and two Marines question a local inhabitant in the town of Arraijan on Panama's Pacific coast. The Marines are members of the First Fleet Anti-Terrorist Security team (FAST). FAST companies have proved very useful and have been deployed in every US operation in the 1990s

PART 2

OPERATIONS

MODERN BATTLE HONORS have been earned in places as far apart as Entebbe, Djibouti, Grenada, the Iranian desert, the Falklands and Mogadishu. What these battles have in common is that they were all conducted by special/elite forces and were all conducted in so-called "low intensity" environments. It is importqant to study such operations by special/elite units, since the operation is the pay-off, where they carry out the job they were created and trained to handle. Of course, many lessons can be learnt from successes, but by no means all speical/elite operations have been unqualified triumphs, and it is important not to shy away from these. In other words, lessons must be learnt from failures as well as from successes.

The prestigious Combat Studies Institute at the US Army's Command and General Staff College at Fort Leavenworth, Kansas, has studied special/elite force operations in great depth. It concluded that, "Many factors determined the conduct of such operations...and of these there are four that are important enough to merit special emphasis. These are: surprise; the quality of opposing forces; the success of friendly forces with which the elite forces were cooperating; and popular support." Of these, the study concluded that surprise was paramount.

Basic tenets and tactics must be studied over and over again, since, taken as a general rule, they are sound and they work. It would, however, be a great mistake to assume that what works in one situation will work in another. The tactics used by Britain's Special Air Service during the siege of the Iranian Embassy in London, for example, or those used by GSG 9 in Mogadishu were very successful on those two occasions, but may well not be suitable in future incidents. Nor, as the 1993 Mogadishu operations show, should the same tactical plan be used over and over again.

One thing all these examples show is that the men and women in special/elite force units must be very adaptable and able to respond effectively to novel situations in unfamiliar places at very short notice. In other words, they must be high caliber people, not only physically but mentallly as well.

Two of the 12-man team of Britain's SAS make their move across the roof during the most publicized rescue operation by special forces to date, when terrorists held 29 hostages at the Iranian Embassy in London in 1980

RESCUE AT ENTEBBE

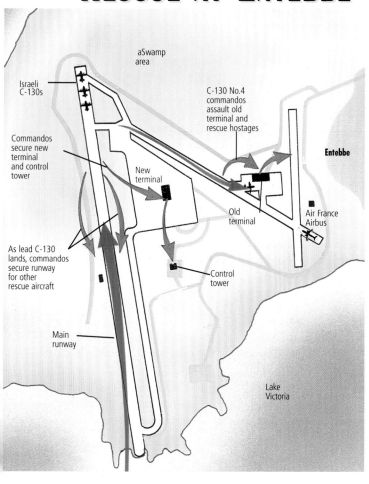

Israeli
C-130s

aSwamp
area

C-130 No.4
commandos
assault old
terminal and
rescue hostages

Commandos
secure new
terminal
and control
tower

New
terminal

Entebbe

Old
terminal

Air France
Airbus

As lead C-130
lands, commandos
secure runway
for other
rescue aircraft

Control
tower

Main
runway

Lake
Victoria

AT 0900 HOURS JUNE 27 1976, Air France flight AF 139 left Tel Aviv airport en route for Paris with 254 passengers and crew aboard. The A300 Airbus aircraft staged through Athens and it was on the second leg of its flight when, at 1210 hours, it was sky-jacked by a combination of Palestinian and Baader-Meinhof terrorists led by a German called Wilfried Boese. The pilot succeeded in pressing the "hijack button" as he turned for Benghazi, where, after a 6-hour delay, the plane was refueled; it then flew on to the terrorists' destination – Entebbe, Uganda, which was under the erratic rule of "Field Marshal" Idi Amin Dada.

Amin purported to maintain an apparently neutral posture, but covertly he supported the terrorists in their demands that unless 53 Palestinians or other terrorist prisoners held in a number of countries were released the hostages aboard the Air France flight would be shot at 1200 hours on July 1. Ugandan troops were deployed to Entebbe airport, supposedly to "keep the peace," but they in fact assisted in guarding the hostages. Amin even visited the hostages and, after he had left, the Israelis and Jews of other nationalities were segregated, although the Air France aircrew insisted on joining them.

On the morning of July 1, the Israeli government, playing for time, announced that it was willing to consider the release of Palestinian prisoners. The hijackers, increasingly confident of eventual success. responded by extending their deadline by three days. They also released all the non-Jewish hostages, who were flown to Paris, where they were debriefed by French and Israeli intelligence.

From the beginning, the Israeli planners had many problems. The first clearly was shortage of time to set up any form of rescue operation before the terrorists killed any of their hostages. The second was to find out just where the hostages were being held and under what conditions. Third, there was the problem of getting a rescue force to Entebbe and back. Fourth, there was the problem of what to do with the non-Jewish hostages.

Fortunately, the problems resolved themselves one after another. The Kenya government agreed to the use of Nairobi airport, and a coup in Sudan resulted in the closure of that country's air control radars. Intelligence on Entebbe airport and the local situation began to be processed, aided considerably by the debriefing of the released non-Jewish hostages. This

ABOVE: The map of Entebbe airport as it was at the time of the Israeli raid. The Air France Airbus was parked at the end of the taxi-way (right), a short distance from the old terminal building, in which the hostages were being held. The main runway was on the left; the new terminal and control tower in the center.

RIGHT: Reconstruction of the scene outside the old terminal building at Entebbe. Speed and deception were essential to the operation's success. Heavily armed jeeps and a Mercedes sedan were disguised to resemble the transport used by Ugandan dictator Idi Amin, and thus temporarily mislead the airport security guards. C-130 No.1 and No.2 (with the command team) landed several minutes apart and deployed troops, while No.3 carried reserves and touched down after the runway lighting had been extinguished. The task of No.4, which contained further reserves, was to taxi to the old terminal building and to pick up the rescued hostages.

LEFT: Israeli chief-of-staff General Mordecai Gur briefs the press, following the commandos' return. On his left is Brigadier-General Dan Shomron, who commanded the operation, but Lieutenant-Colonel "Yoni" Netanyahu, the ground force leader, was killed.

eased the problem of consulting foreign governments. US sources made inform-ation, including satellite photographs of Entebbe, available, and France remained involved not only because it had been an Air France airliner that had been hijacked but because its courageous crew had insisted on staying with the Jewish hostages.

THE RESCUE

Lieutenant-General Mordecai Gur, Israeli chief-of staff, considered that a raid on the airport was feasible, and at 0730 hours on July 3 Prime Minister Rabin reviewed all the facts and then gave the political go-ahead for the operation. Later that morning a full-scale dress rehearsal was held in northern Israel. Drawn from the 35th Parachute Brigade and the Golani Infantry Brigade, the 100-plus force, commanded by Brigadier-General Dan Shomron, aged 48, performed well in an attack on a dummy layout manned by Israeli troops, and all seemed to augur well for the real thing, which was scheduled for the next day. The dress rehearsal lasted just 55 minutes from the time the rescue aircraft landed to the time it took off again (the actual rescue was to take just 53). The primary weapons selected for the raid reportedly were the MAC-10 and Galil assault rifles, the latter equipped with night sights. The force to enter the airport terminal and rescue the hostages was to be led by Lieutenant-Colonel Jonathan Netanyahu, known throughout the Israeli Army as "Yoni."

ABOVE: The C-130 carrying the rescued hostages taxis towards dispersal at Lod airport, following its return from Entebbe. When the ramp was lowered the passengers rushed out into the arms of their tearful relatives; a successful outcome none had anticipated 24 hours earlier.

At 1600 hours that afternoon (July 3), two hours after the full Israeli government cabinet had been made aware of the "go" decision, four Israeli C-130 Hercules took off for the long flight to Entebbe. The route took them down the middle of the Red Sea at high altitude in the hope that Saudi Arabian radars would treat them as unscheduled civil flights. There was, in fact, no reaction, so they were able to turn and fly down the Sudan-Ethiopia border and into Uganda.

Two Boeing 707s were also involved, leaving two hours after the slower C-130s. One was a flying command post fitted with special communications gear; it caught up with the four C-130s near Entebbe and remained in the area throughout the operation with Major-Generals Benny Peled and Yekutiel Adam aboard. The other 707, fitted out as an emergency hospital, went straight to Nairobi, arriving just before midnight; it then waited, its medical staff ready for any wounded from the operation just across the border in Uganda.

The four C-130s arrived at Entebbe without incident and landed at precisely 0001 hours. The first aircraft landed close to the control tower, disgorging its paratroops in a Mercedes car and three Land Rovers while still moving. The men charged into the tower and succeeded in preventing the controllers from switching off the landing lights; even so, emergency lights were deployed, just in case. These were not needed and the second and third aircraft taxied up to the terminal where the hostages were being held and discharged their paratroops straight into action. The fourth C-130 joined the first near the control tower.

The main Israeli squad brushed aside the ineffective resistance from the Ugandan Army guards and charged into the terminal building. The second group destroyed Ugandan Air Force MiG fighters to prevent pursuit when the raiders took off again and also as a noisy and obvious diversion.

The third group went to the perimeter to cover the approach road, since it was known that the Ugandan Army had a number of Soviet-built T-54 tanks and Czech OT-64 armored personnel carriers some 20 miles (32km) away in the capital, Kampala. Had this force appeared, it could have had a major effect since the Israelis had no heavy weapons. The fourth group was made up of 33 doctors who, being Israelis, were also well-trained soldiers and brought down covering fire from the area of the C-130s.

With Shomron in control in the tower and satisfied that the first phase had been successful, it was now "Yoni" Netanyahu's turn to lead the crucial assault on the terminal building to rescue the hostages. The terrorist leader, Boese, behaved with surprising indecision, first aiming at the hostages and then changing his mind, going outside, loosing off a few rounds at the

ABOVE: The celebrations continue at Lod airport. The spectacular and very successful hostage rescue was devised, organized and executed within one week, and, according to some reports, the Israelis took the concept of the US raid on the Son Tay prison in North Vietnam as the start point for their plan.

Israelis and then heading back for the lounge; as he returned he was shot and killed. His fellow German, Gabrielle Tiedemann, was also killed outside the building.

The Israeli soldiers rushed into the lounge where the hostages were being held, shouting at everyone to get down on the floor; in the confusion, three of the hostages were hit by stray bullets, an almost inevitable consequence in such a situation. While some of the soldiers rushed upstairs to kill the two terrorists remaining there, the hostages were shepherded out to the waiting C-130s. At this point "Yoni" Netanyahu emerged from the terminal to supervise the loading and was killed by one shot from a Ugandan solider in a nearby building, a sad loss.

At 0045 hours the defensive outposts were called in as the first C-130 roared off into the night with its load of rescued hostages on their way to Nairobi, with the fourth and last leaving at 0054.

Apart from the loss of Colonel Netanyahu, three Israeli rescuers were wounded. Three hostages were killed in the rescue, while a fourth, Mrs Dora Bloch, who had been taken off to a local hospital earlier, was murdered by the Ugandans in revenge for the raid. On the other side, in addition to the terrorists, there were 20 Ugandans killed and more than 100 wounded.

The whole operation was a brilliant success, mounted on short notice and in a most unexpected direction. It confirmed the Israeli reputation for quick and determined "ad hoc" action, conducted with great dedication and skill. The Ugandans could not be described as substantial foes, but the terrorists had obviously been trained for their task. Interestingly, it later became known that Colonel Ulrich Wegener of Germany's GSG 9 was with the Israelis on the operation, possibly because of the known presence of the two Germans with the terrorists.

The first rescue attempt of its type – unless one considers the US raid on Son Tay Prison in Vietnam, which the Israelis reportedly used as a model – the Entebbe rescue caught the terrorists and Ugandans completely off guard. Following Entebbe, all terrorists have to take into account the possibility that a rescue mission could be carried out in hostile territory over great distances.

MOLUCCAN TRAIN INCIDENT

THROUGHOUT THE NETHERLANDS in the 1970s, repeated terrorist incidents by South Moluccans grabbed headlines. The incidents were used by the terrorists to press demands that the Dutch government support independence for their homeland - the Moluccan Islands, now a part of Indonesia, but formerly a Dutch colonial possession. (They were at one time known as the Spice Islands.) The radicals spearheading the terrorist activity were generally the Dutch-born children of Moluccan immigrants, and had begun forming guerrilla squads in the late 1960s and accumulating arsenals of weapons.

Violence included the killing of a policeman in 1973 when South Moluccans seized the Indonesian embassy in The Hague; the following year, South Moluccans stormed and damaged The Hague Palace itself; and in 1976, they killed three hostages during a train hijacking.

But on May 23 1977, two groups of South Moluccan terrorists launched their most spectacular attack yet in the opening phase of what was to become a three-week drama. The groups simultaneously hijacked a Dutch train and occupied an elementary school in a northern part of the Netherlands,

The raid began when two terrorists pulled an emergency cord to stop Express Train 747 as it traveled between Assen and Groningen. Five masked gunmen rushed aboard, herding 49 hostages into the first-class compartments.

Minutes later and a few miles away, seven terrorists invaded an elementary school, forcing 110 hostages into the main classroom. Of the 110 hostages, 106 were released unharmed a few days later after a virus struck the children.

In addition to demanding assistance in their independence efforts, the Moluccans insisted that they, as well as 21 other South Moluccans jailed for various assaults (including the planned kidnapping of Queen Juliana), be allowed to leave the country. Dutch officials handling the situation steadfastly refused to meet the terrorist demands, but continued to negotiate with them. There was a reluctance to use force, despite the previous train seizure only 18 months earlier.

However, the order for the June 10 rescue assault came only after negotiations dragged on for three weeks with no progress ... and as the Dutch public grew increasingly impatient and bitter over the stalemate. What was to follow was later characterized, appropriately enough, as a switch from psychology to technology.

ABOVE: On December 8 1975 a previously unheard-of group of Moluccan terrorists seized the Indonesian Consulate in Amsterdam. Here a masked terrorist armed with a sub-machine gun forces one of the hostages to retrieve food left for them by the authorities.

LEFT: The setting for the most spectacular operation conducted by the South Moluccan terrorists. In a two-pronged attack, one group seized the Assen-Groningen express train and held 49 hostages, while a second group held 110 children and teachers in an elementary school some miles away. The Dutch authorities played for time, but eventually had to use force.

ABOVE: Dutch troops await the call for action. Special forces must be prepared to spend much time waiting for negotiations to break down before they can strike.

BELOW: Following the 1977 train/ school sieges the terrorists struck again in 1978. Here Dutch marines ring the building where 70 hostages were being held.

EXECUTION

Even though the Dutch government was reluctant to use force, contingency plans had been put in place from the start. To break the dual siege, it was determined that a dual attack would be required. If either the train or the school were taken individually, the terrorists at the remaining location seemed certain to exact vengeance on the hostages in their custody.

Throughout the siege, the specially picked Royal Dutch Marines, and civilian and military police had been rehearsing assaults on an empty train at the nearby Gilze Rijin Air Force Base. Eight combat swimmers had approached the train by way of a canal that ran within 15 yards (5m) of the tracks and had put sensitive bugging devices in place.

Special radar that could detect the heat differences in hot and cold surfaces had also been put in place; this allowed the Marines to monitor the movements of the terrorists through the metal in their weapons. Other sophisticated devices were used so that the Marines would know where the terrorists and hostages were likely to be should the "go" decision be made for the assault.

When it came, Marines wearing night-vision goggles approached the train, and launched what was to be a 20-minute attack. Six F-104 Starfighter aircraft immediately flew in crisscross patterns just a few feet above the train, kicking in their afterburners in an attempt to distract the terrorists and encourage the hostages to keep their heads down. As the jets roared overhead, a force of Marine and police sharpshooters raced across a 100-yard (30m) field and opened up with their weapons on areas of the train where the terrorists normally slept. Shortly before 0500, the assault force blew the doors off with framing charges and went in with Uzis blazing.

Six of the nine terrorists were killed during the assault; two hostages who had panicked and stood up as bullets blazed about were killed also. Seven other hostages, two Dutch Marines, and one terrorist were wounded.

Simultaneously with the assault on the train, Marines assaulted the school at Bovensmilde, rushing the building with armored personnel carriers from all four sides, one of them bursting through a wall. The 10-minute attack met no resistance; four terrorists were captured (three were asleep in their underwear) and the four hostages were rescued unharmed.

ASSESSMENT

The assault demonstrated that the Dutch would resort to force if necessary to counter terrorism. This was particularly important to the government since the belief had been prevalent among South Moluccans that force would not be used, no matter how hard the Dutch were pushed. Perhaps another salutory effect of the split-second, high-tech and successful attack was that it helped temper some of the derogatory remarks directed at long-haired Dutch troops by their more conventional colleagues from other European nations.

Another point was eventually driven home: terrorism would not go unpunished in the courts either. Seven of the terrorists, aged 18 to 28, received prison terms ranging from six to nine years, while another received a one-year term for helping plan the dual seizure.

ABOVE: A classroom window in the school-house of the normally quiet Dutch town of Bovensmilde, the breeching of its tranquillity symbolized by the drawn curtains and the protruding rifle muzzle (lower left). Inside, the terrorists held 110 hostages, but had to release 106 children after a few days when they were struck by a mystery virus.

LEFT: Two terrorists sit in the open doorway of Express Number 747 awaiting their fate after the Dutch special forces had broken their siege. The Dutch experience with the South Moluccan terrorists proved once again that the use of force and heavy penalties for any terrorists that survive the final assault are the only way of dealing with the problem and preventing future occurrences. Giving in to terrorist demands and allowing them to go free after the incident is over only result in further problems. Another price to be paid is the maintenance of special forces units and ensuring that they are always ready to react to the unexpected.

MOGADISHU RESCUE

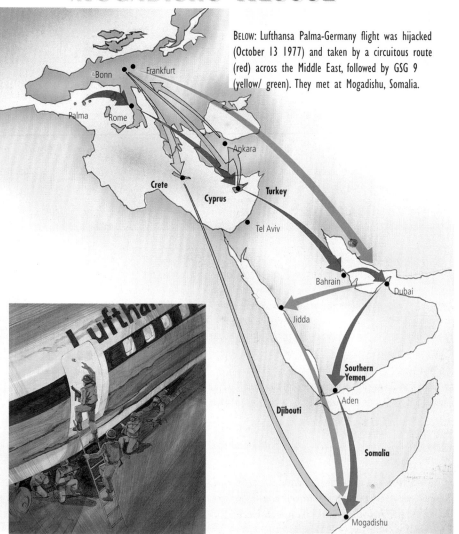

BELOW: Lufthansa Palma-Germany flight was hijacked (October 13 1977) and taken by a circuitous route (red) across the Middle East, followed by GSG 9 (yellow/ green). They met at Mogadishu, Somalia.

ON OCTOBER 13 1977 a Lufthansa 737 airliner en route from Palma in the Balearic Islands to Germany was hijacked by terrorists over the French Mediterranean coast. On board the aircraft were five aircrew (two pilots, three stewardesses), 86 passengers, and four terrorists, two of them women. The hijackers' leader called himself "Captain Mahmoud," and was subsequently identified as a notorious international terrorist, Zohair Youssef Akache. He ordered the aircraft captain to fly to Fiucimino airport in Rome, where the airliner was refueled.

From Rome, the airliner set off eastwards and landed at Larnaca in Cyprus at 2038. Here, "Mahmoud" demanded that the aircraft be refueled again, or he would blow it up, the first of many threats to use explosives. After refueling, the airliner took off and overflew various Middle East countries. Permission to land at Beirut was denied and the runways were blocked, so it was taken on to Bahrein in the Persian Gulf where the same thing happened. It was flown on to Dubai, where, despite being refused permission to land, the crew were forced to do so for lack of fuel.

At one point at Dubai the airliner lost power and the temperature inside rose to over 120°F (49°C); many of the

ABOVE: GSG 9 operators, assisted by two British SAS men, blasted open the airliner's doors, threw in stun grenades, and shot the hijackers. The British involvement, only admitted later, symbolizes the close operational liaison between many special forces units.

RIGHT: Boeing 737, Lufthansa Flight LH 747, sits forlorn and apparently abandoned on the runway at Mogadishu Airport. Inside are 5 aircrew, 86 passengers, and 4 terrorists, with heat increasing, hunger pangs growing, conditions worsening and the terrorists becoming increasingly agitated, and unpredictable. The pilot had already been murdered at Aden and the future seemed bleak.

passengers, some of them quite elderly, became very distressed. While here, the crew managed surreptitiously to signal that there were four hijackers.

Then on Sunday, October 16, the airliner suddenly took off, only 40 minutes before the first deadline for blowing it up. It was refused permission to land in Oman and arrived over Aden airport with sufficient fuel for another 10 minutes' flying. Despite warnings from air traffic control, the aircraft was brought down safely on the taxi track.

PILOT EXECUTED

By now conditions inside the aircraft were very bad, and "Mahmoud" was acting in an increasingly unpredictable and unstable manner. Jürgen Schumann, the pilot, was allowed to leave the airliner to check the undercarriage, and disappeared for a few minutes. When he returned he was taken to the first-class cabin and made to kneel on the fllor; "Mahmoud" then shot him in the head, killing him instantly, directly as a result of Schumann's earlier, successful effort to feed information about the terroists to authorities.

The next morning the co-pilot, Jürgen Vietor, took off and flew the airliner to Mogadishu, the capital of Somalia. There, German government spokesmen contacted the hijackers and said that they were prepared to release 11 terrorists held in jail and fly them to Mogadishu; "Mahmoud" postponed his deadline to 0145 hours the next morning (October 18).

THE RESCUE

A 30-strong contigent from GSG 9 was in the air within hours of the hijacking and arrived in Cyprus just as the Boeing 737 was taking off. Following a brief discussion with the Cypriot police, the GSG 9 team took off in their aircraft again and returned, via Ankara, to Frankfurt. Meanwhile, a second aircraft containing Hans-Jürgen Wischenewski, West German Minister

ABOVE: The body of Lufthansa Captain Jürgen Schumann is carried away from the Boeing 737 after his murder by the terrorist leader "Mahmoud." His "crimes" were passing information over the radio and "disappearing" briefly while inspecting the undercarriage.

BELOW: Still defiant, the sole terrorist survivor, Suhaila Sayeh, is carried away. She now lives quietly in Norway and is resisting extradition to Germany for trial on charges arising from Mogadishu.

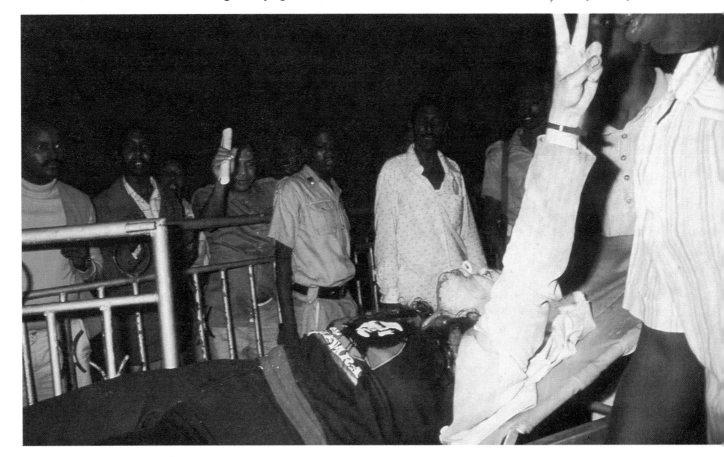

of State, psychologist Wolfgang Salewski, and another 30-strong group from GSG 9, led by their commander Ulrich Wegener, had left West Germany and gone to Dubai. From there they went to Mogadishu, where they were given permission to land.

In Mogadishu, Wischenewski took over discussions with the hijackers. As the 1600 hours deadline approached and it was clear that "Mahmoud" would in all probability carry out his threat to blow up the aircraft, the German minister said that the 11 prisoners would be released. "Mahmoud" gave them until 0245 hours the following morning to produce the 11 at Mogadishu. At 2000 hours the first group of GSG 9 who had gone to Cyprus and then returned to Germany arrived in Mogadishu and the rescue briefings began.

At 0205 hours, just 40 minues before the deadline, Somali troops lit a diversionary fire ahead of the aircraft. Two hijackers went to the cockpit to assess its significance, whereupon the tower contacted them by radio and started to discuss the conditions of the exchange. They said it would commence in the near future, when the aircraft arrived from Germany with the released prisoners on board.

Right: GSG 9 members sprint past the welcoming band on their return to Frankfurt following the completely successful operation at Mogadishu, thus relegating the fiasco of the attempted hostage rescue at the Munich Olympic Games to a distant memory.

Below: Welcoming VIPs disperse following the welcome for GSG 9 at Frankfurt Airport. Note the man with rifle in the center of the picture. GSG 9 continues to have an extremely high reputation over 20 years later.

At 0207 precisely the emergency doors over the aircraft wings were blown open and members of the rescue party tossed in some "stun grenades." The men of GSG 9, with two British SAS men lent by the British government, had reached the aircraft and climbed onto the wings completely undetected; the hijackers (and the hostages) were taken by surprise.

The men of GSG 9 rushed into the aircraft shouting to the hostages to keep down on the floor, and opened fire on the hijackers. "Mahmoud" was fatally wounded in the first few seconds, but managed to throw two hand-grenades before he died; fortunately, their effects were cushioned because they rolled beneath seats. One of the women terrorists died also and the second man was wounded inside the aircraft but died outside it a few minutes later. The second woman, Suhaila Sayeh, was wounded but did not die. Meanwhile, the passengers were herded off the aircraft through the doors and emergency exits; three hostages had been wounded, but none was killed.

The operation ended at 0212 hours and was entirely successful. GSG 9 had proved itself and the men received a well-merited heroes' welcome when they returned to Germany.

Mogadishu was, at the very least, a tribute to the intensive physical and mental training undertaken by the GSG 9, as well as to that unit's attention to technological back-up, examples being the special rubber-coated-alloy assault ladders used, and the stun grenades. At its best, it formed a new standard for rescue operations in that no hostages were killed during the assault – unlike at Djibouti and Entebbe which, though outstandingly successful in their own right, had resulted in at least one hostage death.

OPERATION EAGLE CLAW

ON NOVEMBER 4 1979, a group of Iranian "students" poured into the US Embassy compound in Teheran and seized 53 occupants. They were to hold them hostage for 444 days.

From the earliest days of the crisis one of the options under constant review and development was a military rescue, although both diplomatic and military endeavors were constantly bedeviled by the continuing chaos in Iran, the uncertain, ever-changing intentions of the captors, and the vacillating position of the Iranian leadership. An unchanging factor was the remoteness of Teheran from available US bases. The plan that was eventually decided upon centered on Colonel Charlie Beckwith and the elite Delta force, although it obviously involved many more resources both directly and indirectly. The overall codename was "Operation Eagle Claw," its helicopter element "Operation Evening Light." The plan was complicated mainly by the problems of time and space, and comprised some preliminary moves and a three-phase operation.

BELOW: The plan required C-130s to fly to Desert One (red arrows) to meet eight RH-53Ds from USS *Nimitz* (green arrows). The C-130s arrived according to plan but two RH-53Ds aborted; one was abandoned, one returned to *Nimitz*. The survivors flew back to Egypt (brown arrows).

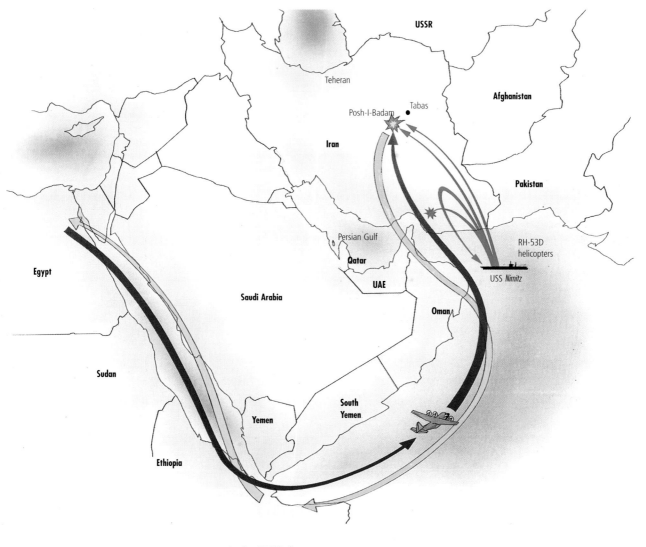

Leading RH-53Ds fly into unexpected "haboobs" - dust storms

RH-53D No. 6 aborts. Crew picked up by RH-53D No. 8

Disaster at Desert One, as RH-53D collides with C-130 tanker, after entire mission had been aborted. Eight servicemen are killed. Remaining servicemen, including Delta Force, flown to Masirah airfield, Oman

RH-53D No. 5 returns to *Nimitz*, aborting mission

LEFT: The helicopter debacle. No.5 suffered equipment malfunction and was forced to return to *Nimitz*, while No.6 had a rotor blade problem, landed, and was abandoned, its crew being picked up by No.8. The worst disaster was at Desert One where No.3 collided with a C-130.

PRELIMINARY MOVES

In the preliminary moves Delta was to fly, via Germany and Egypt, to Masirah airfield in Oman. There they would transfer to C-130s and, flying at very low level to avoid radar, cross the Gulf of Oman and southern Iran to land at Desert One, a remote site in the Dasht-e-Karir Salt Desert, 265 nautical miles (490km) south east of Teheran. Meanwhile, eight US Navy RH-53D helicopters, which had been deployed some weeks earlier via Diego Garcia, would take off from the carrier USS *Nimitz* and, flown (also at very low level) by US Marine Corps crews, join up with the main party at Desert One.

PHASE 1: INSERTION

At Desert One the plan was for the six C-130s (three troop carriers; three to refuel the helicopters) to land and await the helicopters, which were scheduled to arrive some 30 minutes later. Because Desert One was beside a road (judged to be little used), a 12-strong Road Watch Team was the first to deploy to intercept and detain any passing Iranians.

When they had refueled, the helicopters were to load the assault team and fly on towards Teheran, dropping off the men at a landing zone and then proceeding to their helicopter hide some 15 miles (24km) to the north. The assault group was to be met by two agents at the landing zone and guided by them to a remote wadi, some 5 miles (8km) away. Helicopters and men would then rest in their hides through the day.

BELOW: The Sea Stallion was the largest helicopter in the US inventory and the -D version had both the longest range and the greatest carrying capacity, as well as folding rotors and tail-boom, enabling it to be struck-down aboard a carrier. Since its basic role was mine-sweeping, its presence aboard a carrier would not be considered unusual.

PHASE IIA: THE RESCUE

After last light one agent would take the 12 drivers/translators to collect six Mercedes trucks, while the other agent would take Colonel Beckwith on a route reconnaissance. At 2030 hours the complete unit would embus at the hide and drive to Teheran, the actual rescue operation starting between 2300 and 2400 hours. Having disposed of the guards and released the hostages, it was planned to call in the helicopters, either to the embassy compound if an LZ could be cleared (the "students" had erected poles to prevent a surprise landing) or, if this was impracticable, to a nearby football stadium. Once all the hostages were clear the assault party would be taken out by helicopter, the White Element being the last out.

PHASE II: RESCUE AT THE FOREIGN MINISTRY

Concurrently with Phase IIA the 13-man special team would assault the Foreign Ministry, rescue the hostages there, and take them to an adjacent park where they would all be picked up by a helicopter.

PHASE III: EXTRACTION

While the action was taking place in Teheran, a Ranger contingent would seize Manzarieh airfield, some 35 miles (56km) to the south, and several C-141 turbojet transports would fly in. Once everyone had been evacuated from Teheran to Manzarieh they would be flown out in the C-141s, the Rangers leaving last. All surviving helicopters would be abandoned at Manzarieh.

CONTINGENCY PLANS

Various contingencies were foreseen and plans made accordingly; for example, in the event that not enough helicopters were available to lift everyone out of Teheran in one lift. One critically important condition had been agreed throughout the planning, namely that there had to be an absolute minimum of six helicopters to fly out of Desert One, since planners expected at least one to fail during the mission.

COMMAND AND CONTROL

Ground force commander Colonel Beckwith reported to Major-General James Vaught, the Commander Joint Task Force (COMJTF), who was at Wadi Kena airfield in Egypt; they were linked by portable satellite systems. General Vaught had a similar link back to Washington, DC, where General David Jones, then Chairman of the Joint Chiefs of Staff, was in session with President Jimmy Carter throughout the critical hours of the operation. In a last-minute change of plans, Air Force Colonel James Kyle was appointed commander at Desert One.

EXECUTION

The C-141 airlift of the ground party went according to plan, as did the C-130 flights to Desert One. The first aircraft, carrying Colonels Beckwith and Kyle, Blue Element and the Road Watch Team, landed safely and the Road Watch Team deployed, immediately having to stop a bus containing 45 people who were detained under guard,

Minutes later two more vehicles appeared from the south; the first, a petrol tanker, was hit by an anti-tank rocket and burst into flames, but the driver escaped in the second vehicle which drove off at high speed. The first C-130 then took off, leaving those on the ground briefly on their own. The second C-130 then came in and unloaded and, after the remaining four C-130s had landed, took off again for Masirah. The four C-130s and the ground party then waited for the helicopters and waited ....

The eight helicopters were, quite literally, the key to the operation. They had taken off from USS *Nimitz* some 50 miles off the Iranian coast at 1905 hours (local), as scheduled, and headed north for Desert One. At about 2145 hours helicopter No. 6 indicated an impending catastrophic blade failure, one of the two really critical problems requiring an abort. The crew landed, confirmed the problem, removed sensitive documents and were then picked up by helicopter No. 8 which then followed the others some minutes behind.

ABOVE: The impressive bulk of the RH-53D may have led to a misleading confidence in its capabilities. Like all helicopters of its era, it had mechanical weaknesses, which were exacerbated by the unexpected sandstorms.

BELOW: Sea Stallions being readied for Eagle Claw on the deck of USS *Nimitz*. Although the helicopters had good range and payload, lack of proper preparation and non-availability of spares contributed to the failure of the mission.

ABOVE: Colonel Schaefer, US Army, was the senior military hostage held in the 144-day US Teheran Embassy siege. Here he attends the memorial service for the eight men killed during their attempt to rescue him and his fellow hostages in Operation Eagle Claw.

ABOVE RIGHT: Five members of the USAF's 1st Special Operations Wing and three Marines - all aircrew - were killed in the catastrophe at Desert One. This is the scene at the memorial service, April 24 1980, at their home base: Hurlburt Field in the United States.

BELOW: Iranian soldiers inspect a jeep, one of the vehicles abandoned at Desert One, the temporary air-strip, 185 miles (300km) south-east of Teheran.

About one hour later the leading RH-53Ds ran into a very severe and totally unexpected dust storm; all emerged from this, flew on for an hour and then encountered a second and even worse dust storm. (What they encountered was a haboob, a meteorological phenomenon in which gusts generated by thunderstorms kick up masses of dust many miles away. In Iran, where the dust is extremely fine, a haboob can linger in the air for hours.)

The helicopter force commander – Major Seiffert, USMC – had earlier lost his inertial navigation system and, entirely blinded, flew back out of the first dust storm and landed, accompanied by helicopter No. 2. Major Seiffert had a secure radio link to COMJTF, who told him that the weather at Desert One was clear; consequently, after some 20 minutes on the ground both aircraft took off again and followed the others to Desert One.

Meanwhile, helicopter No. 5 suffered several problems, including the loss of its gyro, a burnout of its tactical navigation system, and a radar receiver failure. With no artificial horizon or heading, and with mountains ahead, the pilot was compelled to abort, and barely made it back to the Nimitz, thus leaving six helicopters to continue the mission.

The first helicopter (No. 3) cleared the dust storm some 30nm (56km) from Desert One and, using the burning Iranian petrol tanker as a beacon, landed some 50 minutes late. The remaining aircraft straggled in over the next half-an-hour, all coming from different directions (except Nos. 1 and 2, which were together). The crews were shaken by their experience, but the helicopters were quickly moved to their tanker C-130s, refueling began, and the assault party started to board their designated aircraft.

Colonel Beckwith was fretting on the ground, 90 minutes behind schedule, when he was informed that helicopter No. 2 had had a partial hydraulic failure during the flight; the pilot had continued on to Desert One in the hope of effecting repairs, but these proved impossible. The decision to call the whole thing off was quickly reached. There was no problem in aborting at this stage, even though the rescue team had never practised an abort order. The only minor complication was that helicopter No. 4, which had been on the ground longest, needed to top up with fuel before setting off to the Nimitz. Only one C-130 had enough fuel left and to clear a space for No. 4 helicopter No. 3 took off and banked to the left, but, because of the height (5,000ft/1,525m) and its weight (42,000lb/19,050kg), it could not maintain the hover and banked right into the C-130.

The effect was instantaneous and disastrous: both aircraft exploded, debris flew around and ammunition began to cook off. Five USAF aircrewmen in the C-130 and three Marines in the RH-53D died, but 64 Delta men inside the C-130 escaped quickly from the aircraft and rescued the loadmaster. The decision was then made to abandon the remaining helicopters and the whole party returned to Masirah in the three C-130s.

In hindsight, it can always be said mission planners should have done more, that 10 helicopters should have been sent instead of eight, that much more should have been known about haboobs, and so on. But the Chief of Naval Operations, Adm. Thomas Hayward, summed it up rather cogently in an interview shortly after the attempted rescue. "There had to be some mistakes made," he conceded. But, in the end, the mission was affected at least as much by an incredible string of misfortunes.

IRANIAN EMBASSY SIEGE

THE SIEGE OF THE IRANIAN EMBASSY in London in April-May 1980 caught the imagination of the world and brought the SAS into the limelight because the denouement took place before the gathered press photographers and TV. The eerie, black-clad figures, their efficiency, and the success and sheer drama of the event established for the SAS a public reputation and created an expectation of success which will endure for many years.

The Iranian Embassy at No. 16 Princes Gate, London, opposite Hyde Park, was taken over at 1130 hours Wednesday April 30 by six terrorists armed with three 9mm automatic pistols, one 0.38in revolver, two 9mm sub-machine guns and a number of Chinese-made hand grenades. There were six men directly involved: Oan, the leader (27 years old), and five others, all in their early twenties. They were all from Arabistan, an area of Iran some 400 miles (643km) from Teheran, which had long resisted the rule of the Aryan northerners. Most had supported Ayatollah Khomeini's takeover from the Shah, only to find him as

BELOW Cut-away showing the interior of the five-storey, 50-room Iranian Embassy at Princess Gate, London. The size and complexity of the building added to the difficulties of the rescue mission, but microphones and other sophisticated surveillance devices were essential to discovering the whereabouts of the 6 terrorists and their 26 hostages (3 more escaped in the first few minutes).

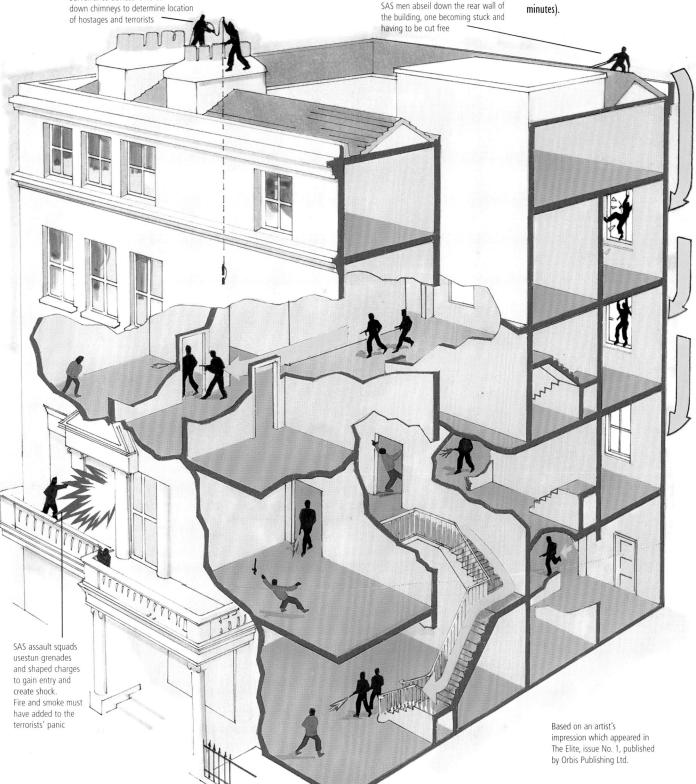

Surveillance devices lowered down chimneys to determine location of hostages and terrorists

SAS men abseil down the rear wall of the building, one becoming stuck and having to be cut free

SAS assault squads usestun grenades and shaped charges to gain entry and create shock.
Fire and smoke must have added to the terrorists' panic

Based on an artist's impression which appeared in The Elite, issue No. 1, published by Orbis Publishing Ltd.

ruthless a suppressor of minorities as his predecessor. The terrorists represented a group entitled the Democratic Revolutionary Movement for the Liberation of Arabistan (DRMLA), a Marxist-Leninist group based in Libya, whose cause was regional autonomy (not independence) for Arabistan.

The occupants of the embassy at the time of the takeover numbered 29: four British and 22 Iranian men and women, three of whom escaped during the early minutes. The terrorists' demands were initially that 91 prisoners in Arabistan be released by the Iranian authorities. The deadline was set for 1200 hours Thursday May 1, and during that night the terrorists had the first of many contacts with the London police and the media.

One sick Iranian woman was released late on Wednesday night and a sick Englishman the following morning. The first deadline was postponed when the police transmitted a message from the terrorists to the press, and a second deadline (1400 hours) passed without a move from either side.

By Friday morning there had been numerous contacts between the terrorists and the police, some direct and some through intermediaries, but by now specific threats were being made against the lives of the hostages. Negotiations continued throughout Saturday and a major advance was achieved when the terrorists agreed to release two hostages in return for a broadcast on the radio of a statement of their aims. One hostage was released in the early evening and after the statement had been broadcast word for word another was released. The atmosphere in the embassy became almost euphoric, helped by a good meal sent in by the police.

Throughout Sunday the British government discussed the situation with various Arab ambassadors, but no agreement could be reached on a possible role for them in reaching a resolution to the crisis. In the embassy the major event in an anti-climactic day was the release of an Iranian hostage who had become ill. On Monday the terrorists were noticeably more nervous and a shouted discussion between two British hostages and the police at noon did little to ease the tension. At about 1330, Oan's patience apparently snapped and he shot Abbas Lavasani, one of the embassy staff, in the course of a telephone discussion with the police. This was the turning point.

Any doubts about whether anyone had actually been killed were resolved just after 1900 when the dead body was pushed through the front door of the embassy.

SAS soldiers had visited the scene on the first day of the siege, and thereafter they stood by in an Army barracks some two miles away. The police had obviously tried their best to identify just where the hostages and their captors were and what they were all doing; many

FAR LEFT, TOP: Two SAS troopers, in nondescript civilian clothes, but wearing balaclava helmets to hide their identity, stand-by ready to give covering fire from the outside wall of the Iranian Embassy. They are holding 9mm Browning pistols, but (unseen in this picture) there are rifles, tear-gas launchers and other weapons at their feet.

FAR LEFT: BELOW: A black-clad SAS man climbs over the balcony at the front of the Iranian embassy. He is armed with a Heckler & Koch 9mm MP5 sub-machine gun. His progress was covered by another squad at street-level (picture above). The entire external operation was conducted under the watchful gaze of TV cameras, which broadcast these events live.

LEFT: Moments before the blasting of the front windows, two SAS men prepare to charge through and rescue the hostages. The success of this operation not only gave a boost to the already high reputation of the SAS, but also served notice to terrorists that the British would not lightly submit to hostage-taking operations, and there have been no more incidents in the UK since.

ABOVE: Witnessed on television screens around the world, the siege at the Iranian Embassy in London ended abruptly on May 5 1980. In a rescue operation lasting just a few minutes, the SAS stormed the building, rescued every hostage and killed five out of six terrorists.

highly classified surveillance devices were used. The SAS were therefore as ready as it was possible to be in the circumstances when, in accordance with British legal practice, the police formally asked the military to deal with the situation.

THE RESCUE

The plan was to use just 12 men in three teams of the customary four-man SAS groups; two teams were to take the rear, descending by rope from the roof, one team to reach the ground and the second the first-floor balcony. Both teams would then break in using either frame-charges or brute force. Team three was to be at the front, crossing from a balcony at No. 15 Princes Gate to No. 16. Once inside all three teams were to rush to reach the hostages before they could be harmed.

Everything that could be done to heighten the impact of the attack was done. The 12 SAS men were dressed from head to foot in black, even including rubber anti-gas respirators, and looked extremely menacing. They would gain entrance using 4ft x 2ft (1.2 x 0.6m) frame-charges, followed by stun grenades ("flashbangs"). Teargas would also be used. The combination of explosions, noise, smoke, speed of action, and the appearance of the men was intended to strike confusion and dread into the minds of the terrorists – and it succeeded brilliantly.

The SAS men had, naturally, pored over the plans of the 50-room building in minute detail and had also spent many hours studying the photographs of the hostages. But, in the end –as every soldier knows – all the training and planning have to be translated into action.

At 1926 hours precisely the men of the rear attack force stepped over the edge of the roof and abseiled down. The first two went down each rope successfully, but one of the third pair became stuck, a hazard known to abseilers everywhere. In the front, SAS men appeared on the balcony of No. 15 and climbed over to the embassy, giving the world's press and the public an image which will last for years.

Simultaneously, police spoke to the terrorists on the telephone and distracted their attention at the critical moment the SAS burst in. Stun grenades exploded, lights went out, and all was noise and apparent confusion. Some parts of the embassy caught fire and the SAS man hanging on the rope at the rear was cut free and dropped onto a balcony - a risk preferable to that of being roasted alive.

The SAS men swept through the embassy. Two terrorists were quickly shot and killed. One started shooting the hostages in an upstairs room, but stopped after causing a few wounds. Within minutes five of the six gunmen were dead, with the sixth sheltering among the newly freed hostages. All survivors were rushed downstairs into the garden, where the remaining terrorist was identified and arrested.

The entire operation took eleven minutes from start to finish. While the SAS is the last organization in the world to seek out publicity, its well-heralded assault had at least two effects: first, it reinforced the message to potential terrorists that their activities could be dealt with in a severe, if effective, manner; and, secondly, it gave the British public a healthy shot of national pride.

BELOW: As flames pour out of a window, a civilian makes his escape along the balconies, moments after being released from captivity by the SAS. One of the primary aims of the operation was to reach the hostages before they could be harmed and in this it succeeded brilliantly, since although the terrorists shot a few, none was seriously wounded.

WIRELESS RIDGE

ABOVE: Three wounded paras show the ugly reality of war: one is receiving a transfusion (right); the second, with a head wound, lies on the rocks (center), and the third lies on the ground, tended by his comrades (left). As this picture was taken an incoming artillery shell had just been heard and the wounded man on the left breathed his last.

RIGHT: It took British forces 10 hours to secure Wireless Ridge, which made the position of the remaining Argentine force in Port Stanley untenable and the commander, General Menendez, surrendered later that day.

THE BATTALION ATTACK by the British 2nd Battalion, The Parachute Regiment (2 Para), on Wireless Ridge, on June 13-14 during the Falklands War in 1982, is an excellent example of an action by a highly trained, fit and experienced infantry unit. This action is of particular interest because 2 Para was the only battalion in the Falklands War to carry out two battalion attacks, and thus the only one to be able to put into practice the lessons learned, in their case at high cost, at Goose Green on May 28.

On June 11, 2 Para was moved by helicopter from Fitzroy on the south coast to a lying-up position west of Mount Kent. At 2300 hours the battalion set off on foot to an assembly area on a hill to the north of Mount Kent, ready to support either 3 Para in their attack on Mount Longdon or 45 Commando Royal Marines, whose mission was to take the position known as Two Sisters. Both attacks were successful, leaving 3 Para, 45 Commando and 42 Commando firmly established.

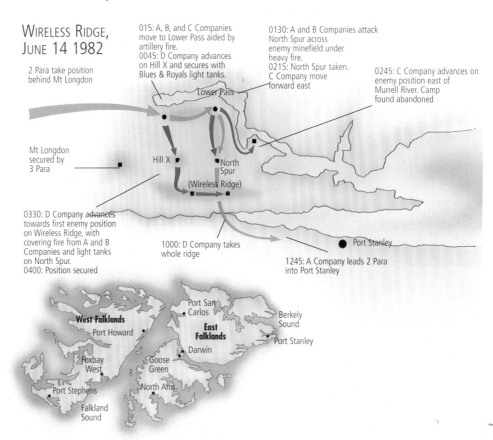

WIRELESS RIDGE, JUNE 14 1982

2 Para take position behind Mt Longdon

015: A, B, and C Companies move to Lower Pass aided by artillery fire.
0045: D Company advances on Hill X and secures with Blues & Royals light tanks.

0130: A and B Companies attack North Spur across enemy minefield under heavy fire.
0215: North Spur taken. C Company move forward east

0245: C Company advances on enemy position east of Murrell River. Camp found abandoned

Lower Pass

Mt Longdon secured by 3 Para

Hill X

North Spur

(Wireless Ridge)

0330: D Company advances towards first enemy position on Wireless Ridge, with covering fire from A and B Companies and light tanks on North Spur.
0400: Position secured

1000: D Company takes whole ridge

Port Stanley

1245: A Company leads 2 Para into Port Stanley

West Falklands

Port Howard

Foxbay West

Port Stephens

Falkland Sound

Port San Carlos

East Falklands

Darwin

Goose Green

North Arm

Berkely Sound

Port Stanley

On June 12, 2 Para moved forward some 9 miles (15km), skirting Mount Longdon on its north-western side, to an assembly area in the lee of a steep escarpment which offered some cover from the sporadic artillery shelling. Orders were received in mid-afternoon for an attack on Wireless Ridge that night, but this was later postponed to the following night.

On June 13 Argentinian Skyhawk attack aircraft flew in low from the west. Intense fire from the ground prevented this attack from being pressed home, but a number of moves in preparation for the forthcoming British battalion action were delayed, especially the registration of targets by the artillery and mortars.

At Goose Green 2 Para had been very short of fire support. In this battle, however, they were to have two batteries of 105mm light guns in direct support, the mortars of both 2 and 3 Para, naval gunfire support from ships within range, as well as the battalion's own machine gun and MILAN anti-tank missile platoons. Last, but by no means least, a troop of Scimitar (1x30mm cannon) and two Scorpion (1x76mm gun) light tanks of The Blues and Royals were an integral part of 2 Para's battle plan.

The battalion moved out at last light (2030 hours local). As they moved to the forming-up places (where the troops shake out into battle formations), the sort of report a commanding officer dreads was received: Intelligence had just discovered a minefield in front of A and B Companies' objective. At this stage, however, there was no alternative but to go ahead.

The artillery supporting fire started at 0015 hours on June 14 and D Company crossed the start-line at 0045 hours. D Company reached its first objective with little trouble, finding that the enemy had withdrawn, leaving a few dead in their slit trenches. While D Company reorganized, enemy 155mm airburst fire began to fall on their position. Meanwhile, A and B Companies began their advance, B Company through the minefield.

Some sporadic fire came from a few trenches, but was quickly silenced, and 17 Argentine prisoners were taken and a number killed in this phase of the battle - the remainder fled. Several radios (still switched on), telephones and a mass of cable suggested that the position had included a battalion headquarters. As A and B Companies started to dig in, accurate and fairly intense enemy artillery bombardment began, which was to continue for some nine hours.

Following the success of A and B Companies, D Company crossed its second start line at the west end of the main ridge, while the light tanks and the machine guns moved to a

ABOVE: A confused, frightened, and hungry Argentinean conscript is led away by a hardened British regular paratrooper. The Argentinean wears a British jersey, probably looted from the stock held in the barracks at Moody Brook, just below Wireless Ridge, which was occupied by the Royal Marines garrison prior to the Argentine invasion.

LEFT: A paratroop company is briefed prior to the Wireless Ridge assault, using a quickly constructed ground model. Such careful and detailed briefings were (and remain) essential to the success of military operations.

ABOVE: A captured and blindfolded Argentine officer is led away for interrogation by Royal Marines. The British marines and paras were tough, fit, well-trained, and very aggressive, which enabled them to overcome numerically superior Argentine forces in every one of the engagements during the brief, hard fought, and bloody 1981 Falklands War.

flank to give covering fire. The ridge itself was a long spine broken in the middle, with each section some 900 yards (300m) in length. The first feature was taken unopposed and there was then a short delay while the British artillery readjusted to its targets for the next phase. During this time the second feature was kept under heavy fire by the light tanks, the machine guns and the MILAN missile being used in a direct-fire artillery role!

Just as the attack was about to start, the commanding officer received a new piece of intelligence, that instead of one enemy company at the other end of the ridge there were two! This was hardly likely to impress the Paras who by this stage of the campaign had established a considerable moral ascendency over the Argentines, but in the early minutes of this final phase of the battle D Company received some casualties as the enemy fought back with unexpected vigor, withdrawing one bunker at a time. As the Paras poured onto the position, however, the enemy suddenly broke and ran, being continuously harassed off the position by the machine guns of the British Scorpions and Scimitars, and chased by the exhilarated Paras.

As D Company began to reorganize they, too, came under artillery fire, as well as remarkably effective small arms fire from Tumbledown Mountain and Mount William to the south, which had not yet been captured by 5 Infantry Brigade. The enemy could be heard trying to regroup in the darkness below the ridge, and to the south in the area of Moody Brook.

At daybreak a rather brave, but somewhat pathetic enemy counterattack developed from the area of Moody Brook, which seems to have been some sort of final gesture. It petered out under a hail of artillery, small arms and machine gun fire.

This seems to have been the signal to many Argentines that the game was up, and shortly afterwards ever-increasing numbers of disheartened and disillusioned Argentine soldiers were observed streaming off Mount William, Tumbledown and Sapper Hill to seek short-lived refuge in Port Stanley.

A and B Companies of 2 Para were now brought forward onto Wireless Ridge, and the battalion's night attack was successfully concluded. The Paras had lost three dead and 11 wounded. Lack of time and opportunity precluded counting the Argentine casualties, but it has been estimated that, of an original strength of some 500, up to 100 may have been killed, 17 were captured, and the remainder fled.

The taking of Wireless Ridge illustrates the standards achieved by a crack unit. In this night battle, it defeated a force of equal strength, which was well prepared and dug-in and occupied a dominant feature. No. 2 Para had learned the lessons of Goose Green well. They had also given the lie to the allegation that parachute units lack "staying power." It is, perhaps, unfortunate that the battle of Goose Green, deservedly famous, has overshadowed this later minor classic at Wireless Ridge.

RIGHT: The key to tactical success in the advance across East Falklands lay in taking and retaining the high ground, which was usually, as here, capped with granite outcrops. As with a surprising number of other troops in the war, one of these smiling and relaxed paras has managed to carry a Union flag throughout the campaign and is now displaying it as a sign of victory.

RESCUE IN GRENADA

LEFT: Officers and men of the US 82nd Airborne Division move out on patrol from Port Salines airfield in Grenada. President Reagan saw the island as "a Soviet-Cuban colony being readied as a major military bastion to export and undermine democracy."

BELOW LEFT: Grenada lies just off the South American coast. President Reagan was determined that it would not become another Cuba. The six-member organization of east Caribbean States voted to intervene with force, although, unsurprisingly, Grenada abstained.

BELOW: The island of Grenada, showing the entry points used by the US paratroops, marines and SEALs in Operation Urgent Fury on October 25 1983. The main reason for the attack was the Port Salines airfield, which was being built by Cuban engineers.

FOLLOWING THE END of the Vietnam War, American forces tried to keep a low profile on the international scene. Two rescue operations were attempted in efforts to secure the release of the crew of the Mayaguez and the Iranian embassy hostages. US troops also took part in various peacekeeping forces such as those in the Sinai and in Beirut. However, major use of force was eschewed for both international and domestic reasons.

But in October 1983 President Ronald Reagan, at the request of the six-member Organization of Eastern Caribbean States, sent troops to the island of Grenada "to restore peace, order and respect for human rights; to evacuate those who wish to leave; and to help the Grenadians re-establish governmental institutions." On October 19, Grenada's Prime Minister, Maurice Bishop, and several Cabinet members and labor leaders had been murdered by former military associates. A 16-man Revolutionary Military Council, headed by Army Chief General Hudson Austin and Deputy Prime Minister Bernard Coard, took power. The council imposed a 24-hour curfew, warning that violators would be shot on sight, and closed the Port Salines airfield.

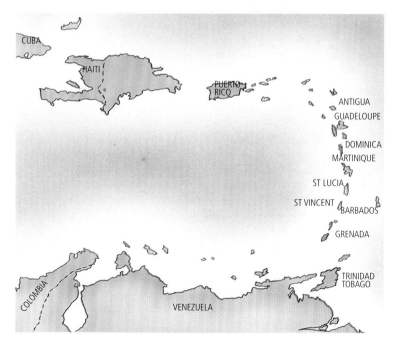

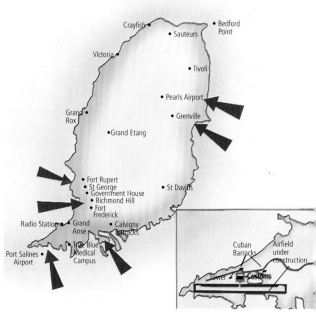

US Intelligence reported Soviet/Cuban backing for the revolutionary regime, with Cubans establishing new fortifications, arms caches and military communications on the island. President Reagan viewed Grenada as "a Soviet-Cuban colony being readied as a major military bastion to export and undermine democracy." Of particular concern was the position of some 1,000 US citizens, especially the 600-odd young Americans at the True Blue Medical School near the Port Salines airfield. The prospect of these youngsters being held hostage by the Marxist government was serious and would have provided a far worse crisis than even that of the Iranian embassy staff. For their part, the Eastern Caribbean States saw the violence and disintegration of political institutions on the island as an unprecedented threat to peace and security in the region.

ABOVE: MC-130E Hercules dropped the first sticks of US Rangers on the morning of October 25 1983. After a short but fierce battle for the airport and control tower (on hill top), aircraft were able to land. This MC-130E stands ready for cargo for the homeward flight.

BELOW: A marine escorts one of 1,100 captured Cuban soldiers into an interrogation center. The US confirmed that the Soviets and Cubans were endeavoring (as Reagan had said) to turn the island into a dangerous military base.

Information on the resisting troops and their disposition in Grenada was fairly sparse, but the US forces had three immediate objectives within the overall mission of capturing the island and restoring a democratic government. These three tasks were the freeing of the 600 medical students, the release of the governor (Sir Paul Scoones) and the defeat of the Cuban troops on the island.

US Navy SEALs were responsible for capturing the governor's residence, and Marines for the Pearls Airport on the island's east coast. The crucial task was, however, the taking of Port Salines airfield, which was being constructed and guarded by Cubans. This task was given to the Rangers.

EXECUTION

The assault by the 24th Marine Amphibious Unit on Pearls Airport began at 0500 hours (local) on October 25, while H-hour for the Rangers was 0536. This was the first major combat operation for the two participating Ranger units - the Fort Stewart, Georgia-based 1st Ranger Battalion, and the Fort Lewis, Washington-based 2nd. The Rangers left the staging airfield on Barbados in the early hours aboard MC-130E Hercules aircraft of 8th Special Operations Squadron, 1st Special Operations Wing, USAF, based at Hurlburt Field in Florida. (The lead planes carried members of the 1st Battalion, with the 2nd following closely behind.) These aircraft were accompanied by AC-130 Hercules gunships (the famous "Spectres" of the Vietnam War) of 16th Special Operations Squadron.

As they came in over Port Salines, searchlights were suddenly switched on, which quickly found the lumbering C-130s and enabled the anti-aircraft guns to open up on the aircraft and descending parachutists. The AC-130s were quickly called into action and silenced most of the Cuban guns. Among the lead elements in the assault was a 12-man team from the 317th Tactical Airlift Wing responsible for combat control of the drop, and these were quickly inside the air traffic control building.

On the ground, the Rangers, told to expect some 500 Cubans (350 "workers" and a "small" military advisory team) found themselves under attack from some 600 well armed professional soldiers. The Cubans were armed with mortars and machine guns, and had at least six armored personnel carriers. A brisk battle developed in which the Rangers quickly gained the upper hand, and by 0700 they were in complete control. The runway was cleared of obstacles (boulders, vehicles, pipes) and at 0715 the first C-130 of the second wave was able to land with reinforcements.

The Rangers then moved out, heading for the medical campus; brushing aside snipers and scattered resistance, they reached their objective by 0830 hours and were greeted by some very relieved students. The campus was secured by 0850, although the other medical school at Grand Anse was not liberated until the following day.

ASSESSMENT

The liberation effort accomplished what it set out to do. The booty of the effort confirmed US intelligence reports that the USSR and Cuba were turning Grenada into a military base in the Western hemisphere. The long-term implications of this were that the island could eventually have become a staging area for the subversion of nearby countries; it would also have considerable value as a transit point for troops and supplies moving from Cuba to Africa and from Europe and Libya to Central America.

Captured documents indicated that the USSR and North Korea, as well as Cuba, had made secret treaties with the Grenada Revolutionary Military Council, and had agreed to provide the leadership with more than $37.8 million in artillery, anti-aircraft weapons, armored personnel carriers, small arms, and ammunition. The Soviet Union had tried hard to keep these arrangements secret. In fact, it wasn't until 18 months after the arms shipments began that they established diplomatic ties with Grenada.

The convincing list of documents found in the aftermath of Grenada included a roster of Grenada's militia; a summary of Political Bureau meetings; a top-secret report from a Grenadian double agent who attempted to infiltrate the CIA operation in Barbados; rosters and correspondence concerning the training of Grenadian troops in the USSR, Cuba and Vietnam; and a training agreement between Grenada and Nicaragua. In all, there was more than enough documentary evidence to still the voices of those who criticized the operation from a political standpoint. From yet another standpoint, the military one, it was a success - and one in which US special forces acquitted themselves well.

ABOVE: Men of 82nd Airborne Division stand watch on a hilltop in Grenada, surrounded by the equipment of their comrades who have gone out on patrol.

BELOW: One of the justifications for the operation was the safety of 600-odd young Americans at the "True Blue Medical School," which was located near Port Salines airfield. In the event, none was harmed and here some of them, happy and smiling, make their way to the waiting aircraft, which will take them back to the United States of America.

ACHILLE LAURO INCIDENT

THE SAGA OF THE ACHILLE LAURO began when four Palestinian guerrillas, armed with Soviet-made machine guns and brandishing hand grenades, took 80 passengers and 340 crewmembers hostage aboard the Italian cruise liner in October 1985. They threatened to kill the passengers, beginning with the Americans, then moving on to Jews and British citizens, if their demands for the release of 50 Palestinians held in Israel were not met.

What followed were 51 hours of threats and violence. Walls and ceilings were sprayed with bullets. The terrorists pulled pins from grenades and tossed them in the air. Gasoline bombs were placed in various parts of the liner. Ultimately, the grisly scenario led to the execution of Leon Klinghoffer, a 69-year-old handicapped American, murdered in his wheelchair.

ABOVE: Aging liner Achille Lauro was seized by four Palestinian terrorists in October 1985. One man, Leon Klinghoffer, an American Jew, was murdered during the incident, with the remainder being released when the ship arrived off Port Said, where the seajackers passed into Egyptian custody.

As these events were unfolding, the *Achille Lauro* wandered along the north coast of Africa seeking haven. Ultimately, the cruise liner anchored off Port Said, Egypt, and the "seajackers" - after negotiations with Palestinian, Italian, and Egyptian officials - went ashore.

Americans, predictably, were demanding that the terrorists be brought to justice, and Egyptian President Hosni Mubarak announced they had already left Egypt allegedly under terms of an agreement struck before the murder of Klinghoffer was known. US intelligence, however, indicated that the four hijackers were still in Egypt and that neither that country nor the PLO had quite figured out what to do with them. This delay provided the United States with an opportunity to shape a plan to help deal with the emerging situation.

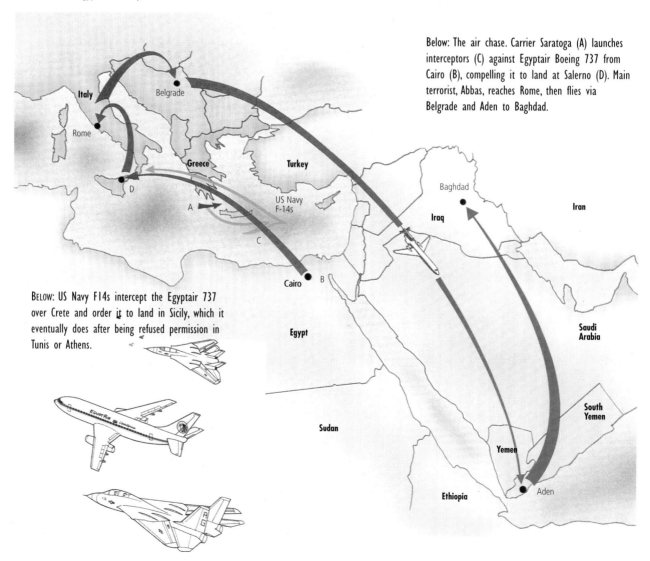

Below: The air chase. Carrier Saratoga (A) launches interceptors (C) against Egyptair Boeing 737 from Cairo (B), compelling it to land at Salerno (D). Main terrorist, Abbas, reaches Rome, then flies via Belgrade and Aden to Baghdad.

BELOW: US Navy F14s intercept the Egyptair 737 over Crete and order it to land in Sicily, which it eventually does after being refused permission in Tunis or Athens.

EXECUTION

The US Navy aircraft carrier USS *Saratoga* was cruising off Albania and was called into action just two hours before the mission. The Italian government, later to play a key role in dealing with the terrorists, was not notified until after the mission had begun,

The plan involved calling in the *Saratoga's* aircraft to surprise the terrorists if they boarded an airliner to fly over the Mediterranean, and force the aircraft to land in Sicily. Intelligence sources had in fact confirmed that the hijackers were still in Egypt, but that they planned to fly to Algiers aboard an Egyptair Boeing 737. Just 45 minutes after the 737 took off from Al Maza Air Base, northeast of Cairo, it was intercepted.

Awaiting it were E-2C Hawkeye radar aircraft, F-14 Tomcat fighters, and EA-6B Prowler electronic warfare aircraft. At first, the F-14s trailed the 737 with no lights on and with cockpits darkened. When they prepared to intercept, they turned on their lights and surrounded the airliner.

The Egyptair pilot desperately tried to radio Cairo for instructions, but his communications had been jammed by the EA-6B aircraft. The airline pilot, recognizing his position, eventually agreed to follow American orders.

The formation approached Sigonella Air Base, a NATO installation on Sicily's densely populated eastern coast. However, Italian air traffic controllers refused the 737 permission to enter their airspace. It was only after the Egyptian pilot declared an in-flight emergency that clearance was finally received.

One F-14 led the 737 into Sigonella while three others stayed in formation up to the traffic pattern. Following the lead F-14, the 737 taxied to an isolated corner of the base, where it was immediately surrounded by Italian carabinieri. Its passengers were taken into custody.

Not only were the four hijackers aboard, but also Abul Abbas, a high-ranking aide to PLO Chairman Yasir Arafat. Abbas was not only the suspected mastermind behind the *Achille Lauro* incident, but the person who was instrumental in getting the terrorists off the liner when it finally docked in Egypt. Abbas later slipped out of Italy before he could be prosecuted. Because an American citizen was killed during the "seajacking," US chagrin at the escape of Abbas was great, creating diplomatic difficulties between Italy and the United States.

ASSESSMENT

In the eyes of many observers, the operation demonstrated that high technology can indeed work well in a counter-terrorist situation. It was considered a triumph of electronics and communications carried out on short notice under cover of darkness and at high speeds.

To this day, a definitive account of all the high tech that went into the operation has not been made available. However, it worked and the United States clearly demonstrated that it had the resolve to back its threats to strike back at terrorists who attacked American citizens. What really counted was that terrorists who took the law into their own hands for whatever motive were ultimately brought before the bar of justice.

ABOVE: In an Italian courtroom, Palestinian terrorist, Abdel Atif Fatyer, one of the four men accused of the "seajacking" of the Italian cruise liner, *Achille Lauro,* listens attentively from inside his cage. No further seajackings have followed the "*Achille Lauro* affair."

LEFT: *Achille Lauro* under guard following the "seajacking."

OPERATION DESERT STRIKE

OPERATION DESERT STRIKE, the 1991 Coalition war against Iraq, saw the largest concentration of international special forces in any combat. Australian and New Zealand provided a combined ANZAC SAS Squadron (133 men), while the French contingent included elements of the Foreign Legion and 6th Parachute Division. The UK sent almost the entire SAS Regiment to Saudi Arabia: some 700 men of A, B, and D Squadrons, plus 15 reservist volunteers from R Squadron; indeed, the only element omitted was G Squadron, which was committed to other operations and on counter-terrorist stand-by in the UK. Also in the Gulf were a squadron of the Royal Marine SBS and RAF special operations aircrew.

By far the largest contribution came from the United States, under the aegis of Special Operations Command (SOCOM) and collectively forming the Joint Special Operations Task Force (JSOTF). The naval

ABOVE: The sky above Tel Aviv as Iraqi Scud missiles attacked the Israeli city, a deliberate attempt by Saddam Hussein to bring Israel into the war. This would have destabilized the Coalition, as several Arab contingents would have withdrawn rather than fight on the same side as the Israelis. Coalition special operations forces played a key role in reducing the Scud threat.

element was commanded by Naval SPECWARGRU (special war group) ONE and included SEAL Teams !, 2, 3, 4, 5, and 8; SDV (special diver) Teams 1 and 2; and SPECBOATU (special boat units) 11, 12, 13, and 20. Largest in terms of numbers was the US Army contribution which comprised: Delta, 1st Special Forces Group, 5th Special Forces Group, and 160th Special Operations Aviation Regiment (SOAR). There were also large elements from 82nd and 101st Airborne Divisions. The US Air Force also deployed large special warfare elements to the Gulf, under the command of 1st Special Operations Wing (1 SOW), which comprised five "special operations squadrons" (SOS): 8th SOS - MC-130E Combat Talon; 9th SOS - HC-130H Combat Shadow tankers; 16th SOS - AC-130H Spectre gunships; 20th SOS - MH-53J Pave Low helicopters; and 55th SOS - MH-60 Pave low helicopters. The US Marine Corps provided reconnaissance specialists.

LAND MISSIONS

The first missions tentatively assigned to both the SAS and Delta were to rescue their national hostages, who had been grabbed by the Iraqis at the outbreak of conflict. The hostages were, however, released before any such operation could be mounted. Then, just before the ground war started, the British commander in the Gulf, General de la Billiére,

RIGHT: The areas deep inside Iraq that were the main zones of activity of the SAS and Delta units as they attacked and reported on Scud missile movements and major supply routes used by Iraqi convoys.

The special forces units destroyed some mobile Scuds and Iraqi lines of communications, laser targeted the missiles or "talked down" air attacks on them, and also tied up Iraqi forces in western Iraq, denying their use against main Coalition forces elsewhere.

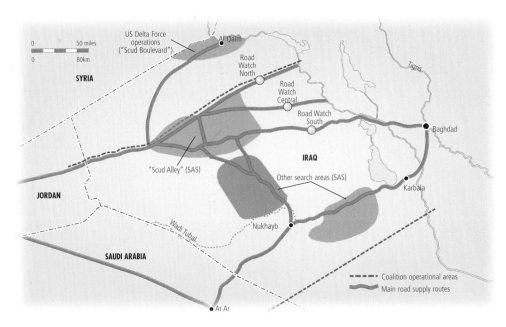

obtained General Schwarzkopf's agreement to deploy special forces behind the Iraqi front line with the aim of distracting the enemy's attention from the forthcoming operations, and two squadrons of SAS duly deployed on January 20 1991. On the 24th, however, their mission was abruptly changed to the anti-Scud role, which it remained for the remainder of the war, and in which they were joined by the remainder of the SAS deployed to the Gulf.

Western intelligence staffs knew that Iraq had received some 820 Soviet R-17 missiles (NATO = "Scud-B") in the early 1980s, of which some 200 missiles were launched against Iran in 1988. By 1990, Iraq had developed a modified version, the al-Hussein, which had greater range, but at the expense of reduced payload (see box). Some 400 of these missiles were built, which, in December 1990 were located in 28 static sites and on some 36 Russian-built 8-wheeled mobile launchers.

Iraq had demonstrated a willingness to use poison gas in artillery shells against both the Iranians and the Kurds, and there was therefore a serious possibility that they had managed to develop chemical warheads for the al-Hussein. The situation became more acute in December 1990, when Saddam launched several demonstration missiles.

Despite this evidence, the threat they posed - particularly psychological - was still not fully appreciated until Iraqi Scuds actually started to impact on targets in Israel on January 18 1991. As a result, Coalition military commanders were suddenly forced to undertake a search-and-destroy battle against the Scud launch sites in order to prevent Israel entering the war in retaliation, which would almost certainly have resulted in most of the Arab contingents leaving the Coalition. The only troops in a position to do this were the elite forces of the British Special Air Service (SAS) and those of US JSOTF, including Delta.

The energetic campaign waged by British and US special forces drove the mobile Scud launchers back out of range of Israel, although sporadic launches took place until the end of the war. Both the SAS and Delta carried out numerous direct attacks on Iraqi Scud sites, but their main task was to locate and report potential targets to Coalition air forces. Initially, the air-tasking system was too slow, with aircraft arriving long after the Scud launchers had departed, but rapid changes, including "cab-ranks" of airborne ground-attack aircraft ready for immediate response, quickly overcame this. In clear daylight the ground troops "talked" aircraft down onto their targets, while at night or against camouflaged targets they used laser

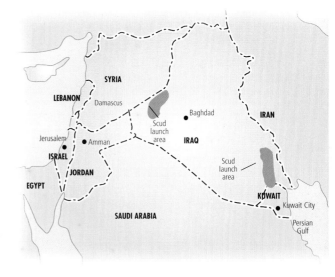

ABOVE: The highly volatile Gulf region showing (shaded) the major concentration of Iraqi Scud sites. A major role of the SAS and Delta was to force Saddam's Scuds to operate far enough away from Iraq's western border so that Israeli cities would be out of range of the missiles.

BELOW: Israeli troops and civil defense personnel view the crater left by an Iraqi Scud. The great fear was that these missiles would be fitted with either chemical or biological warheads but, despite the capability, this was one step Saddam Hussein did not take.

ABOVE: In a scene reminiscent of the original SAS operating in the Western Desert during World War II, a Gulf War SAS Scud-hunting patrol poses for the camera.

BELOW: Based on a US Intelligence map, this shows the Iraqi Air Force's main operating bases (red), dispersal airfields (blue), and the Scud launch areas (shaded).

SYRIA

Scud launch area

IRAN

JORDAN

IRAQ

Scud launch area

KUWAIT

SAUDI ARABIA

● Dispersal airfields
● ○ Main operating bases

target designators.

The SAS's operational area was around Iraq's H-2 airfield, and was designated the "southern Scud Box," although it was more popularly known as "Scud Alley." This was an area some 20 miles (32km) long by 17 miles (26km) wide (340sq miles/830sq km). Into this were placed three 8-man patrols on road watch, staking out the MSRs (Main Supply Routes) to watch for and report on movement by SCUD convoys. The US Joint Special Operations Task Force (JSOTF) arrived in early February and comprised Delta Force, SEALs, and 160th Special Operations Aviation Regiment (SOAR), equipped with MH-60 Black Hawks and MH-47E Chinooks. The JSOTF operated around Al Qaim, in the "northern Scud box," nicknamed "Scud Boulevard."

A second target was the Iraqi fiberglass communications cable system, which had recently been installed and which consisted of one or more cables buried up to 30ft (10m) below the surface. These were used because they provided greater security than microwave systems, since buried cables could not be located, intercepted or destroyed - or so the Iraqis thought.

The weakness was that, for technical reasons, repeaters were required at frequent intervals, which were located at the bottom of manholes and it was these that were found and destroyed by SBS and SAS patrols.

Both Americans and British made use of specialized light vehicles. Delta used Fast Attack Vehicles (FAV) while the British deployed four mobile groups, each consisting of eight Land Rover 110s, a Unimog truck carrying fuel, supplies, and spares, and several motor-cycles. Typical vehicle armament included Browning 0.5 cal machine guns, M19 40mm grenade launchers, and 7.62mm GPMGs, but each group also carried a number of 66mm LAW (light anti-tank weapon) and Milan ATGW (anti-tank guided weapon). Operating so many vehicles gave rise to a need for resupply and repair, so the SAS produced a resupply convoy of some 12 4-ton trucks which was installed in a wadi some 75 miles (120km) inside Iraqi territory, where it carried out maintenance and repairs over a 5-day period and then drove back to Coalition territory without incurring a single loss.

AIR MISSIONS

The majority of special operations air support was provided by the USA and the tasks included transporting and supporting SF teams deployed inside Iraqi territory. This was the task of MH-53Js, which were also able to use their night vision devices to look for Scuds. 1st SOW was also responsible for combat rescue

SUBJECT:
Letter of Commendation for
22d Special Air Service (SAS) Regiment

1. I wish to officially commend the 22d Special Air Service (SAS) Regiment for their totally outstanding performance of military operations during Operation Desert Storm.

2. Shortly after the initiation of the strategic air campaign, it became apparent that the Coalition forces would be unable to eliminate Iraq's firing of Scud missiles from western Iraq into Israel. The continued firing of Scuds on Israel carried with it enormous unfavorable political ramifications and could, in fact, have resulted in the dismantling of the carefully crafted Coalition. Such a dismantling would have adversely affected in ways difficult to measure the ultimate outcome of the military campaign. It became apparent that the only way that the Coalition could succeed in reducing these Scud launches was by physically placing military forces on the ground in the vicinity of the western launch sites. At that time, the majority of available Coalition forces were committed to the forthcoming military campaign in the eastern portion of the theater of operations. Further, none of these forces possessed the requisite skills and abilities required to conduct such a dangerous operation. The only force deemed qualified for this critical mission was the 22d Special Air Service (SAS) Regiment.

3. From the first day they were assigned their mission until the last day of the conflict, the performance of 22d Special Air Service (SAS) Regiment was courageous and highly professional. The area in which they were committed proved to contain far more numerous enemy forces than had been predicted by every intelligence estimate, the terrain was much more difficult than expected, and the weather conditions were unseasonably brutal. Despite these hazards, in a very short period of time the 22d Special Air Service (SAS) Regiment was successful in totally denying the central corridor of western Iraq to Iraqi Scud units. The result was that the principal areas used by the Iraqis to fire Scuds on Tel Aviv were no longer available to them. They were required to move their Scud missile firing forces to the northwest portion of Iraq and from that location the firing of Scud missiles was essentially militarily ineffective.

4. When it became necessary to introduce United States Special Operations Forces into the area to attempt to close down the northwest Scud areas, the 22d Special Air Service (SAS) Regiment provided invaluable assistance to the U.S. forces. They took every possible measure to ensure the U.S. forces were thoroughly briefed and were able to profit from the valuable lessons that had been learned by earlier SAS deployments into western Iraq. I am completely convinced that had the U.S. forces not received these thorough indoctrinations by SAS personnel U.S. forces would have suffered a much higher rate of casualties than was ultimately the case. Further, the SAS and U.S. joint forces immediately merged into a combined fighting force where the synergetic effort of these fine units ultimately caused the enemy to be convinced that they were facing forces in western Iraq that were more than ten-fold the size of those they were actually facing. As a result, large numbers of enemy forces that might otherwise have been deployed in the eastern theater were tied down in western Iraq.

5. The performance of the 22d Special Air Service (SAS) Regiment during Operation Desert Storm was in the highest traditions of the professional military service and in keeping with the proud history and tradition that has been established by that regiment. Please ensure that this commendation receives appropriate attention and is passed on to the unit and its members.

H. Norman Schwarzkopf
General, US Army
Commander in Chief

ABOVE: General Schwarzkopf's acknowledgement of the role played by the SAS in the Gulf War. The US general was at first reluctant to employ special operations forces, but was persuaded by British General De La Billiere — himself an ex-SAS man — that they could be vital, first in reconnaissance and later in Scud-hunting/busting.

and extracted several downed aircrew before the Iraqis could capture them.

One unusual mission was performed by the MC-130 Combat Talons, which dropped a number of BLU-82 "Daisy Cutter" fuel/air bombs. These devices, originally developed during the Vietnam War, contained 6.7 tons (15,000lb/6,804kg) of high explosive and were dropped from the tail ramp at a height of some 6,000ft (1,800m), achieving an accuracy of approximately 50ft (15m). The effect of the enormous explosion was dramatic: the noise was stupefying and the blast caused death up to 3 miles (5km) distant. Indeed, some observers were under the impression that tactical nuclear weapons were being used. British air support for special forces came from RAF Chinook, Army Lynx, and naval Sea King helicopters.

LOSSES

Both American and British special forces incurred losses, some due to Iraqi action, others to the wild terrain and harsh weather. An 8-man SAS team, for example, was detected and pursued by Iraqi troops, during which four men died. The worst US losses occurred on February 21, when an MH-60 helicopter hit a sand-dune in bad visibility, killing all seven occupants: four aircrew and three from Delta. In addition, a USAF AC-130 of 16th SOS was shot down by Iraqi ground fire during the battle to retake the town of Khafji; all 14 aboard were killed.

BELOW: After the war, UN arms inspectors prepare Russian-made MAZ 8x8 trucks for destruction. These Scud launchers proved highly effective, being very mobile, fast and having good off-road capability. Their missiles posed a threat to the Coalition out of all proportion to their numbers.

RUSSIAN R-17/IRAQI AL HUSSEIN MISSILES		
	R-17 SCUD-B	AL HUSSEIN
COUNTRY OF MANUFACTURE	Soviet Union	Iraq
DIMENSIONS		
Length	36.6ft (11.16m)	40.0ft (12.20m)
Body diameter	2.9ft (0.88m)	2.9ft (0.88m)
Launch weight	14,043lb (6,370kg)	15,432lb (7,000kg)
WARHEAD		
Type	HE, chemical, nuclear	HE, chemical
Max weight	2,171lb (985kg)	1,102lb (500kg)
PERFORMANCE		
Maximum range	186 miles (300km)	404 miles (650km)
Accuracy (circular error probable)	492yd (450m)	1,094yd (1km)
Propulsion	Liquid	Liquid
Guidance	inertial	inertial

ASSESSMENT

The attacks on the Scud sites was an excellent example of the use of special forces being used in a strategic role. Had they failed and the Iraqi Scud campaign against Israel been more successful, the outcome of the Gulf War might have been quite different.

One of the problems facing the special forces in the Gulf was poor intelligence, at both strategic and tactical levels. At the higher level this included a serious underestimation of the Scud threat and some very misleading analyses of the Iraqi organization and capability. At the lower level the SF were told it would be warm, so they took thin clothing, only to find it was bitterly cold and they suffered accordingly until Arab coats were sent in to them.

THE BATTLE FOR MOGADISHU

LEFT: A US Marine Corps "Hummer" equipped with loudspeakers takes part in an operation in Mogadishu city. Despite such efforts, the gulf between the hi-tech Western forces and the unsophisticated citizens of Somalia proved so wide as to be unbridgeable.

BELOW: Somalia occupies a strategically important position on the "Horn of Africa".

BOTTOM Center of "downtown Mogadishu". Between the main roads is a maze of tiny streets where US SOF became "lost."

OPERATION RESTORE HOPE shows what happens when missions are unclear and special forces are used in roles for which they were not intended. During the 1980s and early 1990s, unending violence in Somalia led to increasing international frustration as aid was seen to be getting into the hands of gunmen and failing to reach the starving Somali people who were regularly seen on TV. This was hardly surprising as Mogadishu port was held hostage by some 1,000 young gunmen belonging to five separate armed groups, each of which charged aid authorities "protection money" and then stole from the very convoys they were being paid to guard.

In late 1992 international indignation peaked and outgoing US President Bush committed American troops to Somalia in what was planned to be a short, sharp operation, to be completed before incoming President Clinton took office in January 1993. US Marines carried out a tactical amphibious landing on the night of December 9 1992 – to be greeted by waiting pressmen equipped with cameras and floodlights.

The US force quickly became bogged down as troops and the Press corps tried – and failed – to understand Somali politics. Military attention – encouraged by the Press – concentrated increasingly on one warlord: "General" Aidid. Then, on June 5 1993, 24 Pakistani troops of the UN force were killed, resulting in UN Resolution 837 ordering the "arrest and detention for prosecution of those responsible." In practical terms, that meant Aidid, but repeated attempts to capture him failed and matters got worse: Pakistani troops fired into a crowd (20 dead); US gunships attacked suspected arms dumps; Italian soldiers were attacked (3 dead); US helicopters attacked Aidid's command post (70 dead); and Somalis attacked pressmen (4 dead). Meanwhile, Aidid, despite an offer of a US$25,000 reward for his capture, led a charmed existence,

The senior UN administrator, retired US Admiral Howe, requested the despatch of US Special Forces. The 400-man "Task Force Ranger," consisting of Rangers and Delta commandos, arrived, its mission to capture Aidid; in other words, a man-hunt. Intelligence passed to Task Force Ranger was poor: in September they mistakenly arrested eight members of a UN-sponsored development program and later they "snatched" a Somali, thought to be Aidid. Not only was he not Aidid, but he was also a well-known US supporter. Then on September 23, a US helicopter was shot down and its crew of three were killed.

Aidid's men carefully observed US special forces tactics in these actions and noted that raids always consisted of an assault by heliborne troops, roping down in two parties: one (Delta) entering the house, the other (Rangers) forming a cordon outside. Meanwhile, helicopters flew overhead, observing, providing

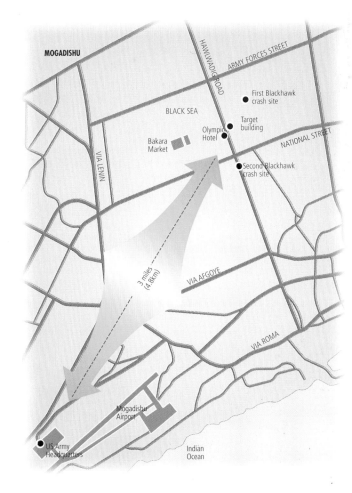

ABOVE: A US Marine supervizes the distribution of urgently needed food to hungry Somalis, which is what Operation Restore Hope was meant to be about. Unfortunately, it all went very seriously wrong and soon the simple survival of the force itself became the primary issue — it is hoped that the lesson has been well learnt.

RIGHT: Italian troops taking part in Restore Hope. Italy was one of the numerous non-US participants in the operation, but as the former colonial power it had more knowledge than most about the country. Their advice to the top command was, however, frequently either deliberately rejected or simply ignored.

covering fire and summoning reinforcements. The Somali gunmen then devised a plan which combined attacks against the helicopters and the use of overwhelming ground forces.

The Somalis were particularly adept at their specialized style of urban warfare. There were a few wide boulevards, but the greater part of Mogadishu was a labyrinth of narrow, twisting alleys, lined on both sides by houses, many with small, high-sided courtyards. The US troops, used to wide open streets and grid patterns of their home towns found these most confusing and frequently got lost. They also found the complex clan structure, which ruled Somali lives, impossible to comprehend, resulting in an enormous gulf between them and the Somalis; the Americans were totally mystified at the way of life and ingratitude of the Somali people, while the latter bitterly resented outside interference in their affairs. On top of all this, Mogadishu was awash with weapons and the Somali clans could mobilize thousands of armed men, women and children in a matter of minutes.

Then US intelligence learnt of a top-level meeting to be held on October 3 1993 in a second-floor room in a building known as the "Aidi house." They were told that Aidid would attend, so a "snatch" was set up, involving AH-1 and OH-6 gunships, UH-60 troop-carrying helicopters, Delta hit squad, Ranger cordon troops and a ground vehicle convoy. Command was exercised by a Delta colonel in a UH-60 command helicopter circling at some 3,000ft (1,000m), with a US Navy P-3 Orion surveillance aircraft about 900ft (300m) above that.

The battle started with Cobra gunships firing TOW missiles into the Aidi house, where some 90 men had assembled, although not Aidid himself. Then 120 Delta men and Rangers roped down beside the smouldering building: the Delta force stormed inside, while Rangers set up the cordon. Inside, many Somalis were already dead. Some managed to escape, but US troops captured 24.

The Somali militia mobilized and the US troops were quickly brought under fire. One militiaman fired an RPG-7 miasile at a low-flying UH-60, destroying the tail rotor, and the aircraft spun into a house then tumbled into an alleyway (Crash 1). Another helicopter arrived and its combat rescue troops roped to the ground, but while hovering it, too, was hit by an RPG and the pilot just managed to return to base.

The US ground convoy of HMMMWVs en route to the Aidi house took casualties from close-range fire, responding with rifles, machine-guns and 0.50in cannon. Whenever the vehicles stopped (usually because they had taken a wrong turning) men jumped out to guard them and took yet more casualties. Despite this, the convoy reached the Aidi house and took the 24 prisoners on board, together with some wounded Delta and Rangers; men were packed inside like sardines, the remainder had to walk.

The convoy was about to move off when new orders were received. Instead of heading out of the city the convoy was to go to Crash 1, which was only three blocks distant, and rescue any survivors who could be reached no other way, while the remaining unwounded troops moved to the crash site on foot. Then news was received that a second

UH-60 was down (Crash 2) and they were ordered to proceed there after rescuing the survivors at Crash 1.

Matters then got worse. In the foot party, cooperation between Rangers and Delta became very strained, although, despite being under constant fire, they eventually reached the crash site and joined in a defensive battle. The vehicle convoy, however, repeatedly took wrong turnings and after 45 minutes ended up back where it had started - in front of the Aidi house. Since he had many wounded and virtually all vehicles were seriously damaged, the convoy commander refused to make another attempt to reach either helicopter crash site and he headed back to base.

Meanwhile, a second vehicle convoy (four HMMWVs; three 5-ton flatbed trucks) was hastily assembled at the base 2 miles (3km) down the beach to rescue the crew of the second downed UH-60. This convoy also came under heavy fire and was forced to turn round and take a different route, but that too was blocked. They then decided to go right around the city but en route they met the original convoy and the two commanders joined up to return to base, abandoning the rescue of the troops in the city.

By nightfall there were some 90-odd men in and around Crash Site 1, scattered between various buildings. A UH-60 had dropped some medical supplies and ammunition, but their situation was desperate. At this point it was decided to commit the UN Quick Reaction Force (QRF). The force that was cobbled together comprised some 300 men from US 10th Mountain Division, with some Rangers and Delta men, desperately eager to rescue their comrades. Multinational contributions including four Pakistani tanks and 28 Malaysian armored personnel carriers, the latter painted UN white. The convoy rolled at 2320 and made its way slowly into the city, drawing heavy fire and encountering several roadblocks. However, part of the convoy eventually reached Crash 1, where it took some time to locate and load all the dead and wounded and then to reorganize for the journey out. This was finally achieved and the weary survivors of Delta and the Rangers reached the assembly temporary field hospital in a football stadium in the early hours of the morning.

US losses were 18 dead, 73 wounded and one wounded helicopter pilot held prisoner. Somali losses were far greater: some 500 dead and 1,000 wounded, many of them women and children. This was not peace-keeping.

Above: A Pakistani Army corporal faces up to a crowd in Somalia. It was hoped that the Pakistanis, being fellow Middle Eastern Muslims, would achieve a rapport with the Somalis, but this failed to happen and they suffered numerous casualties.

BELOW: A heavily armed US patrol in downtown Mogadishu in the early days of the operation, with everyone smiling. Unfortunately, the good humor did not last for long and in the fighting the once-smiling women proved just as dangerous as their menfolk.

PART 3

WEAPONS & EQUIPMENT

To A LARGE EXTENt elite and special forces use standard military equipment, both because it is cheaper for their governments to do so and because it helps avoid the "signature" given by special or "one-off" equipments. Sometimes, however, the requirement for such special equipment cannot be avoided.

Special forces around the world use a vast range of equipment – probably over 50 different types of rifle, for example, and 100 types of sub-machine gun – and only a small selection of typical items can be illustrated here. Thus, the equipment shown here is a combination of:

Standard equipment used by both special forces and conventional forces, such as the US High Mobility Multipurpose Wheeled Vehicle (HMMWV) and the French FA MAS rifle.

Weapons and equipment specifically designed for special forces, such as the Mark 23 (SOCOM) pistol, the armed versions of the Lockheed C-130 Hercules transport aircraft, and the Russian BVD infantry combat vehicle.

Some older weapons often used by terrorist movements and which may also be used by special forces to avoid the "signature" problem. These include some sub-machine guns (British Sten and Sterling, and Danish Madsen SMG), and the Russian RPG-7V anti-tank rocket launcher.

The final pages are devoted to submarines, because it is important to remember that these are among the most effective means of delivering and recovering special forces, and it will not be often that a target lies so far from a suitable coastline that submarine-delivery cannot be used.

The world's special forces are equipped with a wide range of weapons and protective kit, some of it general-issue, some specially developed for their use. Many units train with and use weapons of foreign forces. These are members of Spain's special forces with (left) H&K MP5 silenced submachine gun, and and (right) Mossberg 12-gauge shotgun.

BERETTA 92F/M9 AND 92L 9MM PISTOLS

SPECIFICATIONS

ORIGIN:
Italy/United States.
TYPE:
Double-/single-action, semi-automatic pistols.
DIMENSIONS:
Length overall: 92F/M9 - 8.54in (217mm); 92L - 7.8in (198mm); barrel, 92F/M9 - 4.92in (125mm); 92L - 4.3in (109mm). Width: both, 1.5in (3.81mm). Height: 92F/M9, 5.51in (140mm); 92L, 5.3in (135mm).
WEIGHTS:
Loaded, 92F/M9 - 2.55lb (1.16kg); 92L - 2.40lb (1.09kg).
Empty, 92F/M9 - 2.09lb (0.95kg); 92L - 2.0lb (0.91kg).
CALIBER:
9mm x 19 Luger/Parabellum.
MAGAZINE CAPACITY:
92F/M9 - 15 rounds; 92L - 13 rounds.

T HE BERETTA 92F was the eventual winner of the long and hard-fought, US Army-led competition to replace the Colt M1911A1, which had served the US armed forces for some 70 years. Designated the M9, the new pistol entered service in 1985, the total order amounting to well over 500,000 weapons.

The Beretta M9/92 series pistols use the locked-wedge design pioneered in the Walther P.38 and are loaded in the orthodox manner by inserting a charged magazine into the butt, following which the slide grip is used to pull the action to the rear, cocking the hammer, and then released to chamber a round. On firing, gas pressure drives the barrel and slide to the rear, locked together by a wedge, but, having traveled some 0.3in (8mm), the locking wedge pivots downwards, disengaging from the slide; the barrel immediately stops but the slide continues rearwards to complete the reloading cycle. Unlike many automatic pistols, these Beretta weapons are of an open-slide design: ie, the greater part of the barrel is exposed and not covered by the slide.

The Beretta 92/M9 is the standard sidearm in the US, Italian, and many other armed forces, including special forces. Some special forces, however, also use the Beretta 92 Compact L version, which is slightly smaller and lighter, with a shorter barrel and a magazine which accommodates only 13 rounds.

RIGHT AND BELOW RIGHT: The Beretta 92F was adopted by the US forces as the M9, and is now the standard sidearm in the US, Italian, and many other armed forces. The top example has been fitted with non-standard sights for use in competitions; the lower example is standard "as issued." Unlike many pistols the Beretta has an open slide, leaving the barrel exposed.

SIG P-229 AND P-239

SCHWEIZERISCHE INDUSTRIE GESELLSCHAFT (= Swiss Industrial Company [SIG]), based at Neuhausen Rhinefalls, Switzerland, manufactured pistols for the Swiss Army for many years, but was prevented from exporting its designs by the strict government regulations covering the export of military small arms. In the 1960s, however, SIG teamed up with the German Sauer company, based at Eckernförde, Germany, with the former doing design and domestic manufacture, while the latter undertook manufacture and marketing of SIG designs for the export

The SIG P-229 is used by numerous special forces. It is a rugged and dependable weapon with a magazine holding: 9mm Parabellum - 13 rounds; or 0.40in S&W or 0.357in SIG - 12 rounds.

SPECIFICATIONS

ORIGIN:
Switzerland/Germany.
TYPE:
Recoil-operated, mechanically locked, semi-automatic pistols.
DIMENSIONS:
Length overall: P-229 - 7.1in (180mm); P-239 - 6.77in (172mm); barrel, P-229 - 3.8in (96.5mm); P-239 - 3.6in (92mm). Width: P-229 - 1.46in (37mm); P-239 - 1.26in (32mm). Height: P-229 - 5.4in (137mm); P-239 - 5.12in (130mm).
WEIGHTS:
Without magazine, P-229 - 1.72lb (0.78kg); P-239 - for 9mm Parabellum, 1.72lb (0.78kg); for 0.40 S&W and 0.357 SIG, 1.81lb (0.82kg).
CALIBER:
Both 9mm Parabellum, 0.40 S&W or 0.357 SIG.
RIFLING:
Both 6-groove, 9mm Parabellum - 1 in 10in (250mm); 0.40 S&W - 1 in 15in (380mm); 0.357 SIG - 1 in 16in (406mm).
MAGAZINE CAPACITY:
P-229 - 9mm Parabellum, 13; 0.40 S&W and 0.357 SIG, 12 rounds. P-239 - 7 rounds.

market. This arrangement has proved so successful that SIG has since acquired Sauer and now operates as SIG-Sauer. A number of designs have been marketed, starting with the P-210, which have established an excellent reputation for reliability and accuracy, being used by many special forces (including those of Denmark, Sweden, Switzerland, and the USA) and law-enforcement agencies (eg, the American FBI, DEA [Drug Enforcement Agency] and the Secret Service).

One of the early models was the SIG P-220, which entered service with the Swiss Army as the Pistole 75. In a trend followed by most subsequent SIG-Sauer designs, the P-220 is manufactured in three separate versions to take the 9 x 19mm, 0.38 Super, and 0.45 ACP rounds, to suit the needs of various customers. SIG-Sauer also entered the US Army's Colt M1911A1 successor program with their 9mm P-226 which became one of the two finalists (the other was the Beretta 92) and was very nearly selected, reportedly matching the latter in accuracy and reliability, but losing out on the grounds of cost.

The P-228, which was introduced in 1988, is essentially a P-225 with a larger magazine, holding 12 rounds of 9 x 19mm, while the P-229 is yet further improved. It uses a machined, stainless steel slide (manufactured in the USA), with an aluminum alloy frame manufactured in Germany. There are three control levers, all on the left side of the weapon. Nearest the muzzle is the release lever for stripping; the middle lever, just below the slide, is the decocking lever. Like all SIG pistols, the 229 has an automatic firing-pin safety, operating without a traditional safety control lever, with the first shot when the hammer is down requiring a double-action trigger pull. On the double-action, trigger pull is 12lb (5.44kg); on the single action, trigger pull is 4.5lb (2.0kg).

SIG-Sauer took a slightly different approach with their P-239. There are increasing numbers of women in both military forces (including special forces) and law enforcement agencies, and the company established that, because most women's hands are smaller than men's, they needed a pistol which packed the same performance in a physically smaller package. The smaller size also makes the pistol easier to conceal, whether being carried by men or women. This size reduction has been achieved by reducing the number of rounds in the magazine from 12 to 7 in order to eliminate the double-stacking of rounds, although a ten-round magazine is available as an optional extra.

The P-239 is a mechanically locked, recoil-operated, auto-loading weapon. The sights are adjustable, the rear sight having six notches, while five different foresight posts are available. Optional SIGLITE nightsights can also be fitted. As with earlier SIG pistols, the P-239 has a machined, stainless-steel slide, with a light alloy frame, and is black anodized. Like the P-229, the P-239 is produced in three versions, to fire standard NATO 9mm parabellum, the American 0.40 Smith & Wesson, or SIG's own, newly developed 0.357 round, which is more powerful and with a higher muzzle velocity than earlier rounds. Trigger pull in double action is 10.35lb (4.7kg) and in single action is 4.63lb (2.1kg).

BELOW: The SIG P-239 has been designed with female users in mind, and is slightly smaller and much easier to hold. The penalty is a reduction in magazine size, reducing the rounds to 7, but a 10-round mag is an optional extra.

HECKLER & KOCH MK23 (SOCOM) PISTOL

Specifications
ORIGIN:
USA.
TYPE:
Self-loading pistol.
DIMENSIONS:
Length without suppressor
- 9.65in (245mm); length
including suppressor
16.56in (421mm).
WEIGHT:
Empty - 2.26lb (1.03kg).
CARTRIDGE:
0.45 ACP Ball M1911.
MUZZLE VELOCITY:
850ft/s (260m/s)

T HE US ARMED FORCES had a long-lived affection for the Colt Model 1911 .45 pistol which, together with the slightly modified Colt Remington Model 1911A1, served from World War I to the 1990s. Discussions over a possible replacement lasted over many years, but eventually US Special Forces Command (SOCOM) issued a new operational requirement in February 1990 for an Offensive Handgun Weapon System (OHWS), which was to consist of three sub-systems: a handgun; a Laser Aiming Module (LAM); and a sound/flash suppressor. The main operational scenario was for a weapon which could be used to take out a sentry without alerting his comrades.

The program was divided into three phases: Phase I design and testing; Phase II full development; Phase III production. The stated criteria included:

- 45 ACP caliber, with a magazine holding at least 10 rounds.
- Loaded weight less than 5.5lb (2.5kg) and length under 9.84in (25cm) without and 15.75in (40cm) with the sound/flash suppressor.
- Only one firing malfunction every 10,000 rounds and one materiel malfunction every 30,000 rounds were allowed.
- A 5-round group inside a 2.5in (6.35cm) circle at a range of 27.34yd (25m) using a fixed firing stand.
- The ability to mount the LAM and the sound/flash suppressor, both of which, in their turn, had to meet tight criteria.

Any arms company world-wide was eligible to compete, but only two actually submitted bids for this very demanding

ABOVE: The Heckler & Koch 0.45in Mk 23 Mod 0 automatic pistol — usually known as the "SOCOM pistol" — with its Knight's suppressor attached. These weapons are in the process of being distributed to all US special forces, initial orders having been placed for 7,500 handguns and 1,950 suppressors.

requirement. The first of these was the US firm of Colt, which offered a modified version of its Double Eagle pistol, with a Knight's suppressor, while the Heckler & Koch bid was a development of their USP handgun, with a Heckler & Koch suppressor. Both companies received a contract to produce 30 Phase I prototypes, which were delivered in 1992 and at the end of a very taxing testing program, the Heckler & Koch entry was declared the winning handgun. However, the Knight's design was declared the winning suppressor, even though it was most unusual for a component of a losing system to be selected. The winning LAM was made by Insight Technology Incorporated of Londonderry, New Hampshire.

The Heckler & Koch design exceeded the reliability requirements by a wide margin, averaging in excess of 6,000 MRBS. It also comfortably met the accuracy requirements, and in just under 500 test firings from a stand, Heckler & Koch pistols averaged a group of 1.44in (3.66cm), with 65 groups being less than 1in (2.54cm) and 4 groups of 0.5in (1.77cm), with 5 rounds actually going through the same hole.

Heckler & Koch's success was crowned in July 1995, when their pistol was adopted under the official designation "Pistol, Caliber .45, Mark 23 Mod 0" although it is more usually known as the "SOCOM pistol." The Pentagon duly placed a US$12.1 million production contract for 7,500 handguns and 1,950 suppressors, the first deliveries being made on May 1 1996. The pistols are being issued to all SOCOM units, including Navy SEALs, Army Delta and Rangers, and Air Force Special Operations Wings and Combat Control Teams.

The Knight's suppressor consists of a straight tube with a special internal surface. The device gives 32dB noise suppression in the "dry" mode and 36dB in the "wet" mode (for comparison,

TOP: The complete SOCOM pistol with its Knight's suppressor and the Laser-Aiming Module (LAM). The LAM is mounted in front of the trigger-guard and was designed and manufactured by Insight Technology Inc, of Londonderry, NH. It enables the weapon to be used with great precision.

ABOVE: The bare weapon, showing the three levers for (from front-to-rear) disassembly, safety and holding open. Note also the screw thread around the muzzle for attaching the suppressor.

FAR LEFT:: A Special Forces trooper with the SOCOM pistol. The Knight's suppressor enables the pistol to be fired with a suppression of 32dB, resulting in no more noise than that of an air rifle. Fitting the suppressor restricts the weapon to single rounds, but the benefits of virtual silence far outweigh the loss of the automatic facility.

normal conversation has a sound level of approximately 65dB). Silencing the Mk 23 pistol is made easier by the fact that the .45 ACP round has a muzzle velocity of approximately 850ft/s (260m/s), somewhat less than the speed of sound (approximately 1,100ft/s [340m/s]). This avoids the characteristic "crack" of a supersonic bullet. With the suppressor fitted the pistol can only fire single rounds, but the benefits of quietness far outweigh the loss of the automatic facility.

HECKLER & KOCH MP5 SUB-MACHINE GUN

SINCE ITS INTRODUCTION in the 1960s, Heckler & Koch's MP5 has enjoyed a reputation as a weapon sophisticated enough to satisfy the requirements of the world's most elite military units - the British SAS for example - as well as many police anti-terrorist squads. Using the same roller delayed blowback operating principle as its bigger brothers, the G3 and G41, the MP5 features good handling qualities coupled with parts that are interchangeable with those in a wide range of heavier assault weapons.

The MP5 fires in one of three modes: semi-auto, full-auto or three-round burst. Similar to the FN FAL's trigger, the H&K's safety acts as its fire selector.

Three-shot bursts are accomplished through a small ratchet "counting mechanism" interacting with the sear. Each time the bolt cycles to the rear, the ratchet advances one notch until the

ABOVE: The MP5K (= Kurz [short]) is a compact version of the MP5, firing standard 9x19 Parabellum rounds. It is small enough to fit into a briefcase and is only marginally larger than an automatic pistol, but the forward handgrip makes much greater accuracy possible.

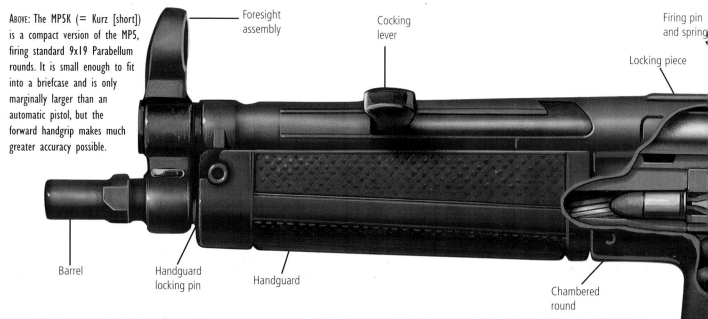

Foresight assembly — Cocking lever — Firing pin and spring — Locking piece — Barrel — Handguard locking pin — Handguard — Chambered round

SPECIFICATIONS

ORIGIN:
Federal Republic of Germany.
TYPE:
Sub-machine gun.

DIMENSIONS:
Barrel (MP5A2 and MP5A3) - 9in (225mm); (MP5SD1, MP5SD2 and MP5SD3) - 6in (146mm); (MP5K) - 5in (115mm)
overall length (MP5A2) - 26.8in (680mm); (MP5A3) - 19.3in (490mm); (MP5SD1) - 21.7in (550mm); (MP5SD2) - 30.4in (780mm); (MP5SD3) - 24in (610mm); (MP5K) - 12.8in (325mm).
WEIGHTS:
(MP5A2) - 5.6lb (2.5kg); (MP5A3) - 6.3lb ((2.9kg); (MP5SD1) - 6.2lb (2.8kg); (MP5SD2) - 6.8lb (3.1kg); (MP5SD3) - 7.5lb ((3.4kg); (MP5K) - 4.4lb (2kg).
CALIBER:
9mmx19 parabellum.
FEED:
10/15/30 round box magazine.
MUZZLE VELOCITY:
1,320ft/s (400m/s).
RATE OF FIRE:
(MPSA2) - 750rpm; (MP5A3) - 750rpm; (MP5SD1) - 650rpm; (MP5SD2) - 650rpm; (MP5SD3) - 650rpm; (MP5K) - 840rpm.
SIGHTS:
Rear, four operative rotating barrel; front, hooded blade, non-adjustable.

third cycle allows re-engagement of the sear or the trigger is released, circumventing the "counter" and ending the cycle before three shots are fired.

These arms have great appeal to Third World countries, not only for their reliability and maintainability but also for their ease of manufacture. The receiver, constructed of stamped sheet steel in 19 operations (several combined), is attached to the polygonal rifled barrel by a trunnion which is spot welded to the receiver and pinned to the barrel. The trigger housing, buttstock, and fore-end are high impact plastic. H&K utilizes metal stampings and welded sub group parts.

The MP5 has an impressive list of accessories. These include: a magazine loader; a .22 cal. conversion kit; a blank firing device; a muzzle-mounted tear gas grenade launcher; and various optical devices. The MP5 has various configurations. The MP5A2 has a fixed buttstock and the MP5A3 features a retractable stock - they are interchangeable.

ABOVE: The MPA5 has an extendable stock and the selector includes a 3-round option. It is seen here with a 15-round magazine.

Bolt head carrier

Recoil spring and guide rod

Hammer

Rear sight assembly

Compression spring

Stock (retracted)

Ejector

Magazine catch lever

Follower and spring

Magazine

Selector

The MP5K was introduced in 1976 and is designed for special operations; the barrel is shorter, a vertical foregrip is added, and the rear-sight apertures are replaced with open notches. There is no butt-stock, only a receiver cap.

The MP5SD is a silenced weapon and is identical to the MP5A2/A3 with regard to functioning principle and bolt system. MP5SD1 is the weapon with receiver cap; SD2, weapon with a fixed stock; and SD3, weapon with retractable stock. The primary feature of the silenced version is that it fires below the speed of sound, thus preventing bullet blast.

Left: The cutaway shows the working parts of the MP5. It uses the same roller-delayed blowback system as the Heckler & Koch rifles and the simplicity of operation is matched by ease of manufacture. It can be fitted with 10, 15 or 30 round magazines.

Far left: The MP5SD is fitted with a silencer and a special laser sight, which enables the firer to lay a laser beam on the target, thus knowing precisely where the rounds will hit.

UZI UZI/MINI-UZI SUB-MACHINE GUN

A YOUNG ISRAELI ARMY MAJOR named Uziel Gal, an arms expert, designed and produced a new sub-machine gun - the Uzi - which has become one of the most prolific SMGs in the western world today. Gal based his design on the Czechoslovakian postwar 9mm Models 23 and 25 sub-machine guns, a major departure from prewar and wartime designs. Early sub-machine guns were not known for accuracy, and to overcome this Czech designers developed a concept wherein the bolt actually telescoped the rear end of the barrel, enclosing the cartridge. Major Gal kept this and another clever Czech design as well: the magazine was inserted through the pistol grip. This meant that the bolt face/breech was at the point of balance, but also just forward of the shoulder axis for more accurate point-fire from the hip.

The Uzi is a simple blowback design. The bolt is cocked by drawing it to the rear. The sear rotates up to engage and hold it open. The trigger mechanism is also simple. A coil spring is used to tension the sear; pulling the trigger to the rear allows the sear to move down and rotate out of engagement with the bolt. The bolt's own coil spring drives it forward, stripping a cartridge from the magazine, chambering it and firing it as the striker in the bolt face impacts the primer. The momentum generated by the exploding cartridge then drives the bolt to the rear, extracting and ejecting the fired case – until it comes up against the bolt stop. Its spring then drives it forward again in a repeat cycle.

In all the years that Major Gal's 9mm Uzi has been in production, there have only been two significant changes made. A grip safety, which blocks the trigger unless depressed, has been added, and the Uzi is now available to fire the .45 Automatic Colt Pistol Cartridge.

SPECIFICATIONS
ORIGIN:
Israel.
TYPE:
Sub-machine gun.
DIMENSIONS:
Length 25.2in (640mm).
WEIGHT:
7.7lb (3.5kg).
CALIBER:
9mm and .45cal.
RIFLING:
4 groove r/h (9mm); 6 groove l/h (.45cal).
FEED:
25/32/40 round box (9mm); 16 round (.45cal).
MUZZLE VELOCITY:
1,280ft/s (390m/s).
RATE OF FIRE:
Cyclic 600rpm (9mm); cyclic 500rpm (.45cal).
SIGHTS:
Flip, 110-219yd (100-200m).
[Specifications for Uzi SMG.]

ABOVE: The Mini-Uzi, with its wire folding stock extended. When the stock is retracted the weight is symmetrically disposed about the pistol-grip, making one-handed firing much easier. It is so small that it can easily be hidden under clothing or in a brief-case and is ideal for use on clandestine and special operations.

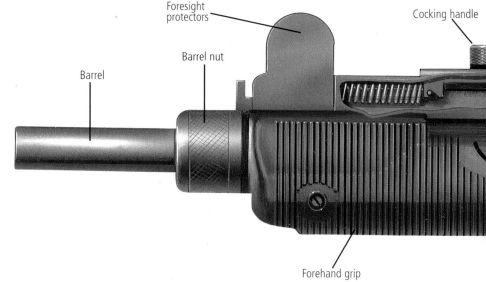

Foresight protectors

Cocking handle

Barrel nut

Barrel

Forehand grip

Trigger

In addition to Israeli forces, the Uzi is in use in Belgium, Germany, Iran, the Netherlands, Thailand, Venezuela, and other countries. It has been ordered in the hundreds of thousands and is probably the most widely used sub-machine gun in the western world. Optional attachments include a short bayonet and a barrel-mounted searchlight. A grenade launcher may be screwed to the front of the receiver in place of the barrel locking-nut. Two 32-round magazines, if clipped together, increase fire capacity.

Israeli Military Industries has produced a smaller version and designated it the Mini-Uzi. In operation it exactly resembles its larger "parent," differing only in size, weight (only 5.9lb/2.7kg), and firing characteristics. It will accept a 20-round magazine for its 9mm parabellum pistol ammunition, as well as 25- and 32-round magazines.

It can easily be concealed under ordinary clothing, and carried in the minimum vehicle space, which makes the Mini-Uzi particularly useful for security and law enforcement personnel, and in commando operations. It can be fired full- or semi-automatic from the hip or, with stock extended, from the shoulder, and is said to maintain the high standards of reliability and accuracy set by the Uzi.

There are three models - open bolt, closed bolt, or heavy bolt – to meet specific requirements. The heavy bolt model offers a reduced rate of fire (750rpm) for situations

A stripped Uzi, showing the small number of components. From top to bottom: slide cover with cocking handle; bolt, with return-spring rod; and body; and on the left, barrel and barrel nut.

requiring easier control.

Even newer is the smallest Uzi ever offered, which is designed to be used when the situation requires maximum concealment without sacrificing 9mm firepower. This new Micro-Uzi is less than 10in (254mm) long with shoulder stock folded, and has a 1,200rpm rate of fire.

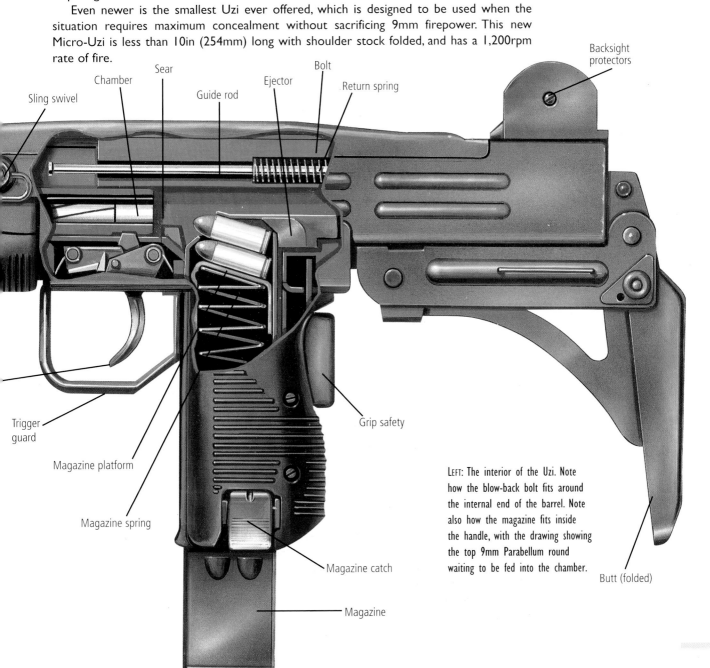

Sling swivel

Chamber

Sear

Guide rod

Ejector

Bolt

Return spring

Backsight protectors

Trigger guard

Magazine platform

Magazine spring

Magazine catch

Grip safety

Magazine

Butt (folded)

LEFT: The interior of the Uzi. Note how the blow-back bolt fits around the internal end of the barrel. Note also how the magazine fits inside the handle, with the drawing showing the top 9mm Parabellum round waiting to be fed into the chamber.

9MM STERLING L2A3/L34A1

SPECIFICATIONS

ORIGIN:
United Kingdom.
TYPE:
Sub-machine gun.
DIMENSIONS:
Length (stock extended) -
28in (690mm); (stock folded) ·
- 19in (483mm); barrel -
77.9in (198mm).
WEIGHTS:
Empty - 6.0lb (2.72kg);
loaded - 7.6lb (3.47kg).
CALIBER:
9mm parabellum.
FEED:
34-round box magazine.
RIFLING:
6 grooves r/h.
MUZZLE VELOCITY:
1,287ft/s (390m/s).
RATE OF FIRE:
Cyclic, 550rpm.
[Specifications for L2A3.]

DESIGNED BY A TEAM headed by G W Patchett of the Sterling Engineering Co, England, the Sterling began life at the end of World War II as the successor to the Sten. It took the same magazine as the Sten, but the design was much more efficient and effective. It was formally adopted by the British forces in 1954.

Well made and finished, the gun has a normal blowback mechanism, but is unusual in having a ribbed bolt which cuts away dirt and fouling as it accumulates and forces it out of the receiver. This allows the gun to function well under the most adverse conditions. The magazine, which sticks out of the left side of the action (similar to the Sten), holds 34 rounds, although a 10-round version is also available.

Sights comprise a rear flip-type aperture that graduates to 110 and 220 yards (100 and 200m), and a narrow blade (almost a post) front. The gun is capable of selective fire, either semi-automatic or fully automatic. It is also fitted for a blade bayonet.

In addition to Britain, some 90 nations use the Sterling. The weapon was particularly useful to British special forces in the Falklands War and in Northern Ireland. Sterlings were also a favorite weapon for use in the Mau Mau uprisings in Kenya. A special forces operator who has used the Sterling in operations has commented, "It flows like syrup when fired. It is a nice field sub-machine gun, simple, reliable and easy to control." Many of these weapons have also been found in terrorist arsenals.

The L34A1 is the silenced version. It is somewhat longer than the L2A3 and tops the Mk 4 version's weight, unloaded, by almost 2lb (1kg). Many of its parts are interchangeable with those of the L2A3, thus keeping down replacement costs and ensuring availability. The barrel jacket is covered by a silencer casing, with front and rear supports. The barrel has 72 radial holes drilled through it, which permits propellant gas to escape, thus reducing

the muzzle velocity of the bullet. The barrel has a metal wrap and diffuser tube; the extension tube goes beyond the silencer casing and barrel.

A spiral diffuser beyond the barrel is a series of discs, which has a hole through its center that allows passage of the round. Gas follows the round closely and is deflected back by the end cap; it mingles with the gases coming forward - with the result that the gas velocity leaving the weapon is low.

The silenced Sterling is used by many countries, and by terrorist groups.

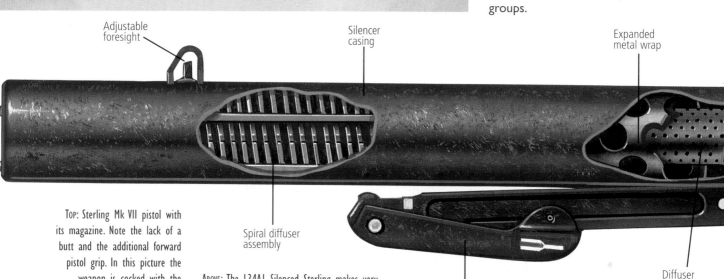

TOP: Sterling Mk VII pistol with its magazine. Note the lack of a butt and the additional forward pistol grip. In this picture the weapon is cocked with the working parts to the rear. The change lever has three positions: safe (as shown here); single rounds; and fully automatic.

ABOVE: The L34A1 Silenced Sterling makes very little sound, but the gas escapes in the diffuser reduce the muzzle velocity of the round making it a close-range weapon.

Adjustable foresight

Silencer casing

Expanded metal wrap

Spiral diffuser assembly

Folded butt

Diffuser tube

STEN GUN

ORLD WAR II dictated an urgent requirement for a simple, British-produced sub-machine gun, and by the middle of 1941 a weapon had not only been designed but was in limited production and undergoing user trials. This was the famous Sten, which took its name from the initial letters of the surnames of the two people most closely concerned with its development - Major R V Shepherd and H S Turpin, allied to the first two letters of Enfield, the location of the factory where it was first produced. In its various forms the Sten provided an invaluable source of additional automatic fire power to the British forces.

The Sten works on a simple blow-back system using a heavy bolt with a coiled return spring and fires either single shots or bursts, the change lever being a circular stud above the trigger.

The main production versions were the MkII, MkIII, MkV and MkVI. The Sten Mark II has a short barrel and barrel jacket, and a simplified buttstock. The second pattern (MkIIS) has a shorter barrel, silencer, a lighter bolt, and a shorter recoil spring. MkIII does not have the detachable barrel of the other models and is probably the most cheaply made of the Sten guns. Its receiver and barrel jacket are made of a single welded steel tube, with the housing of the magazine welded to the receiver. The MkV has a number of features that were not in the earlier models; among them are wooden pistol grip and stock, a front sight with protective ears, and lugs on the barrel for bayonets. The MkVI is the MkV fitted with a shortened barrel and a silencer.

Sten guns were manufactured in millions. Later models are still widely used throughout the world, but are no longer standard weapons in the UK. Built in the UK, Canada, and New Zealand, the Sten gun will be encountered for years to come in the hands of irregulars around the globe.

SPECIFICATIONS

ORIGIN:
United Kingdom.
TYPE:
Sub-machine gun
DIMENSIONS:
Length overall, MkII - 30.5in (762mm); MkIIS - 34.3in (857mm); MkIII - 30.5in (762mm); MkV - 30.5in (762mm); MkVI - 34.3in (857mm); barrel, MkII - 7.9in (197mm); MkIIS - 3.7in (91.4mm); MkIII - 7.9in (197mm); MkV - 8.0in (198mm); MkVI - 3.8in (95mm).
WEIGHTS:
Loaded, MkII - 7.6lb (3.4kg); MkIIS - 9.lb (4.14kg); MkIII 8.4lb (3.82kg); MkV - 10.0lb (4.54kg); MkVI - 10.9lb (4.96kg).
CALIBER:
9mm parabellum.

RIFLING:
6 grooves r/h, one turn in 10.2in (254mm); MkII has two grooves.
MUZZLE VELOCITY:
1,205ft/s (366m/s); MkIIS and MkVI - 1,007ft/s (304m/s).
RATE OF FIRE:
Cyclic, 550rpm.

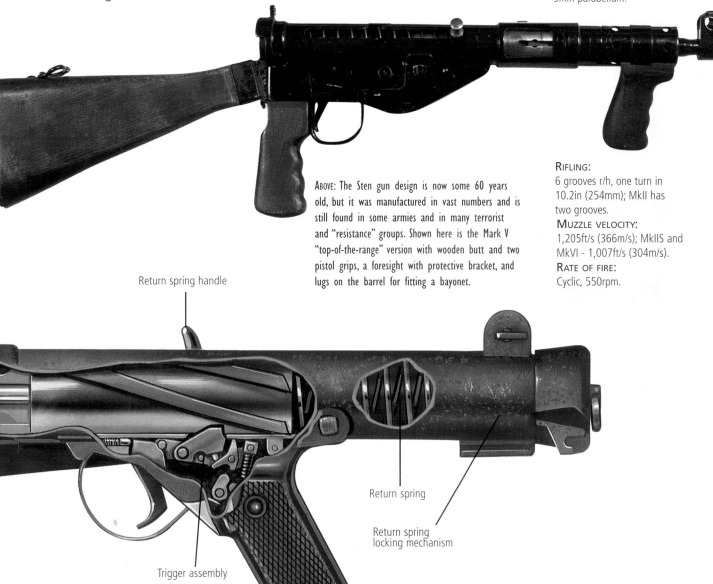

ABOVE: The Sten gun design is now some 60 years old, but it was manufactured in vast numbers and is still found in some armies and in many terrorist and "resistance" groups. Shown here is the Mark V "top-of-the-range" version with wooden butt and two pistol grips, a foresight with protective bracket, and lugs on the barrel for fitting a bayonet.

Return spring handle

Return spring

Return spring locking mechanism

Trigger assembly

MADSEN MODEL 53

SPECIFICATIONS

ORIGIN:
Denmark.

TYPE:
Sub-machine gun.

DIMENSIONS:
Length (stock extended) -
31.8in (794mm); (stock folded) - 21.2in (528mm); barrel
- 8.0in (198mm).

WEIGHT:
Empty - 7.0lb (3.2kg).

CALIBER:
9mm parabellum.

FEED:
32-round box.

RIFLING:
4 groove r/h.

MUZZLE VELOCITY:
1,287ft/s (390m/s).

RATE OF FIRE:
Cyclic, 550rpm.

ABOVE: Danish Madsen Model
1953. Note the 'grip safety' just
behind the magazine housing
and the tubular stock, which
pivots onto the right side of
the weapon.

BELOW: The unique stripping
configuration, with the weapon
splitting in half, pivoting on the
same bolts as the stock.

THE FIRST SUB-MACHINE GUN to be made in Denmark was a type of Finnish Suomi, made under license by the Danish Madsen Industrial Syndicate in 1940. Production continued throughout World War II, with the gun being used by the Danes, the Germans and the Finns. This same syndicate has made all Danish sub-machine guns since then.

The first weapon of the present series was the Model 1946, and the Danes, profiting from wartime advances in mass production, made sure it was designed in such a way as to be able to take advantage of these improved techniques.

One of the most unusual sub-machine guns ever designed and produced, the Model 53 is designed to lend itself to high speed production at extremely low cost. The main body, including the pistol grip, is made from two side pieces, hinged together at the rear so that the weapon can easily be opened for repair, cleaning or inspection. It does, however, have the disadvantage that the springs are liable to fall out unless care is taken. The Madsen works on the normal blowback system and will fire single rounds or bursts.

One of its unusual features is a grip safety behind the magazine housing which (with the magazine itself) acts as a forward hand grip. Unless this safety is in, the gun will not function, which makes it impossible to fire it one-handed. The tubular metal stock is on a pivot and folds onto the right side of the weapon.

The Model 53 has been used by Danish police forces and in some South American and Southeast Asian countries, as well as by several terrorist groups. It was made under license in Brazil in .45 caliber. Many of the design and manufacturing features lend themselves to ready application to other small arms designs.

9MM MAT49

THE M1949 SUB-MACHINE GUN, which was built by Tulle (Manufacture d'Armes de Tulle), has a good reputation among French troops. First adopted by the French Army in 1949, it saw considerable service in Indochina and Algeria. A large number of these weapons, incidentally, were captured in Indochina and later converted to fire the Soviet 7.76mm Type P round, and the cyclic rate was increased to 900 rounds per minute. These weapons can be recognized by their longer barrel and 35-round magazine.

Of conventional blowback design, the MAT49 has several unusual, but useful, features. The magazine housing (with magazine attached), for example, may be folded forward and clipped under the barrel - and has only to be swung back and down to be used instantly. Combined with a telescopic steel stock, this feature makes the weapon particularly usable by parachute troops. A pistol-grip squeeze safety is fitted, and this prevents accidental discharge by dropping. The ejection port cover helps keep dirt out of the internal mechanism of the gun.

The weapon is used by French forces and the armies of many former French colonies. It has also been found in terrorist arsenals.

SPECIFICATIONS

ORIGIN:
France.
TYPE:
Sub-machine gun.
DIMENSIONS:
Length (stock extended) - 28.8in (720mm); (stock folded) - 20.2in (460mm); barrel - 9.1in (228mm).
WEIGHTS:
Unloaded - 7.9lb (3.6kg); loaded - 9.2lb (4.2kg).
CALIBER:
9mm parabellum.
FEED:
32- or 20-round box magazine.
RIFLING:
4 grooves l/h.
MUZZLE VELOCITY:
1,287ft/s (390m/s).
RATE OF FIRE:
Cyclic, 600rpm.

LEFT: These French soldiers show the two configurations of the French MAT49 sub-machine gun. The soldier on the left has the magazine in the operating position, while the man in the center has the magazine housing folded forward, out of the way.

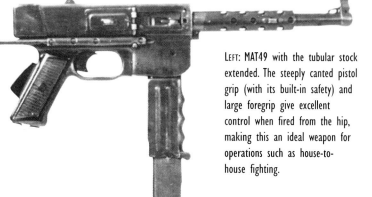

LEFT: MAT49 with the tubular stock extended. The steeply canted pistol grip (with its built-in safety) and large foregrip give excellent control when fired from the hip, making this an ideal weapon for operations such as house-to-house fighting.

ABOVE: MAT49. A large "squeeze safety" is located on the rear of the pistol grip. The picture shows the stock retracted and six representative 9mm rounds. There are two magazines; one takes 20 rounds, the other 32. Note also the clip on the underside of the cooling sleeve, which is used to retain the magazine housing in its forward position. This is an excellent and reliable weapon.

5.56MM FA MAS RIFLE

RIGHT: French trooper wading through a river with his MAS rifle at the ready. Its short length and light weight make this an easy weapon to carry and handle.

BELOW RIGHT: The MAS with its bipod legs, which are a standard feature of the weapon, extended. The design of the weapon looks futuristic even today, but it has, in fact, been in service for 20 years. The prominent "bridge" serves as a carrying handle and also houses the sights.

THE FA MAS (FUSIL AUTOMATIQUE, Manufacture d'Armes de St. Etienne) is France's current service rifle and has proved to be a highly effective and generally well-conceived piece of ordnance for general service and special forces use. First introduced in 1973 (and subsequently modified), the rifle was placed into production in 1979. Delivery of the first complement of 148,000 rifles was completed in 1983.

Firing from the closed-bolt position, the method of operation is by means of delayed blowback, the system having been adopted from the French AA52 general purpose machine gun. A black

SPECIFICATIONS
ORIGIN:
France.
TYPE:
Assault rifle.
DIMENSIONS:
Without bayonet - 30.28in (757mm); barrel - 19.51in (488mm).
WEIGHTS:
Without magazines, sling or bipod - 7.94lb (3.61kg); magazine - 0.33lb (0.15kg) empty; 0.99lb (0.45kg) loaded with 25 rounds; bipod - 0.374lb (0.17kg).
CALIBER:
5.56mm x 45mm NATO; M193-type ammunition.
EFFECTIVE RANGE:
330yd (300m).
MUZZLE VELOCITY:
3,168ft/s (960m/s).
RATE OF FIRE:
Cyclic, 900-1,000rpm.

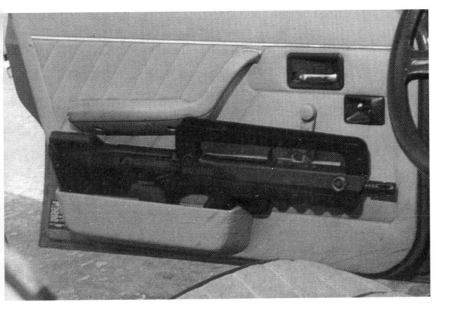

plastic lower handguard, pinned to the barrel and receiver, extends to the magazine well and cannot be removed.

Because it has a "bullpup" configuration, the trigger mechanism and pistol grip have been mounted to the lower handguard, forward of the magazine well. The pistol grip is ergonomically designed, with three finger grooves and a storage trap that contains a bottle of lubricant, The sheet metal trigger guard can be pulled away from the rear retaining pin and rotated for firing with gloves under arctic conditions, an obvious advantage to mountain forces. The trigger is connected to a long, thin strip of sheet metal which rides in a slot on the right side of the receiver and reaches the hammer mechanism.

To remove a magazine, a spring-loaded plastic catch must be pressed back. Magazines are inserted by pushing them straight into the well.

Among the interesting features of the FA MAS are optional right- or left-side ejection and three-round burst mode as an alternative to single shot or fully automatic. With its high cyclic rate (900-1,000rpm), the three-shot burst mode is a real boon in controlling the weapon. Each weapon is equipped with an ambidextrous web sling. The foresight is mounted on a column pinned to the barrel; the rear sight is also on a column, above the return spring cylinder.

Versions of the FA MAS have scopes integrated into the carrying handles, as are short barreled models with 16.5in (419mm) barrels. A new carrying handle that will accept any NATO STANAG scope is under development. The weapon is widely used among elite troops such as France's naval infantry, Foreign Legion and paratroops.

A short version - the FA MAS Commando - is intended for use by commando and similar special forces. The barrel has been shortened to 16.2in (411mm), but in other respects is the same as the main service weapon.

LEFT: An MAS rifle with a telescopic sight mounted in the carrying handle. This is not intended to convert the weapon into a sniper rifle, but enables special forces to identify targets when hostages or non-combatants are in the killing zone. Note that the bipod makes the firer adopt a high profile firing position, which is a possible disadvantage.

FAR LEFT: The MAS is a compact weapon as shown by this example fitted in a car door.

5.56MM STEYR AUG

The Steyr AUG looks as futuristic in the late 1990s as it did when it first appeared in the early 1980s. This weapon was designed by Steyr-Daimler-Puch AG of Steyr, Austria, to meet an Austrian Army specification and was designated the Armeé Universal Gewehr (AUG = universal army rifle). It uses a "bull-pup" design in which the working parts are in the stock at the rear and the magazine is behind the trigger, which combine to enable a full-length barrel to be mounted in the shortest possible overall length.

The AUG is gas operated, with gas-cylinder mounted on the barrel and a short-stroke piston. The gas-regulator has three settings: one for normal operation; the second for adverse conditions; and the third for firing blank rounds or rifle grenades. The safety also has three settings: semi-automatic; safe; and three-round bursts.

There are four versions of the AUG - sub-machine gun (SMG), carbine, rifle and light machine gun (LMG) - which differ mainly in the lengths of the barrel, which are 13.8in (350mm); 16in (407mm); 20in (508mm); and 24.6in (626mm), respectively. The SMG, carbine and rifle use a 30-round magazine, which is made of clear plastic so that the firer can see exactly how many rounds remain to be fired, while the LMG is fitted with a light bipod and uses a 42-round magazine.

ABOVE: The AUG-P is a sub-machine gun version of the AUG firing 9mm Parabellum ammunition. Note the short barrel, the used cartridge ejection slot and the revised magazine housing, which is different from that on the 5.56mm version.

RIGHT: Austrian paratrooper with his Steyr AUG in the hip firing position. Note the use of the sling, left hand on the forward grip, right hand on the pistol grip and stock firmly held by the forearm and elbow. The AUG can be used by either left- or -right-handed firers, needing only the most basic adjustments.

SPECIFICATIONS

ORIGIN: Austria.

TYPE:
SMG, carbine, assault rifle, sustained-fire machine gun.

DIMENSIONS:
SMG: barrel - 13.8in (350mm); overall - 25in (632mm).
Carbine: barrel - 16in (407mm); overall - 27in (690mm).
Assault rifle: barrel - 20in (508mm); overall - 31in (790mm).
Sustained fire: barrel - 24.6in (626mm); overall - 36in (908mm).

WEIGHTS:
SMG: empty - 6.5lb (2.95kg): loaded 7.16lb (3.25kg).
Carbine: empty - 7.3 lb (3.3kg); loaded - 8.05lb (3.65kg).

Assault rifle: empty - 7.9lb (3.6kg) loaded 8.5lb (3.85kg).
Sustained fire: empty - 10.8lb (4.9kg).

CARTRIDGE:
NATO standard 5.56mm ball round - M193 and M885 (SS109).

FEED:
SMG/carbine/rifle: 30 round, clear plastic.
Sustained-fire: 42-round plastic.

RIFLING:
6 groove, r/h, 1 turn/9in (23cm).

SIGHT:
Sworowski 1.5X optical.

EFFECTIVE RANGE:
Assault rifle - 328yd (300m).

RATE OF FIRE (cyclic):
680rpm.

The AUG has been designed so that it can be fired with equal ease by right- or left-handed firers. Thus, the bolt is replaceable and the ejection port can be set on either side of the receiver. Even the sling swivels can be adjusted to either side of the weapon, according to the requirements of the firer.

The stock is a one-piece, greenish-colored unit, fabricated from a very strong, durable plastic; it accommodates the receiver group, the hammer mechanism and the magazine housing. The pistol grip is integral with the stock, and a transverse safety is located where it can be operated by the firer's right thumb.

The cold hammer-forged barrel is chrome-lined and locks into the receiver by rotating it 1/8th turn; it can safely be cooled by direct immersion into cold water. The cylindrical pistol grip can be folded away, if required, and can also be used to protect the firer's hand when removing a hot barrel. A flash hider is attached to the muzzle.

The carrying handle is fixed and incorporates a 1.5X sight which is fully adjustable for windage and elevation.

There is a wide range of accessories, including such standard items as a carrying sling, cleaning kit, blank-firing attachment, and a muzzle cap. There are also two types of bayonet: one is a multi-purpose tool which incorporates a wire-cutter and a screw-driver; the other is a light bayonet. In addition, a grenade-launcher, designated AUG-8, can be attached under the barrel and is similar in operation to the US Army's M-203.

The AUG has been adopted by numerous armies and many special forces, including those of Australia, Austria, New Zealand and the Oman.

ABOVE: Three versions of the AUG, all 5.56mm caliber. Top is the standard rifle, with long barrel and flash suppressor. Center is the carbine, basically the same as the rifle, but with a slightly shorter barrel. Bottom is the sub-machine gun, with an ultra-short barrel, designed for paratroops.

LEFT: An NCO of the Austrian Army shows how light and handy is the AUG. Note that the forward hand-grip is folded forward out of the way. Note also the bayonet/combat knife which is carried on his webbing.

5.45MM AK-74 AND AKS-74 ASSAULT RIFLES

Receiver catch
Selector lever
Hammer
Return spring
Bolt carrier
Rears
Rearsight assembly
Bolt
Stock (folded)
Safety sear
Magazine catch
Magazine spring and follower
Plastic magazine

BELOW: A Polish elite paratrooper armed with the Russian AK-74 5.45mm assault rifle, which was widely exported to members of the Warsaw Pact before the end of the Cold War. Note the firing position, with the left hand grasping the magazine rather than the forward hand-guard.

ABOVE: An AKS-74 with a folding stock, for use by paratroops and other special forces. The weapon is an AKM rechambered and rebored to take the Russian 5.45mm round. Note the cleaning rod and the new type of blast compensator, which is intended to reduce the recoil forces on the firer.

AS INDICATED BY ITS DESIGNATION, the AK-74 assault rifle was developed in 1974 and probably entered service around 1977. The folding stock AKS-74, sometimes referred to as the AKD, was first seen with Soviet airborne troops in the Red Square Parade in Moscow on November 7 1977.

The AK-74 is basically an AKM rechambered and rebored to fire a 5.45mm cartridge. Externally, it has the same general appearance as the AKM, with two notable differences: the AK-74 has a distinctive, two-port muzzle brake (giving it a slightly greater overall length than the AKM), and a smooth plastic magazine which is slightly shorter and is curved to a lesser extent than the grooved metal AKM. It uses the same type bayonet as the AK series weapons. The folding stock version, designated AKS-74, has a Y-shaped tubular stock with an extremely narrow buttplate, as opposed to the T-shaped, stamped-metal buttstock of the AKMS.

The muzzle brake on the AK74 uses a fluidic

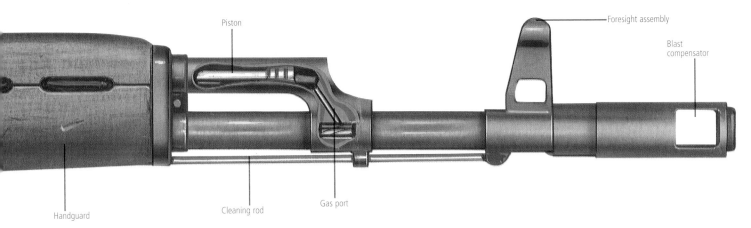

Piston

Foresight assembly

Blast compensator

Handguard

Cleaning rod

Gas port

device to minimise recoil and muzzle climb. Although the AK-74 is somewhat heavier than the AKM when empty, its loaded weight is slightly less, primarily because of the plastic magazine and its smaller caliber ammunition, which can inflict a particularly nasty wound. The AKS now has a Russian version of the US M203 grenade launcher.

Among limitations of the rifle are that the gas cylinder is in a vulnerable position and, if dented, may cause weapon malfunction, and that the reddish-brown or orange color of the plastic magazine does not lend itself to camouflage,

SPECIFICATIONS

ORIGIN:
Russian Federation.
TYPE:
Assault rifles.
DIMENSIONS:
Length (AK-74) - 37in
(930mm); (AKS-74, with butt
folded) - 28in (690mm);
barrel - 16in (40mm).
WEIGHT:
Unloaded (AK74/AKS-74)
7.9lb (3.6kg).
RIFLING:
4 grooves r/h; 1 turn in 7.8in
(196mm).
CALIBER:
8.45mm x 39.
FEED:
30-round plastic box
magazine.
EFFECTIVE RANGE:
495yd (450m).
MUZZLE VELOCITY:
2,970ft/s (900m/s).
RATE OF FIRE:
Cyclic, 650rpm.

LEFT: Russian paratrooper takes aim with his 5.45mm AKR sub-machine gun (SMG). This is a shortened, lighter version of the AKS-74, with a Y-shaped, tubular metal folding stock. Note that this Russian soldier uses the conventional grip with his left hand holding the forward handguard, as opposed to that used by the Polish soldier opposite. Note the coveted blue beret and the paratrooper badge on the soldier's left sleeve.

M16A2/COLT COMMANDO

BELOW: Special Operations training at the John F. Kennedy Special Warfare Center, Fort Bragg, North Carolina, with a trainee aiming a 5.56mm Colt Commando assault rifle. The Commando is essentially a shorter and lighter version of the M16, and the changes include a telescopic butt.

THE M16 (PREVIOUSLY THE AR-15) was designed by Eugene Stoner. It was first adopted for use by US forces in Vietnam. When first used in combat, numerous faults became apparent, most of them traceable to a lack of training and poor maintenance. The M16 then replaced the 7.62mm M14 as the standard rifle of the United States forces.

Millions have been manufactured, most by Colt Firearms. The weapon was also made under license in Singapore, the Republic of Korea, and the Philippines. The M16A2 was also adopted in Canada, which built 80,000 under license, but with full-automatic capability in place of the burst-control option.

The weapon is gas-operated and the user can select either full-automatic or semi-automatic. Both 20- and 30-round magazines can be fitted, as can a bipod, bayonet, telescope,

Flash suppressor

Foresight assembly

Sling swivel

Plastic handguard

SPECIFICATIONS

ORIGIN:
United States.
TYPE:
M16A2 - rifle; Commando -
sub-machine gun.
DIMENSIONS:
Length overall
(with flash
suppressor) -
40in (1,000mm);
barrel - 19.8in (508mm).
WEIGHTS:
7.5lb (3.4kg); with standard
30-round magazine - 8.2lb
(3.72kg); sling - 5.3oz
(182g).
CALIBER: 5.56mm.
FEED:
20- and 30-round box
magazine.
MAXIMUM EFFECTIVE
RANGE:
300yd (274m).
Muzzle velocity:
3,280ft/s (1,000m/s).
RATE OF FIRE:
700-950rpm (cyclic);150-
200rpm (auto); 45-65rpm
(semi-automatic).
[Specificataions for M16A2.]

and night sight. The weapon can also be fitted with the M203 40mm grenade launcher (q.v.).

The Commando sub-machine gun model of the M16 is a special version with a shorter barrel, telescopic butt, flash suppressor, and a telescopic sight; the overall length is 27.9in (710mm). It is in use with US Special Operations Forces.

The M231 is a special model with no butt or sights, and can be fired from within the M2 Bradley Infantry Fighting Vehicle.

There was much dissatisfaction with the M16A1 in the US Army and US Marine Corps, one of the major complaints being its lack of effectiveness at ranges above 340 yards (300m). This came to a head with the increased emphasis on desert warfare. Combined with the high average age of stocks at the time, this led to a major review in 1981. The resulting M16A2 is a rifle that is actually a throwback to the 1950s; it is a weapon that has finally come full circle to where it should have begun in the first place. It entered inventories in 1987.

The barrel of the M16A2 is heavier, with a thicker profile. It weighs 8.15lb (3.69kg) with

sling and empty 30-round magazine compared to the 7.9lb (3.58kg) of the M16A1. Other major changes include a three-round burst device, intended to cut down ammunition waste from the full-automatic operation on the A1; a new rear sight with a windage knob; a square-edged front sight post to give better target definition; a buttstock and handguard made of stronger materials; a flash suppressor that doubles as a muzzle compensator; and a wedge-shaped projection at the rear of the ejection port to deflect hot brass away from the face of the left-handed shooter.

Most importantly, the requirements for a longer-range weapon have been met by rebarreling to use the new NATO 5.56mm round more effectively. The longer, heavier bullets of these rounds are fully stabilized by the M16A2's barrel, which is rifled with a twist of one turn in 7in (177mm). This improves the maximum effective range to about 550 yards (500m).

ABOVE LEFT: USAF guard on duty during the 1991 Operation Desert Storm, armed with a 5.56mm M16A2 assault rifle, complete with grenade launcher and night sight. The device immediately to the left of the foresight is the sight for the grenade launcher.

ABOVE RIGHT: US Army soldier with M16A1 assault rifle, the original production version, which was criticised by the US Army, mainly for its limited effective range of 340yd (300m). M16A2 has a heavier barrel, revised rifling and fires the NATO standard 5.56mm round, increasing the effective range to about 550yd (500m).

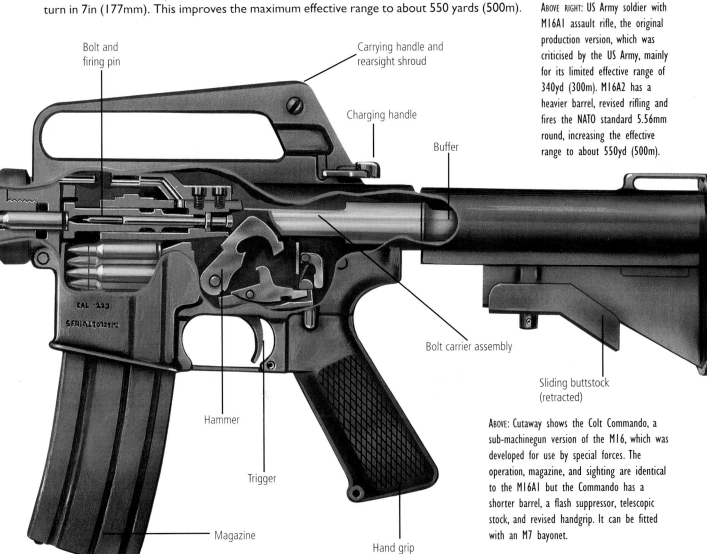

Bolt and firing pin

Carrying handle and rearsight shroud

Charging handle

Buffer

Bolt carrier assembly

Sliding buttstock (retracted)

Hammer

Trigger

Magazine

Hand grip

ABOVE: Cutaway shows the Colt Commando, a sub-machinegun version of the M16, which was developed for use by special forces. The operation, magazine, and sighting are identical to the M16A1 but the Commando has a shorter barrel, a flash suppressor, telescopic stock, and revised handgrip. It can be fitted with an M7 bayonet.

5.56MM & 7.62 GALIL ASSAULT RIFLE

SPECIFICATIONS

ORIGIN:
Israel.
TYPE:
Assault rifle.
DIMENSIONS:
Length (stock extended, 5.56 model) - 38.6in (979mm); (7.62 model) - 41.3in (1,050mm); (stock folded, 5.56 model) - 29.2in (742mm); (7.62 model) - 31.9in (810mm); barrel - (5.56 model) 18.1in (460m); (7.62 model) - 21in (533mm).
WEIGHTS:
5.56 model - 8.6lb (3.9kg);
7.62 model - 8.7lb (3.95kg).
CALIBER:
5.56 model - .233; 7.62 model - .308.
MAX EFFECTIVE RANGE:
5.56 model - 550yd (500m);
7.62 model 660yd (600m).
MUZZLE VELOCITY:
5.56 model - 3,230ft/s (980m/s); 7.62 model - 2,800ft/s (850m/s).
RATE OF FIRE:
Cyclic, both models, 650rpm.

ABOVE RIGHT: An Israeli soldier aims the 5.56mm Galil. Note that the large capacity magazine causes a high prone position to be adopted, reducing the firer's accuracy and increasing threat from return fire.

BELOW: The Galil's selector switch is located above the pistol grip; "safety" not "fire" is engaged by the natural forward push of the thumb.

CREDIT FOR THIS RIFLE'S development is given to an Israeli ordnance officer with the surname of Galili, along with Israel Military Industries (IMI). They realized that by combining the full-scale Finnish Valmet M-60/62 receiver with a stout but not-too-heavy barrel a system could be developed which would serve both the 5. 56 NATO cartridge and the 7,62 NATO round as well,

The operating system is a rotating bolt gas system and, with the exception of the stamped steel breech cover, the Galil is fully machined. The handguard is wood, lined with Dural, and has ample clearance around the barrel for heat dissipation. When extended, the buttstock has a positive latching system which prevents wobble by wedging the hinge end's tapered latching lugs into corresponding slots.

These are released by the simple expedient of squeezing with the right hand and folding the stocl< outward. The bipod folds and rotates into a slot on the underside of the handguard, where the legs then spread apart by spring tension to latch into retaining slots.

The ambidextrous safety switch on the left side is a small lever, but its reciprocal rightside member also acts as an ejection port cover. The magazine is held by a catch in front of the trigger guard. To operate, the lever is taken off "safe" and the cocking handle pulled to the rear. When released, the carrier is driven forward and the top round pushed from the

magazine into the chamber. The bolt comes to a halt and the cam pin (engaged in a slot in the carrier) rotates the bolt, which forces the cartridge forward, whereupon the extractor slips over the rim and the gun is ready to be fired.

The system used for the trigger and firing mechanism is that employed in the M1 Garand rifle, the AK series and many others.

Some 35 rounds are held in the 5.56 magazine and that for the 7.62 holds 25 rounds, but 50-round magazines have been produced for it. On consequence of having large numbers of rounds is a long magazine, forcing the firer to adopt a high firing position.

Sights for the Galil are folding "L" rear with two peeps, one for 330yd (300m), and a second for 550yd (500m). Unique to the system is its set of folding night sights which use tritium for illumination. For close quarter work at night or in a dark jungle, these sights are undetectable

The Galil has been adopted by a number of armies and has been produced in South Africa, with some modifications, as the R-4.

TOP: Israeli paratrooper with Galil assault rifle, a versatile weapon developed using Eastern European technology allied to Israeli ingenuity.

ABOVE : The 7.62mm Galil section machine gun, which fills the gap between the rifle and the belt-feed medium machine gun. Apart from the straight magazine, it has more than a passing resemblance to the Russian-built AK-47, which the Israelis captured in large numbers. However, it is in every way a superior weapon.

LEFT : Israeli troops at the ready in front of an APC. The soldier on the right is armed with a Galil rifle.

ROYAL ORDNANCE ARWEN 37

SPECIFICATIONS

ORIGIN:
United Kingdom.

TYPE:
Anti-riot weapon.

DIMENSIONS:
Arwen length: 29.9in-
33.1in (750mm-840mm).
Arwen Ace length: 30in-
33in (762-838mm).

WEIGHTS:
Arwen 37 empty - 6.8lb
(3.1kg); loaded - 8.4lb
(3.8kg).
Arwen Ace empty - 4.6lb
(2.1kg); loaded - 5.1lb
(2.3kg).

CALIBER:
37mm.

TYPE OF FIRE:
Arwen 37 - automatic/
single rounds.
Arwen Ace - single rounds.

RATE OF FIRE:
Arwen 37: cyclic - 60rpm;
single rounds - 12rpm.
Arwen Ace: cyclic - n/a;
single rounds - 12rpm.

MAXIMUM EFFECTIVE
RANGE:
Standard rounds - 110yd
(100m).

BELOW: The Arwen ACE is a British-designed, single-shot weapon, developed specifically to fire the Royal Ordnance 37mm baton and smoke anti-riot rounds. The weapon itself is 33in (838mm) long and weighs 5.1lb (2.3kg) with a round loaded. A skilled operator can fire the weapon at up to 12 rounds per minute.

IN THE 1970s BRITISH SOLDIERS were facing hostile crowds in Northern Ireland equipped with either rifles or the totally inadequate L67A1 38mm Riot Gun, an adaptation of the Verey Pistol, which had originally been designed to launch illuminating flares. The L67A1 had a very short effective range, forcing the firer to get dangerously close to a crowd, and was a single-round weapon which had to be broken to extract the used case and replace it with a new cartridge. In addition, the existing plastic bullet was unsatisfactory.

As a result, the British Ministry of Defence issued a requirement in 1977 for a multi-shot "Crowd Control Weapon System" for use in Northern Ireland. By 1979 the (then) Royal Small Arms Factory at Enfield had produced three different systems: a pump-action weapon with a four-shot capacity; a five-shot, revolver-action weapon; and a self-loading weapon with a box magazine. Prototype baton rounds were developed in parallel with the launchers.

Following trials, it was decided in early 1981 to produce yet another version, which combined the barrel and action of the five-shot revolver with the trigger/pistol grip and stock of the self-loader. After some other and more minor modifications this was eventually placed in production as the Arwen 37 (= Anti-Riot Weapon, ENfield). The 37mm caliber was selected as offering the optimum combination of energy and velocity, while the new barrel had a rifled twist of one turn in 21in (540mm), giving the greatest accuracy.

Safety is a primary consideration. The pistol-grip/trigger-housing contains an integral safety lever, which is operated with equal ease by right- or left-handed firers. The trigger is designed for operation by both index and middle fingers and has two pressures. The weapon only becomes fully cocked when the firer takes up the first pressure on the trigger and if it is released the action returns immediately to the uncocked state. Taking up the second pressure and releasing it fires the weapon and revolves the feeding mechanism, bringing the next round into line with the breech. Recoil is not heavy.

An aperture on the right-hand side of the weapon serves as both a loading and ejection port and the weapon can be fired from right or left shoulder without modification. The weapon also has an adjustable stock with six settings and a forward pistol grip with a variety of radial settings, which combine to offer the firer a wide choice of adjustments to suit his/her requirements. The weapon is also easy to clean and the revolving feed mechanism can easily be removed. The number and type of rounds in the magazine can be checked visually.

A number of versions have been developed from the

LEFT: The ARWEN 37 is a multi-shot, self-loading, semi-automatic, anti-riot weapon, fitted with a 5-round magazine. ARWEN is an acronym of the full name — Anti-Riot, ENfield — the last being the name of the former small arms factory at Enfield where it was designed.

BELOW: Special forces troops show firing positions for the ARWEN 37. The advantage of this weapon is that it can place 37mm baton or smoke rounds with great precision out to the maximum effective range of 110yd (100m). The AR5 round can even be used to penetrate windows or plywood before releasing its payload of CS chemical smoke.

basic Arwen 37. The Arwen 37 Multi-S very close-quarter 5-shot revolver has no stock and a shorter (165mm) barrel, while the Arwen 37 Multi-V, also stockless, is designed for use on a ball-mounting in an anti-riot vehicle. These all used the revolver-principle, but Royal Ordnance have also developed a single-shot version, the Arwen Ace, which weighs only 5.1lb (2.3kg) loaded, but can achieve the same 12 aimed rounds per minute firing rate as the Arwen 37.

In any of its different configurations, Arwen provides military, paramilitary ,and police forces with a highly effective and flexible method for containing situations involving riots and civil disturbances. It is in wide-scale service around the world.

AMMUNITION

A family of 37mm rounds was developed for use from the various Arwen weapons.

- AR1 KE (KINETIC ENERGY) BATON ROUND. This uses a specially developed polyurethane baton, which is sufficiently stable to be able to hit a man-sized target at 109yd (100m).
- AR2 MULTI-SOURCE IRRITANT SMOKE ROUND. This airburst projectile contains four CS-filled canisters within a plastic sabot which is discarded one second after leaving the muzzle. The canisters then disperse and the CS gas is intended to cover a circular area approximately 5.5yd (5m) in radius at a range of 98yd (90m). The irritating CS smoke is emitted for approximately 12 seconds.
- AR3 FRANGIBLE-NOSE BATON ROUND. The AR3 is intended to assist in arresting people in or near buildings and consists of a polyurethane baton, with soft nosecap (expanded polystyrene-Styrofoam). This contains 0.07oz (2gm) of CS powder which is dispersed on impact.
- AR4 SMOKE SCREENING ROUND. This is similar in construction and performance to the AR2, but contains ordinary smoke instead of CS.
- AR5 BARRICADE-PENETRATING, IRRITANT ROUND. This round is designed for use against such targets as car windscreens/windows and interior doors, as well as plywood up to 0.5in (13mm) thick, albeit at lesser ranges. It uses a higher velocity projectile with a cutting edge around a hollow nose. The cutter penetrates the target and the micronized CS power is then dispersed.
- SPECIAL VERSIONS. Special versions of the AR1 and AR2 rounds are available, which have the same terminal effects, accuracy and payload, but with a much reduced range. Practice versions of the AR1 and AR2 are also available.

ITHACA 37

SPECIFICATIONS
ORIGIN:
United States.
TYPE:
Slide-action repeater shotgun.
DIMENSIONS:
Length - 18.8 to 20in
(470-508mm).
WEIGHTS:
6.5 to 7lb (2.94-3.06kg).
CALIBER:
12-guage, 2in (69.85mm).
FEED:
5- or 8-shot tubular
magazine.

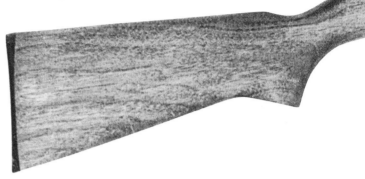

THIS SHOTGUN IS THE FAMED basic "Featherlight" Model 37 pump action repeater manufactured by the Ithaca Gun Company of Ithaca, New York. It is a weapon that is uniquely free of stamped steel components, even to the trigger group.

The solid steel receiver does not have the usual ejection port on the right because it pops empty shells straight out of the bottom. Its unique action is centered around a dual-duty shell carrier that lifts live shells up to feed straight into the chamber.

RIGHT: The Ithaca Model 37 pump action has been one of the most commonly issued shotguns in the USA. Its light weight, fast action, and 18in (525mm) barrel make it ideal as a police weapon, and it has also been found in the arsenals of terrorists.

Its pistol grip affords greater control while firing from the shoulder, and makes it practical to fire from a hip position.

The type of barrel in Ithaca's "Deerslayer" model (a trademark of the company to indicate precision-bored cylindrical barrels for general hunting uses) has been fitted to a combat shotgun. The objective is to provide a weapon capable of firing rifle slugs with optimum accuracy as well as being capable of handling the usual loadings.

A number of short-barreled cylinder-bored configurations have been put in use by military and police forces in the US.

MOSSBERG 500 ATP

RIGHT & FAR RIGHT: Mossberg 500 ATP8 carried at the ready and snapped into firing position. A common fallacy with modern firearms is that they should be fired from the hip. In fact, over 80 percent of all firearms training given to special forces personnel involves obtaining a flash sight picture at minimum.

BELOW: The 500 ATP8 is regarded as one of the most reliable pump-action shotgun designs issued. Because of its stock angle and generous-sized fore end, three aimed shots a second are possible.

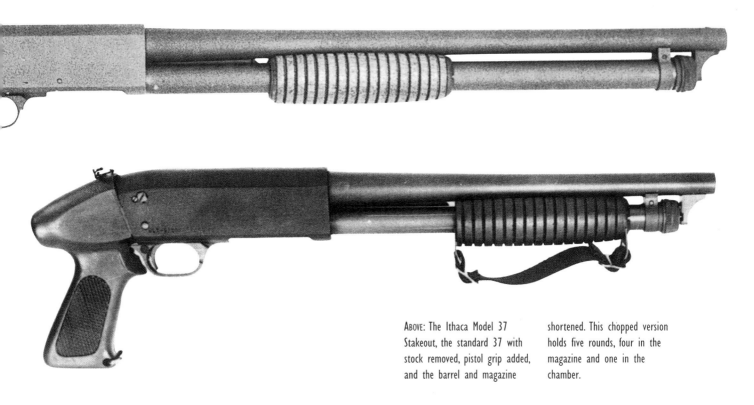

ABOVE: The Ithaca Model 37 Stakeout, the standard 37 with stock removed, pistol grip added, and the barrel and magazine shortened. This chopped version holds five rounds, four in the magazine and one in the chamber.

THE BASIC SERIES OF THE MOSSBERG 500 shotguns are specially modified for police and military use. They have been described by some, as have other shotguns, as "reloadable Claymoores".

There are two main types - the six-shot and eight-shot models but it is the latter which is used by elite forces. Its design is such as to ensure maximum reliability in use. It has an aluminum receiver for good balance and light weight. A cylinder-bored barrel, which is proof-tested to full magnum loads, provides optimum dispersion patterns and permits firing of a variety of ammunition.

The shotgun has twin extractors and the slide mechanism has twin guide bars that help prevent twisting or jamming during rapid operation. A recent addition is that the muzzle has been formed into a muzzle brake by cutting slots in the upper surface. Gas can then be expelled in such a way as to exert downward force, thus permitting easier pointing. In its pistol grip form, the Mossberg ATP8 is extremely compact and can thus be stowed more easily inside vehicles.

There is an almost infinite variety of options available.

SPECIFICATIONS
ORIGIN:
United States.
TYPE:
Shotgun.
DIMENSIONS:
Length (ATP8) - 40.3in (1,009mm); (ATP8, pistol grip) - 30.9in (762mm); barrel - (20.3in (308mm).
WEIGHTS:
ATP8 - 6.7lb (3.06kg); ATP8 (pistol grip) - 6.1lb (2.72kg).
CALIBER:
12-guage, 2 or 3in (69.85 or 76.2mm).
MAGAZINE CAPACITY:
Eight.

HECKLER & KOCH PSG-1 SNIPER RIFLE

SPECIFICATIONS

ORIGIN:
Germany.
TYPE:
Sniper rifle.
DIMENSIONS:
Length overall - 47.5in
(1,206.5mm); barrel -
25.6in (650.2mm).
WEIGHT:
17.8lb (8.07kg).
CARTRIDGE:
7.62 x 51mm NATO.
FEED:
Roller locked, delayed
blowback, semi-automatic.
MAGAZINE CAPACITY:
5 or 20 rounds.
RANGE:
Maximum effective range
1,968ft (600m).
RIFLING:
Polygonal; twists: 12in
(304.8mm) r/h.
SIGHTS:
Hensoldt 6x42 telescopic
with reticle illumination. Six
settings covering 110-
650yd (100-600m).

T HE PRÄZISIONSSCHÜTZENGEWEHR-1 (marksman's precision rifle [PSG-1]) was developed specifically for use by military and police marksmen and was not an adaptation of a service rifle. Unusually among sniper rifles, it is a semi-automatic, using the Heckler & Koch's roller-locked, delayed blowback system. The PSG-1 is built around a polygon-bored heavy barrel which, according to the makers, results in the world's most accurate semi-automatic rifle. Most sniper rifles have a bipod, but the PSG-1 uses an unusual fore-end rest, consisting of a single tube let into a platform which is supported by three short legs. The stock can be adjusted for length and there is also a vertically adjustable cheek-piece, to meet the requirements of the most demanding user.

The PSG-1 is fitted with the Hensoldt 6x42 scope, with an LED-enhanced manual reticle. This is factory-fitted as an integral part of the receiver and no other sight can be fitted, which is seen as a limitation by some. The manufacturers test every rifle off the production line to ensure that it can place 50 rounds of match-standard ammunition into a 3.14in (80mm) circle at 325yd (300m), a very demanding test by any standard.!

RIGHT: Trooper of Brazil's 1o Batalhao da Forces Especials with Heckler & Koch 7.62mm PSG-1 semi-automatic sniper rifle. Many special forces around the world use this weapon, which is noted for its accuracy, reliability, and ease of use. Note how the unusual short-legged tripod has adjusted to the profile of the corrugated roof covering.

RIGHT: The PSG-1 design is based on that of the very successful G1 assault rifle and is a semi-automatic, single-shot weapon firing 7.62mm NATO ammunition. The butt stock can be adjusted in length to fit the individual sniper's requirements and the cheek-piece can be adjusted vertically. The weapon is fitted with a Hensoldt 6x42 scope.

DRAGUNOV SVD

THE SVD WAS DEVELOPED in 1965 and entered service in 1967. It is the standard Russian sniper weapon. One squad in each motorized rifle platoon has an SVD, and selected riflemen receive regular, centralized sniper training. Largely due to its open buttstock, the SVD is lighter than older sniper rifles.

Both the bolt mechanism and the gas recovery system are similar to those of the AK and AKM assault rifles; however, because of the difference in cartridges, parts of it are not interchangeable with these weapons. The most distinguishing features of the SVD are the open buttstock, which is fitted with a cheek pad for ease in sighting, and the telescopic sight mounted over the receiver.

It has a combination flash suppressor/compensator, four magazines, a cleaning kit, and an extra battery and lamp for the telescopic sight. It is equipped with a bayonet, although the rifle would not be an ideal weapon for close combat.

The Russian Army has always set great store by sniping and in World War II men were specially trained to spot German officers by their badges of rank and then shoot them.

SPECIFICATIONS
ORIGIN:
Russian Federation.
TYPE:
Sniper rifle.
DIMENSIONS:
Length (overall) - 48.22in (1,225mm); barrel - 24.4in (620mm).
WEIGHTS:
With PSO-1M2 sight , empty - 9.4lb (4.3kg); loaded - 10.5lb (4.78kg).
CALIBER:
7.62 x 54mm rimmed cartridge.
RANGES:
Max - 2,734yd ((2,500m); effective - 1,422yd (1,300m).
MUZZLE VELOCITY:
2,725ft/s (830m/s).
RATE OF FIRE:
Semi-automatic - 30rpm; effective - 4rpm.

LEFT: Hungarian paratrooper with a Russian Dragunov 7.62mm x 54 sniper rifle. This weapon is widely used by special forces of the former Warsaw Pact and is an effective, reliable, and accurate weapon, although one disadvantage is that it uses different ammunition from other rifles in the squad.

ACCURACY INTERNATIONAL L96A1 SNIPER RIFLE

IN THE 1970s the British infantry used a mix of Lee Enfield 0.303in L42s and 7.62mm L4A1s, while special forces used a variety of rifles which had been acquired at different times to meet specific needs. Virtually all of these were basically service rifles adapted to meet snipers' requirements. It was therefore decided to design and develop one weapon to replace all of these and that it should be specifically designed for use by snipers, not a modified service rifle. The result was a weapon developed by Accuracy International, which, after extensive trials, was accepted for service as the L96A1 sniper rifle.

The initial design was supplied to the British Army as the L96A1 between 1984 and 1990. Two very similar models were also exported as the PM Infantry and the PM Counter Terrorist to 19 other special forces and police. A new version was developed for the Swedish Army as the PSG-90, which was also purchased by the Belgian, Canadian, Irish, New Zealand, and Omani armies, and by several police forces. Total sales have been: L96/PM – 2,000+; PSG-90/AW - 3,000+.

ABOVE: The Accuracy International L96A1 sniper rifle, fitted with PM 6x42 telescopic sight. This is a bolt-operated, single-shot weapon firing either 7.62mm NATO, .243 Winchester or .338 Lapua Magnum ammunition. There is a bipod forward and a single spike in the butt, which can be used to maintain the weapon in the aim during a long wait.

RIGHT: Traveling sniper's outfit with a brief case containing a complete Accuracy International Moderated (ie, noise suppressed) Model PM, firing .308 Lapua ammunition. The suppressor is a 'Thundertrap' manufactured in the USA and gives a reduction in excess of 35dB.

All models are available in 7.62 x 51mm NATO (.308 Winchester), .243 Winchester and .338 Lapua Magnum calibers and the barrel can be changed in five minutes using three allen keys and a screw-driver. The rifle is fitted with a modified Parker-Hale LM6 bipod, with adjustable legs which permit the rifle height to be varied between 8.5 and 12in (216 and 304.8mm). The Thundertrap sound suppressor is 8.5in (216mm) long and 1.6in (40mm) in diameter and is fabricated from non-magnetic stainless steel. Made by AWC of Phoenix, Arizona, it gives a reduction in sound pressure in excess of 35dB. Where the sniper has to spend long periods in the aim a retractable spike can be fitted to the butt, enabling the sniper to maintain the aim without excessive fatigue. The magazine holds 10 rounds.

SPECIFICATIONS

ORIGIN: United Kingdom.	**FEED:** Bolt action.
TYPE: Sniper rifle.	Magazine capacity: 10 rounds.
DIMENSIONS: Length overall - 45.8in (1,163mm); barrel - 25.8in (655mm).	**MAXIMUM EFFECTIVE RANGE:** 1000yd (914m)
WEIGHT: 13.67lb (6.20kg).	**RIFLING:** 20in (508mm), 1-12 twist, stainless steel barrel.
CARTRIDGE: 7.62 x 51mm NATO.	**SIGHTS:** Schmidt and Bender 3-12x50 optical sight or iron sights.

LEFT: US Army sniper (center) with M24 Sniper Weapon System (SWS), which fires NATO standard 7.62mm x 51mm ammunition.

SPECIFICATIONS
ORIGIN:
United States.
TYPE:
Sniper rifle.
DIMENSIONS:
Overall length - 48in (1,219mm); barrel - 24in (609.6mm); 1 twist in 11.2in (284.5mm).
WEIGHT:
Empty - 12.1lb (5.49kg).
CALIBER:
7.62 x 51mm NATO (.308 Winchester).
OPERATION:
Bolt action.

FEED:
5-round internal magazine.
Max effective range:
875yd (800m).

M24 SNIPER WEAPON SYSTEM

THE US ARMY'S current sniper rifle is the M24 Sniper Weapon System (SWS). This bolt-action weapon uses the Remington 700 action, a composite stock, aluminum bedding block, adjustable butt plate, and a detachable bipod.

M40A1 SNIPER RIFLE

THE US MARINE CORPS' current sniper rifle is the 7.62mm M40A1 which is a modified Remington Model 700 which has been remanufactured by hand by specially trained USMC armorers at Quantico, Va. The M40A1 has a heavy barrel made of competition-grade heavy barrel and a bolt action, and is equipped with a special 10x sniper scope.

SPECIFICATIONS
ORIGIN:
United States.
TYPE:
Sniper rifle.
DIMENSIONS:
Overall - 44in (1,117.6mm); barrel - 24in (609.6mm).
WEIGHT:
With scope - 14.5lb (6.58kg).
CARTRIDGE:
7.62mm x 51mm (NATO) (.308 Winchester).
MAXIMUM EFFECTIVE RANGE:
1,000yd (914m).
MUZZLE VELOCITY:
2,550ft/s (777m/s).
MAGAZINE CAPACITY:
5 rounds.

LEFT: Range practice for a US Marine Corps sniper, firing the M40A1, which is essentially a Remington 700 that has been completely rebuilt by Corps' armourers.

M60 GENERAL-PURPOSE MACHINE GUN

RIGHT: US Army general-purpose machine gun (GPMG) team trains in urban warfare; note the blank-firing attachments on the muzzles of the two weapons in the picture. The M60 is a gas-operated, belt-fed, air-cooled weapon, firing NATO standard 7.62mm ammunition, which was required to be used from a bipod, as shown here, and from a tripod in the sustained-fire role.

Below: US paratrooper with the greatly improved M60E3. The original M60 suffered from shortcomings, including a lack of a gas-regulator, and to run-away if dirt got into the mechanism.

THE M60 WAS THE STANDARD GPMG of the US Army but is now being replaced. The weapon is gas-operated, air-cooled and is normally used with a 100-round belt of ammunition. To avoid overheating the barrel is normally changed after 500 rounds have been fired. Its fore sight is of the fixed blade type and its rear sight is of the U-notch type and is graduated from about 656ft to 3,937ft (200 to 1,200m) in about 328ft (100m) steps. The weapon is provided with a stock, carrying handle and a built-in bipod. The M60 can also be used on an M122 tripod mount, M4 pedestal mount and M142 gun mount for vehicles, Other versions include the M60C remote for helicopters, M60D pintle mount for vehicles and helicopters and the M60E2 internal model for AFVs.

The original M60 was not a complete success, perhaps because too much was expected of a general purpose gun. This inevitably results in a system that is too heavy for the light role and too light for the heavy. However, the M60 was used extensively by US forces in Vietnam and, partly because of the practical experience obtained there by regular and special forces, was improved considerably and issued as the M60E1. It is still widely used and can be found in service in the armed forces of Australia, El Salvador, the Republic of Korea and Taiwan among others.

SPECIFICATIONS

ORIGIN:
United States.
TYPE:
General-purpose machine gun.
DIMENSIONS:
Gun length (overall) – 44.2in (1,105mm); barrel - 22.4in (560mm).
WEIGHTS:
With bipod and gas cyclinder, gun - 23.1lb (10.51kg); barrel - 8.2lb (3.74kg).
CALIBER:
7.62mmx51mm (NATO cartridge).
EFFECTIVE RANGES:
On bipod - 1,100yd (1,000m); on tripod - 1,980yd (1,800m).
MUZZLE VELOCITY:
2,820ft/s (855m/s).
RATE OF FIRE:
Cyclic, 650rpm.

PK7.62MM GENERAL-PURPOSE MACHINE GUN

THE RUSSIAN PK WAS INTRODUCED into service in 1960 and is a fully automatic, gas-operated general-purpose machine gun (GPMG) which seems to have been designed by taking the best elements of other Russian weapons, including a Kalashnikov rotating bolt, Goryunov cartridge extractor and barrel-change, and Degtyarev feed system and trigger. There are four known variants in the basic PK series: PK - standard GPMG with bipod; PKB - PK without stock and with revised trigger for use in a pintle mounting (eg, on the roof of a vehicle); PKS - PK on light tripod for sustained fire or AA; PKT - vehicle version, without sights or stock and with trigger mechanism replaced by a solenoid.

The PKM is a later, lighter version of PK with a bipod and a hinged butt rest, and with weight reduced to 18.5lb (8.4kg). The PKMS is a PKM on a tripod and the PKB does not have a stock.

The PK-series weapons are easy to handle, have little recoil, and do not tend to climb when fired on automatic. They are also lighter, more reliable and easier to maintain than the US M60, although their maximum effective range is some 109yd (100m) less. They are likely to be found in any Russian or former Warsaw Pact army or special forces unit, as well as in numerous foreign armies.

SPECIFICATIONS
ORIGIN:
Russian Federation.
TYPE:
General-purpose machine gun.
DIMENSIONS:
Length overall - 45.7in (1,173mm); barrel - 25.9in (658mm).
WEIGHTS:
Gun on bipod 19.8lb (9.0kg); gun on tripod 36.3lb (16.5kg).
CARTRIDGE:
Russian 7.62 x 54R full-power, rimmed.
FEED:
50/250 round belts.
RATE OF FIRE:
Cyclic 650rpm; practical 250rpm.
MAXIMUM EFFECTIVE RANGE:
1,093yd (1,000m).
MUZZLE VELOCITY:
2,707ft/s (825m/s).

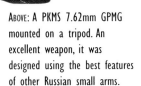

ABOVE: A PKMS 7.62mm GPMG mounted on a tripod. An excellent weapon, it was designed using the best features of other Russian small arms.

BELOW: Another widely used Russian machine gun, the RPK is a development of the 7.62mm AK-47 assault rifle. Range is 875yd (800m) and it uses either 30-round box or 70-round drum magazines.

5.56MM M249
SQUAD AUTOMATIC WEAPON (SAW)

WHEN THE 5.56MM M16 (Armalite) rifle entered service during the Vietnam War it gave every man in the squad an automatic weapon, but with a maximum effective range of little more than 330yd (300m). It was quickly realized, however, that both fire teams needed a weapon of greater all-round capability, but lighter than the contemporary 7.62mm M60 and one which used the same ammunition as the riflemen. This gave rise to a US Army requirement for a 5.56mm Squad Automatic Weapon (SAW), with the US Marine Corps joining the program later.

After considering all suitable weapons in the Western world, the US forces selected a "product improved" development of the Belgian Fabrique Nationale's (FN) "Minimi" which was placed in production as the M249, with initial supplies coming from the FN factory in Herstal, although a US line was subsequently established. The product improvements in the US version include minor changes to the barrel, buffer, handguard, pistol grip, stock and sights.

BELOW: The standard model FN Minimi firing NATO standard 5.56x45mm ammunition. The weapon shown here is fitted with a 200-round plastic magazine. In action, the carrying-handle would be twisted down beside the body out of the way of the firer.

SPECIFICATIONS

ORIGIN: Belgium.
TYPE:
Light machine gun.
BORE DIAMETER:
0.233in (5.56mm).
DIMENSIONS:
Length overall - 40.87in (1,038mm);
barrel - 18.4in (466mm).
WEIGHTS:
Gun empty, with bipod and tools -
15.16lb (6.88kg);
30-round magazine: 1.07lb (0.49kg);
200-round box magazine: 6.92lb
(3.14kg).
CARTRIDGE:
5.56mm x 45mm (NATO)/M193 (US).

FEED:
30-round box, or 100- or 200-round belts; gas-operated, disintegrating link belt.
RANGES:
Effective range against area target -
1,093yd (1,000m);
maximum range: 2.23 miles (3.6km).
MUZZLE VELOCITY:
SS109 - 3,000ft/s (915m/s); M193
3,166ft/s (965m/s).
RATE OF FIRE:
Cyclic -- 725rpm; sustained -- 85rpm.
RIFLING:
6 grooves, r/h.

RIGHT: The Minimi showing its various ammunition feed systems. In the front is a traditional pattern 30-round box, while between the bipod legs is a pre-loaded 200-round plastic box magazine. Aligned underneath the weapon is a belt, which is issued in either 100- or 200-round lengths. The weapon accepts either magazines or belts without any modification.

The M249 is smooth in operation and is very reliable. Fully combat ready and complete with 200 rounds, bipod, sling and cleaning kit it weighs just 22lb (9.97kg) which is 1lb (0.4kg) less than an empty M60. The M249 can accept either magazine or belts without modification and is normally fired from a bipod, although a tripod for the sustained-fire role is also available. The gunner normally carries 600 rounds of linked ammunition, which can be loaded into either 30-round magazines or pre-loaded 200-round plastic magazines or fed trough as a belt.   A parachute model with a sliding stock and other modifications, such as a shorter barrel, is also available. This weapon is 35.5in (900mm) long with the stock extended and 28.5in (725mm) long with it folded. Overall weight is marginally greater: 15.7lb (7.1kg) compared to 15.2lb (6.875kg).

ABOVE: Paratroop version of the Minimi, which has a number of modifications, including shorter barrel, sliding stock (retracted in this picture) and canted carrying-handle. It has the same facilities as the standard version for firing either belt-fed, boxed or magazine-fed NATO standard 5.56x45mm ammunition.

LEFT: In the background is the FN Mimimi with the stock in the retracted position, with the two types of magazine in front and a belt on the gun. In front is the FNC (Fabrique Nationale Carabine) a 5.56x45mm (.223 Remington) weapon, which uses Kalashnikov-type working parts to provide very smooth operation. It is 40in (102cm) long (30in [76cm] with stock folded), empty weight is 8.4lb(3.8kg) and the magazine contains 30 rounds. It has been adopted by Indonesia and Sweden

M2HB 0.50IN HEAVY MACHINE GUN

SPECIFICATIONS
ORIGIN:
United States.
TYPE:
Heavy machine gun.
DIMENSIONS:
Length overall - 65.2in
(1,656mm); barrel - 45in
(1,143mm).
WEIGHT:
Empty - 84lb (38.15kg).
CARTRIDGE:
0.50 Browning (12.7 x
99mm).
FEED:
Short recoil; disintegrating
link belt.
RIFLING:
8 grooves, right hand.
MUZZLE VELOCITY:
Standard rounds - 2,900ft/s
(883m/s); SLAP rounds -
3,985ft/s (1,215m/s).
RATE OF FIRE:
485-635rpm
MAXIMUM EFFECTIVE
RANGE:
Standard rounds - 2,600yd
(2,380m); SLAP rounds –
1,640yd (1,500m).

THE BROWNING M2HB is quite simply one of the greatest machine guns ever designed, being efficient and very effective; easy to use and to maintain; and as suitable for installation in a tank turret as on a ground tripod or an aircraft. Further, it has been in front-line service for five decades and there is a large range of widely available ammunition.

Like all weapons, the design started with the cartridge. When the United States Army arrived in France in 1917 it found a need for a machine gun firing a larger round than that used in contemporary rifles, which was required not only for use against troops but also for new tasks such as attacking tanks, balloons, and aircraft. It proved impossible to convert any US weapon to take the 0.43in (11mm) round then being tested by the French, but at that point the US Army happened to capture some new Mauser anti-tank rifles with their ammunition. The excellence of the round was quickly recognized and a new United States 0.50in cartridge was rapidly developed along the same lines. At the same time John Browning, one of the most famous gunsmiths in history, was called in to develop a weapon to take this new round, which resulted in the M1921A1 machine gun. The design was refined in the early 1930s which led to the M2, but this was limited by barrel life, and a new, much sturdier barrel was quickly produced, resulting in the definitive M2HB (HB = heavy barrel).

The M2HB has seen service in fixed-wing aircraft; helicopters; a multitude of trucks and field cars such as jeeps, Land Rovers, fast strike vehicles and HMMWVs; as well as APCs and tanks. It has been manufactured in vast numbers and is still widely used, since its 0.50in high velocity round has both considerable range, greater carrying capacity than the 5.56mm rounds now used in rifles and light machine guns, as well as great accuracy since it is highly resistant to wind drift.

The ammunition is widely available, having been manufactured in some 30 countries, and is still in production in at least 10 of them. There is also a vast range of natures (ie, different types) with some countries still devoting research effort to producing new 0.50 caliber rounds. One of the most recent of these developments was the Saboted Light Armor Penetrator (SLAP) round developed by the US Marine Corps in the middle and late 1980s. This uses a sub-caliber (0.30in [7.62mm]) tungsten carbide penetrator carried in a 0.50in (12.7mm) sabot, which breaks away as the round exits from the muzzle. This results in the penetrator having a much increased velocity (3,985ft/s [1,215m/s] compared to 2,900ft/s [883m/s]) giving it a very flat trajectory, thus enhancing both hit probability and armor

RIGHT: US Army 0.50in M2HB machine gun post during Operation Desert Storm in 1991. The only major change since it entered production in the 1920s is the heavy barrel, which replaced the earlier version in the 1930s. It fires a 0.50in (12.7mm) round, which is accurate and possesses considerable hitting power, and ammunition is widely available, being manufactured in many countries around the world.

penetration. SLAP rounds were used with great success during their operational debut in Operation Desert Storm in 1991. SLAP ammunition is completely interoperable with M2 machine guns, but requires one of the new type of chrome-plated, stellite-lined barrels.

Upgrade kits are also being marketed, mostly concentrating on quick-change, longer-life barrels fitted with noise suppressors. Indeed, the only challenge of any significance to the M2HB is coming from the new heavy cannon, such as the McDonnell Douglas ASP 30mm, although these are very much larger and considerably heavier.

ABOVE: A version of the 0.50in M2HB from Fabrique Nationale of Belgium, featuring a quick-change barrel (QCB) and a number of minor improvements. Despite its age, much effort is being put into refining the M2 rather than developing a totally new weapon, since it is very good at its job and, just for once, the principle of "if it ain't broke, don't fix it" is being applied.

GRENADES

GRENADES ARE A FORM of local artillery which range in purpose from high-explosive, through fragmentation, stun and smoke, to illuminating. They are extremely valuable for giving the individual soldier effective firepower, under his own control. They are easily carried and are used by both terrorists and anti-terrorist forces. For hand grenades the only criterion is that their lethal radius must be less than the distance an average man can throw, but this does not apply to those fired from a grenade launcher.

Mk19 40mm Machine Gun, Mod 3

The Mk19 grenade launcher was developed to provide effective fire support weapon for US Navy riverine patrols in Vietnam and has proved to be an outstanding success in both offensive and defensive roles, delivering rapid and accurate firepower against enemy troops and lightly armored vehicles. It is a gas-operated, air-cooled, belt-fed, blowback weapon, firing a variety of 40mm grenades from 20- or 50-round magazines. A Product Improvement Program (PIP) in the 1970s resulted in the current Mk19 Mod3, which is more reliable and simpler to maintain than earlier versions. The Mk19 Mod 3 can be mounted on a ground tripod, or in almost any vehicle, including HMMWV, M113FOV and 5-ton trucks, and has been used by special forces in combat situations such as the 1991 Gulf War.

ABOVE: The Mk 19 Mod 3 grenade launcher mounted on a HMMWV ("Hummer") vehicle. It fires dual-purpose anti-personnel and anti-armor 12oz (340gm) grenades to a range of 1,800 yards (1,650m).

RIGHT: The Russian AGS-17 Plamya is an automatic grenade launcher. Because of its weight, it (like the US Mk 19 Mod 3) requires a vehicle for mobility.

30mm AGS-17 Plamya Automatic Grenade Launcher

The Plamya (= flame) is a Russian-produced weapon that fires small grenades of three types: anti-tank with HEAT warhead; ant-personnel, containing iron needles fatal over a 4.4-5.5yd (4-5m) radius; and a phosphorous round. The drum magazine contains 30 rounds and the cyclic rate of fire is 100 rounds per minute. Effective range is 770-870yd (700-800m). The weapon is, however, rather heavy, weighing 77lb (35kg) including the tripod.

M203 40MM GRENADE LAUNCHER

The M203 was developed by the AAI Corporation to meet a US Army requirement for a lightweight, single-shot, breech-loading, pump-action, shoulder-fired weapon. It can be attached under the barrel of any version of the M16 rifle, and has its own trigger and sight. The M203 fires a wide variety of 40mm low-velocity grenades, including: high explosive; high-explosive airburst; buckshot; anti-armor; smoke; illuminating; and riot control. Two sighting systems are used. The primary sight consists of an aperture and post system, and has ranges marked on a quadrant scale. The secondary sight is a folding, graduated, lead sight, mounted on the forestock, and which uses the rifle's foresight blade as a front-aiming reference. M203s are widely used by US forces, including SEALs, Delta and Rangers, as well as by many foreign forces.

RGD-5

Widely used in the former Warsaw Pact, the Russian RGD-5 comprises a 2.42oz (110g) HE charge, housed in a serrated fragmenting liner, which is surrounded by a thin, sheet-steel casing. The grenade weighs 0.68lb (310g) and is 2.2in (56mm) in diameter.

RKG-3M

The RKG-3M was the standard hand-thrown anti-armor grenade of the former Warsaw Pact forces. It comprises a 2.2in (55.6mm) diameter hollow-charge (HEAT) warhead, containing 1.24lb (567g) of explosive, housed in a metal case and mounted on a wooden handle which also contains a drogue parachute. The earlier RKG-3 had a steel liner inside the hollow charge but this was replaced in the RKG-3M by a copper liner, which increased armor penetration from 5in (125mm) to 6.5in (165mm). When the grenade is thrown the drogue automatically deploys, thus completing the arming process and ensuring that the grenade hits the target armor plate as near to the optimum 90 degrees as possible.

HALEY & WELLER E182 STUN GRENADE

When conducting anti-terrorist operations in closed spaces such as rooms, cabins or aircraft, anti-terrorist forces quickly found that explosions and flashes of light disoriented the terrorists, but that conventional fragmentation grenades were highly unsuitable. An alternative was, therefore, found in "stun" grenades, which are designed to emit a loud explosion but to cause minimal damage. Typical of these is the Haley & Weller E182, which is 2.2in (50mm) in diameter, 4.1in (104mm) long and weighs 9oz (250g). The safety-pin is on a ring which is pulled in the normal way and on being thrown the firing lever is released but does not fly off. The grenade contains a small electric cell and the firing lever closes a circuit, which, after a 0.5sec time delay, then initiates the main 0.4oz (12g) charge. This releases 16 sub-munitions, the first of which detonates after 2sec, followed by the others at 3-4sec intervals. Each sub-munition explodes with a very loud noise and emits a 22 million candela flash.

ABOVE: The M203 launcher clips underneath the M16 rifle and has its own trigger. It launches a 40mm grenade out to a maximum range of 380 yards (350m).

LEFT: Haley & Weller's E182 multi-burst stun grenade, a disorientating grenade employing high candela and decibel levels. It weighs just over 1/2lb (250gm).

RPG-7V AT ROCKET LAUNCHER

THE STANDARD ANTI-ARMOR WEAPON of Russian infantry, the RPG-7 replaced an earlier weapon derived from the World War II German Panzerfaust which merely fired a hollow-charge projectile from a shoulder-rested tube. The original, and heavier, version of this weapon was introduced in 1962 and was known simply as the RPG-7. The RPG-7V is a later variant which made its appearance in 1968.

RPG-7V fires a projectile which, a few feet beyond the muzzle, ignites an internal rocket to give shorter flight-time, flatter trajectory and better accuracy. The HEAT or HE warhead has improved fuzing, the HEAT round penetrating to 12.6in (320mm) of armor. The PGO-7 and PGO-7V optical sights are frequently supplemented by the NSP-2 (IR) night sight. There is also a special folding version used by airborne troops, designated RPG-7D.

During the Cold War this launcher was standard issue for Soviet Union and Warsaw Pact forces - as well as forces in North Korea, North Vietnam, and other satellite countries.

Even in the hands of unskilled and illiterate troops, it is known to be highly effective against bunkers and buildings, troops, vehicles of all types, and even helicopters when properly employed. Like many other Soviet weapons, the

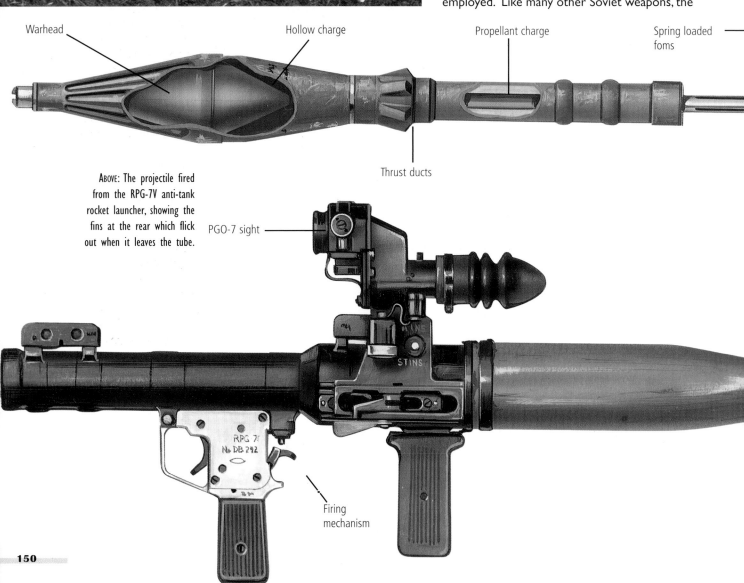

Warhead

Hollow charge

Propellant charge

Spring loaded foms

Thrust ducts

ABOVE: The projectile fired from the RPG-7V anti-tank rocket launcher, showing the fins at the rear which flick out when it leaves the tube.

PGO-7 sight

Firing mechanism

SPECIFICATIONS
ORIGIN:
Russian Federation.
TYPE:
Rocket launcher.
DIMENSIONS:
Length - 38.5in (990mm).
WEIGHTS:
Launcher - 15lb ((7kg);
grenade - 4.95lb (2.25kg).
CALIBER OF TUBE:
40mm.
CALIBER OF PROJECTILE:
85mm.
EFFECTIVE RANGES:
Moving target - 328yd
(300m); stationary target -
550yd (500m).
MASS OF PROJECTILE:
4.95lb (2.25kg).
MUZZLE VELOCITY:
984ft/s (300m/s).

FAR LEFT:: At one time issued to former Soviet special forces and regular troops of Warpac nations, the RPG-7V is less effective nowadays against modern tank armor, but is nevertheless a devastating weapon in the hands of guerrillas and terrorists.

ABOVE The Chinese have made their own version of the RPG rocket launcher, known as the Type 56 grenade launcher, the grenade being the Type 50. Both this and the RPG-7 were developed from the RPG-2, itself derived from the World War II German Panzerfaust. The RPG-7V is a small, lightweight anti-tank weapon with a big punch. The grenade is percussion-fired, the rocket motor igniting after 33 feet (10m). As the grenade is fired from the tube, four large fins toward the rear flick out. At the very end of the weapon small offset fins give slow rate of roll to maintain stability.

Spin inducer

RPG-7V was widely distributed to and is still used by a variety of guerrilla and subversive organizations and it is hardly possible to see a photograph or telecast concerning small internal conflicts without being able to pick them out, slung casually from the bearer's shoulder with the body of a rocket protruding menacingly from the top. A few even appeared in Ulster in the hands of the Provisional IRA, but do not seem to have been used with any great success.

A new disposable, single-shot, man-portable anti-tank weapon designated RPG-16 replaced the RPG-7 in the Russian Army in the 1980s, but RPG-7 will doubtless be used in other hands for many years to come.

STINGER FIM-92 B/C GROUND-TO-AIR MISSILE SYSTEM

STINGER WAS DEVELOPED for the US Army and US Marine Corps in the 1970s as a replacement for the first-generation Redeye missile. Designated FIM-92 MANPADS (man-portable air defense system) the new missile was intended to provide an air defense capability for even the smallest detachment, such as an infantry platoon or a special forces patrol.

In a ground-air engagement the Stinger gunner acquires the target visually, or, if equipped with the latest, third-generation sight, by use of an image intensifier, which enables him to acquire targets at night or in bad weather. The gunner then operates the friend-or-foe (IFF) device, which, if it confirms hostile status, allows the missile seeker to lock-on to the target. The missile then informs the gunner by an audio signal that it has locked-on and the gunner then presses the launch button, activating the eject motor which fires in a very short burst (burn-out is completed before the missile leaves the launch tube), propelling the missile out of the tube.

SPECIFICATIONS

ORIGIN:
United States.
TYPE:
Man-portable air defense system (MANPADS).
DIMENSIONS:
Missile length 60in (1,524mm); body diameter 2.75in (69.8mm); wing span 0.5in (166mm).
WEIGHT:
Launch - 22.3lb (10.1kg); package - 35lb (15.6kg).
PROPULSION:
Two stage; solid propellant eject motor; solid propellant boost/sustainer motor.
GUIDANCE:
Stinger – optical aiming; passive IR homing; Stinger POST – dual mode infra-red/ultraviolet (IR/UV).
MAXIMUM EFFECTIVE RANGE:
In excess of 3.1miles (5km).
FLIGHT SPEED:
Supersonic, about Mach 1.7.
WARHEAD:
Magnavox high-explosive fragmentation; with smooth fragmenting casing; impact fuze.

On leaving the tube the four spring-loaded control surfaces (two fixed, two movable) deploy and when the missile is at a safe distance the boost/sustainer motor fires, the fuzing circuit is armed and the missile accelerates to its cruise speed of approximately Mach 1.7. The missile homes on IR energy emitted by the target and computes a proportional navigation course to intercept. It can be fired from any angle relative to the target and has a very high hit probability, but should it miss there is a self-destruct capability.

Stinger is stored and issued as a certified round of ammunition in a sealed storage/launch tube. When required it is attached to the gunner's sighting/aiming unit and following launch the empty tube is discarded and another one fitted. The tubed missile requires no field maintenance.

Stinger has been adapted for launch from helicopters for self-protection (for example, by AH-64) and from pedestal mounts on vehicles such as HMMWV. The USMC uses Pedestal Mount Stinger (PMS) on its eight-wheeled LAV vehicles.

The two current versions of this system are: Stinger POST (passive optical seeker technique), and Stinger RMP (reprogrammable microprocessor). Stinger Post entered service in 1987 and uses a dual mode IR/UV seeker to improve performance against decoys, countermeasures, and background clutter.

Stinger RMP (entered service in 1988 and uses the Stinger POST seeker, but with an added digital information processing system, incorporating an external software reprogramming function, thus enabling software changes to be made to meet a changing threat.

Well over 50,000 Stingers are in service with many nations including: Germany, Israel, Italy, Japan, Netherlands, Saudi Arabia, Turkey, and the USA. It was also used with some success by the British in the Falklands War. The Stinger system has been used in combat by the mujahideen in Afghanistan, the British SAS in the Falklands, as well as in Nicaragua and Angola.

LEFT: Stinger missile powers away, propelled by its Atlantic Research Mk 27 booster/ sustainer rocket motor. Top speed is approximately Mach 2, range is in excess of 3.1miles (5km), and the missile is sufficiently maneuverable to counter any jinking by the target.

AGM-114 HELLFIRE ANTI-TANK MISSILE

ELITE AND SPECIAL FORCES are likely to be used in advance of other troops where they will be vulnerable to attack by enemy armored vehicles, such as tanks, armored cars and armored personnel carriers. It is therefore essential that they should have some anti-tank protection, of which the most flexible is an attack helicopter such as the AH-64, AH-1 or Lynx. TOW is already widely used in this role, but Hellfire is much faster and has a more powerful warhead.

The latest version is Hellfire II, which is based on the earlier Laser Hellfire, in which the target is "designated" by a laser aimed by the launching aircraft, ground observers or other aircraft. The missile seeker then homes on the reflection, using four canard surfaces to control the flight. The missile can also be launched without target acquisition, in which case it either follows a line of sight or a programmed trajectory, until a target has been acquired.

The missile is powered by a single-stage, solid-propellant motor which accelerates the missile at some 10g until it reaches its maximum speed of some 950mph (1,52km/h). Arming takes place some 500-1,000ft (150-300m) from the aircraft. The missile is fitted with tandem warhead, which enables it to defeat the latest "reactive armor." The missile can also be used against concrete bunkers.

The Longbow Hellfire missile provides the AH-64D with a "fire-and-forget" anti-armor missile which can be used in poor weather conditions. The Longbow Hellfire fire control radar works in the millimeter wave (MMW) band and will locate, classify, and prioritize targets for the Longbow Hellfire missile. The Longbow system will be integrated into both the Apache attack helicopter and the Comanche armed reconnaissance helicopters.

The advantages of the Longbow missile include a capability to operate in rain, snow, fog and smoke; MMW countermeasures survivability; and "fire-and-forget" guidance, which allows the Apache Longbow to launch and then return to cover, thus minimizing exposure to enemy fire. The missile also has an advanced warhead capable of defeating reactive armor

BELOW: One of the primary weapons systems for the US Army's AH-64D Apache longbow is the AGM-114 Hellfire II, of which 16 are seen under the stub wings of this aircraft. Using millimetre wave (MMW) band radar, the Hellfire II gives the AH-64D's crew a 'fire-and-forget' capability and enables them to attack targets in rain, snow, fog and smoke. The missile has a tandem warhead, enabling it to attack armoured vehicles protected by 'reactive armor.'

and its software is reprogrammable, thus enabling it to be adapted to changing threats.

Delivery of the first service missiles began in September 1984 and known versions of the Hellfire include:

AGM-114A, no longer in service.

AGM-114B, designed for shipboard use with additional electronic arm/safety device.

AGM-114C, with a low smoke motor, lower trajectory and an improved semi-active laser seeker with an improved low visibility capability.

AGM-114F, with a tandem warhead to defeat vehicles equipped with reactive armor.

AGM-114K, with the same tandem warhead as the -F but with electro-optical countermeasures hardening, semiactive laser seeker, and a programmable autopilot for trajectory shaping.

RBS-17, Swedish designation for the Hellfire used in the ground-based coastal defense role.

Hellfire is in service in the USA, the Netherlands and Sweden, and will enter service in the UK with the AH-64D Apache Longbow.

SPECIFICATIONS
ORIGIN:
United States.
TYPE:
Heli-borne anti-armor missile.
LENGTHS:
Active seeker version - 70.4in (1.78m); laser-seeker version - 64.6in (1.64m).
DIAMETER:
7in (178mm).
WING SPAN:
13in (330mm).
PROPULSION:
Morton Thiokol TX-657 single-stage, solid propellant, smokeless rocket motor.
WARHEAD:
Firestone tandem conical charges, 16lb (7.25kg); impact fuze.
LAUNCH WEIGHT:
105.6lb (47.88kg).
SPEED:
Mach 1.17 - 950mph (1,530km/h).
RANGE:
4.5 miles (7,000m).

ABOVE LEFT: An early model Hellfire missile, showing the semi-active laser homing head and four steerable canard surfaces, which control the missile in flight. Behind the nose electronics package is the tandem warhead, with an impact fuze.

LEFT: A Westland Longbow Apache of the British Army Air Corps, showing its weapons load of 16 Hellfire II missiles. These well-armed, well-equipped aircraft have great potential for the support of special forces and for special operations of their own.

HIGH MOBILITY MULTI-PURPOSE WHEELED VEHICLE (HMMWV)

SPECIFICATIONS
ORIGIN: United States.
TYPE:
High mobility, multi-purpose, wheeled vehicle.
DIMENSIONS:
Length - 15ft (4.57m); width - 7.08ft (2.16m); height - 6.00ft (1.83m) [can be reduced to 4.5ft (1.37m)].
ENGINE:
General Motors 6.5l; V-8; liquid-cooled, diesel, with fuel-injection; 150hp at 3,600rpm.
DRIVE:
4 x 4; 3-speed, automatic transmission; 2 speed, locking, chain driven transfer.
TRANSMISSION:
Allison, fully-automatic; 3 speeds forward/1 reverse.
TRANSFER:
Permanently-engaged all-wheel drive, with integral transfer case.
ELECTRICS:
24 volt; negative earth (ground); 60 amps.
SPEED:
55mph (89km/h), governed at gross weight.
FORDING DEPTH:
No preparation - 2.5ft (0.76cm); with deep water fording kit -- 5ft (1.5m).
GROUND CLEARANCE:
16in (406mm) loaded.
FUEL:
Diesel; 25 gallons (94.63l).
ROAD RANGE (MAXIMUM):
350 miles (563km).
SLOPE LIMITS:
Maximum slope (grade) - 60 percent; side slope -- 40deg.

ABOVE: HMMWV "Hummer" armed with a tank-busting TOW missile system. The 1-ton vehicle replaced a large number of different types.

RIGHT: The Hummer provides a platform for a wide variety of missiles, including the Avenger system, seen here.

FAR RIGHT Hummer armed with a Mk 19 40mm grenade launcher. The Hummer range provides the standard vehicle platform for all four US Services and new uses are regularly being found.

The High Mobility Multi-Purpose Wheeled Vehicle (HMMWV) (popularly known as the "Hummer" or "Hum-V") is the workhorse of the US armed forces and is found in most elite units. Its importance lies in its light weight and small size which enable it to be parachuted or air-landed into operational areas, while its large carrying capacity means that it can carry relatively heavy weapons.

The HMMWV was the outcome of an early 1980s competition for a new, all-purpose, field-car to replace a variety of light vehicles, including: M151-ton "Jeep;" M274-ton Mule; M8780 1-ton pick-up; M561 Gama Goat articulated vehicle; and the M792 1-ton ambulance. With vast numbers to be ordered, the competition was hard fought, the eventual winner being American Motors, General Division.

The HMMWV is required to provide the standard vehicle platform for a whole series of light tactical vehicles for all four US services for roles which include: cargo and troop carriers; command and control; shelter carriers; weapons platforms; and ambulances. The HMMWV is powered by a General Motors V-8 diesel engine, and has automatic transmission and permanently-engaged, four-wheel drive. Many versions of the HMMWV are equipped with a self-recovery, 6,000lb (2,722kg) capacity

Additional armor is fitted to the weapons and TOW missile carriers, and the M1109 is an up-armored version, produced in limited quantities, mainly for use by Scout Platoons. Other versions carry the AN/TRC-170 Radio Digital Terminal and the pedestal-mounted Stinger missile system.

New uses are contantly being found for the HMMWV and among current US Army developments are:

- The Long-Range Advanced Scout Surveillance System #3 (LRAS3), which incorporates forward-looking infrared (FLIR), TV camera, laser rangefinder and GPS, mounted on a HMMWV, which will enable reconnaissance units to locate direct fire weapons, by day or night, from outside the range of those weapons.
- The Line of Sight Anti-tank (LOSAT) weapon system which will consist of a kinetic energy weapon launcher with four missiles, mounted in an expanded-capacity HMMWV with the mission of defeating advanced AFVs, helicopters, bunkers and other targets. The HMMWV-based LOSAT would provide early entry forces with an air-mobile and parachute droppable, roll-on/off assault weapon.
- The M31 Biological Integrated Detection System (BIDS), which can monitor, sample, detect and identify battlefield biological warfare (BW) agents. Each BIDS team consists of an M31 BIDS, a high-mobility multi-purpose wheeled vehicle (HMMWV) support vehicle, and four soldiers, and a towed 15kv trailer-mounted generator.

SUMMARY OF MAIN CURRENT TYPES OF HMMWV			
TYPE	ROLE	PAYLOAD	KERB WEIGHT
M998	Cargo/troop carrier	2 + 8 or 2,500lb (1,134kg)	7,700lb (3,492kg)
M1038	Cargo/troop carrier, with winch	2 + 8 or 2,500lb (1,134kg)	7,700lb (3,492kg)
M1025	Armament carrier	M60 7.62mm MG or M2 .50in HMG or Mk 19 grenade launcher.	8,200lb (3,719kg)
M1044	Armament carrier, with winch	M60 7.62mm MG or M2 .50in HMG or Mk 19 grenade launcher	8,400lb (3,810kg)
M1035	TOW carrier	TOW launcher + missiles	8,380lb (3,801kg)
M1046	TOW carrier, with winch	TOW launcher + missiles	8,400lb (3,810kg)
M996	Mini-ambulance	2 litter patients, or 6 ambulatory patients or combination	8,380lb (3,801kg)
M997	Maxi-ambulance	4 litter patients, or 8 ambulatory patients, or combination	9,100lb (4,128kg)
M1035	Soft-top ambulance	2 litter patients	7,700lb (3,493kg)
M1037	Shelter carrier	Crew + 3,600lb (1,633kg) inc shelter	8,660lb (3,928kg)
M1042	Shelter carrier, with winch	Crew + 3,600lb (1,633kg) inc shelter	8,660lb (3,928kg)
M1097	Cargo/troop carrier (heavy)	2 + 8 or 4,575lb (2,075kg)	10,000lb (4,536kg)
M1097A1	Cargo/troop carrier, with winch	2 + 8 or 4,575lb (2,075kg)	n/k
M1109	Up-armored armament carrier	M60 7.62mm MG or M2 .50in HMG or Mk 19 grenade launcher	n/k
M1114	Up-armored Armament carrier, with winch	M60 7.62mm MG or M2 .50in HMG or Mk 19 grenade launcher	n/k

BMD-3
AIRBORNE INFANTRY FIGHTING VEHICLE (AIFV)

TWO REQUIREMENTS FOR a parachute-landed force are the ability to move rapidly around the battlefield and to provide defense against armored counterattacks. Western armies meet this requirement by converting standard military vehicles (eg, HMMWV) but the Soviet Army developed a series of vehicles specifically for the airborne forces. The basic vehicle was the "Boevaya Mashina Desantnya - 1" (BMD-1) (= airborne combat vehicle), which was first seen by Westerners in the November 1973 Red Square parade.

BMD-1

Despite its small size BMD-1 bristled with weapons. Turret-mounted armament comprised a 73mm smoothbore gun, 7.62mm PKT coaxial machine gun and a launchrail for 9M14M Malutka (NATO = Sagger) ATGMs, while a further two 7.62mm PKT MGs were mounted in the glacis plate. The paratroops in the rear compartment could use their weapons, with one firing port in each side, while the others fired their personal weapons from the roof hatch. The vehicle could be dropped by parachute from any type of military transport aircraft, although a practical problem was that it usually took some time for the section to assemble after the drop. BMD-1 had an excellent power-to-weight ratio (32hp per ton) making it both agile and fast.

BMD-1 was the base vehicle for two other versions. First was BMD-1KShM, a command-post vehicle identical with BMD-1 except for the installation of two radio sets, an extra external antenna, and a petrol generator; the turret was retained but the bow MGs and side firing ports were faired over. Second was BTR-D, an armored personnel carrier (APC) derivative, based on BMD-1 parts but with a longer hull and one more road-wheel on each side; it did not have a turret, armament being confined to two bow-mounted MGs. BTR-D was also the basis of a number of further vehicles, including: remotely piloted vehicle (RPV) control post; artillery observation post; artillery fire-control center; BTR-RD armored personnel carrier fitted with Fagot ATGMs; command-and-communications vehicles; ambulances; and an armored recovery vehicle (BREM-D).

ABOVE: Soviet-era designers produced some excellent fighting vehicles which were widely admired in the West. One such was the BMD-1 AIFV, designed for the airborne forces, armed with a 73mm LP gun, three MGs and an ATGW, which could carry five paratroops, and was also air-droppable, highly mobile on land, and fully amphibious.

SPECIFICATIONS
ORIGIN: Russian Federation.

	BMD-1	BMD-1P	BTR-D	BMD-2	BMD-3
ENTERED SERVICE	1969	1971	1974	1980	1990
WEIGHT	7.38tons (7,500kg)	7.48tons (7,600kg)	7.87tons (8,000kg)	7.87tons (8,000kg)	12.7tons (12,900kg)
CREW	2+5	2+5	14	2+5	2+5
MAX SPEED ROAD	37mph (60km/h)	37mph (60km/h)	37mph (60km/h)	37mph (60km/h)	43mph (70km/h)
AFLOAT	6mph (9km/h)	6mph (9km/h)	6mph (9km/h)	6mph (9km/h)	7mph (10km/h)
CRUISING SPEED	22mph (35km/h)	22mph (35km/h)	22mph (35km/h)	22mph (35km/h)	28mph (45km/h)
RANGE (KM)	310 miles (500km)	310 miles (500km)	310 miles (500km)	310 miles (500km)	310 miles (500km)
WEAPONS: MAIN GUN	73mm 2A28	73mm 2A28	—	30mm AP 2A42	30mm AP 2A42
ATGM LAUNCHER	9M14M Malyutka	9M111 Konkurs	—	9M111 Konkurs	9M111 Konkurs
COAX MG	7.62mm PKT	7.62mm PKT	—	7.62mm PKT	7.62mm
BOW MG	2x7.62mm PKT	2x7.62mm PKT	2x7.62mm PKT	2x7.62mm PKT	5.45 RPKS-74
GRENADE LAUNCHER	—	—	—	—	30mm AG-17
ENGINE POWER	240hp	240hp	240hp	240hp	450hp
TRANSMISSION	mechanical	mechanical	mechanical	mechanical	hydromechanical with hydrostatic steering
HYDROPNEUMTATIC SUSPENSIONS, WITH ADJUSTABLE GROUND CLEARANCE	100-450mm	100-450mm	100-450mm	100-450mm	130-530mm

BMD-2

Combat experience in Afghanistan showed that the main armament mounted was too weak, leading to development of the BMD-2 (1985) armed with a stabilized 30mm 2A42 automatic gun, which could fire against both ground and air targets. BMD-2 was also fitted with a launcher rail for 9M113 and 9M111 ATGMs. A command version, BMD-2K, was also developed.

BMD-3

BMD-3 which entered service in 1990 is totally new, its most dramatic attribute being that it can be dropped with the full crew inside the vehicle, using the PBS-950 parachuting system. This is claimed to be highly reliable, while the fact that the crew is already together cuts out the assembly time when they parachute down individually.

BMD-3 has a very heavy weapons fit, comprising a turret-mounted 30mm 2A42 automatic gun with twin-belt feed, and 9P135M Konkurs ATGM launcher (four missiles), while in the glacis plate are a 30mm AG-17 grenade launcher (on the driver's left) and a 5.45mm RPKS-74 light machine gun (on the driver's right), both mounted in ball-joints. The BMD-3 hull is of all-welded aluminum construction and all seats are suspended from the roof (as opposed to being mounted on the floor) to give the crew protection against mine injuries. The inside is much roomier and the vehicle has full collective NBC protection using a filter-ventilation unit to overpressurize the combat compartment.

The BMD-3 uses a new power train, with a new diesel engine giving a considerable improvement in performance over BMD-1 and -2 (see table), driving through a new hydromechanical transmission. In addition, there is a new type of hydropneumatic suspension, which enables the driver to alter the vehicle's height without leaving his seat.

ABOVE LEFT: BMD-I drives away from the dropping zone (DZ). It is fully amphibious, being propelled in water at up to 6mph (10kmh) by two hydrojets; the circular flap covering one of these can be seen on the rear plate.

ABOVE RIGHT: Paratroops have no difficulty in exiting over the sides of the vehicle.

BELOW: Cutaway shows the interior of this remarkable vehicle. The turret mounts a 73mm LP gun, a Sagger ATGW launcher and a coaxial 7.62mm PKT machinegun, while a further two fixed PKTs are mounted in the glacis plate, controlled by a gunner who sits beside the driver. Note also the RPG-7 missiles inside the turret, reloads for the man-portable launcher carried by one of the infantry squad. The 5 members of this squad enter and leave the vehicle via overhead hatches; there are no rear doors.

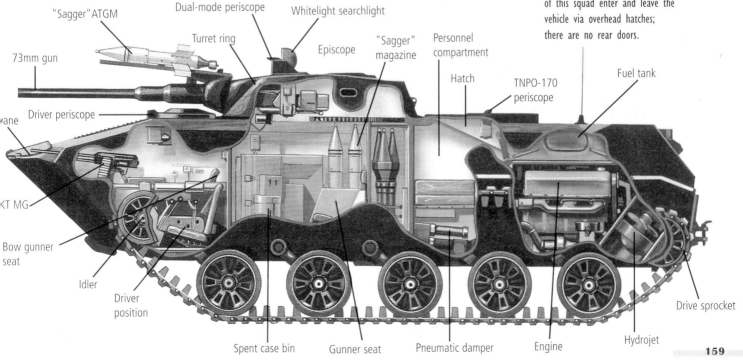

"Sagger" ATGM · Dual-mode periscope · Whitelight searchlight · Turret ring · Episcope · "Sagger" magazine · Personnel compartment · Hatch · 73mm gun · Driver periscope · ...ane · ...KT MG · Bow gunner seat · Idler · Driver position · Spent case bin · Gunner seat · Pneumatic damper · Engine · Hydrojet · Drive sprocket · Fuel tank · TNPO-170 periscope

LAND ROVER DEFENDER/PERENTIE

DEFENDER 4x4

LAND ROVER MULTI-PURPOSE light cargo vehicles have been in production since the early 1950s, with military versions being produced in large numbers for many armed forces. The military model, the Defender, is produced in three basic versions, designated Defender 90, 110, and 130, respectively. The latest, product-improved versions are the Defender 90XD and Defender 110XD (XD = eXtra Duty).

Various Defender models are produced for special forces, the most widely used being the Defender Special Operations Vehicle (SOV), which employs a Defender 110 chassis, but with a cut-down superstructure. It can be fitted with a host of small-arms mounts, including those for: 30mm cannon, 51mm mortar, LAW 80, general-purpose machine guns (12.7mm, 7.62mm or 5.56mm), and 40mm grenade launchers. Crew is up to six including the driver and commander.

The Multi-Role Combat Vehicle (MRCV) is intended as a flexible, air-transportable vehicle for use by rapid reaction forces. It is designed to be adapted within minutes to serve as: pedestal-mount weapons carrier; Milan anti-tank missile-launcher; multi-purpose ring mount; personnel carrier; cargo carrier.

The XD range looks from the outside like standard Defenders (the only external differences are wing-mounted air louvers and the rear lamp clusters), but underneath it is virtually a new vehicle, with redesigned body, suspension, suspension bushes, mountings, chassis, and axles, while Goodyear has produced a totally new 7.50x16 tire. Innovations include longitudinal girders with built-in seat-belt anchorages and beefed-up overhead bars which provide a roll-over cage rather than simply supporting the canopy.

One version, the Defender CAV100 Armored Patrol Vehicle (APV), looks like an innocuous cargo truck - which is precisely what is intended. In many tactical situations, particularly special forces operations in a non-wartime environment, the media and agitators are quick to use the

ABOVE; The air-portable Special Operations Vehicle (SOV), which can also be dropped by parachute, is based on the Defender 110 chassis, and can carry a mix of 30mm cannon, 51mm mortar, LAW 80, 7.62mm general-purpose machine gun, 5.56mm assault rifles, and 40mm grenade pistols.

ABOVE: Defender 110XD Composite Armored Vehicle (CAV) is a low-profile personnel carrier with glass-reinforced plastic armor protection against small arms fire and grenade fragmentation.

arrival of tracked or heavy wheeled armored personnel carriers to escalate the situation. The Defender APV overcomes this since, although it appears to be unaggressive, it is in fact protected by a new Courtauld-made armor, which uses high-performance glass-reinforced composites to give better protection than the equivalent steel armor but with 20 percent less weight. The wind- and sidescreens are made of multi-laminate glass with a polycarbonate inner liner.

PERENTIE 6×6

A MODIFIED VERSION of the Land Rover 4×4, named the Perentie, was developed in Australia. It was generally similar to the British design but with modifications to suit Australian conditions, including a new, 4-speed transmission and the Isuzu 4BD1 3.9L 4-cylinder diesel engine. A further development is the Perentie 6×6, which is a unique and somewhat larger and heavier Australian design, with the same Isuzu 4BD1 engine, but in this case it is turbocharged. Front suspension is by live axle and coil-springs, while the rear bogie employs two leaf springs and a load-sharing rocker on each side. Tires are 750R16LT 10-ply (Dunlop-Olympic Steeltrek 105) on 6Fx16 rims. The long-range patrol/special forces vehicle is open and without doors, and is lighter than the normal Perentie. It is fitted-for-radio (FFR) and standard fittings include a winch, a machine gun mounting, and a 250cc motor-cycle mounted on brackets on the rear bulkhead. Two spare wheels are recessed into the bodywork.

ABOVE: A Perentie 6x6 long-range patrol vehicle. Note low profile, 6x6 drive and heavy armament.

SPECIFICATIONS

ORIGIN: United Kingdom.

TYPE:
High mobility, multi-purpose, wheeled vehicle.

DIMENSIONS:
Lengths: Defender 90 - 12.7ft (3.9m); Defender 110 - 14.4ft (4.4m); Defender 130 - 16.7ft (5.1m); Perentie 6x6 LRP (Long Range Patrol) - 19.7ft (6.0m).
Widths: 90, 100, and 130 - 5.9ft (1.8m); Perentie 6x6 LRP - 7.2ft (2.2m).
Cab heights: 90, 110, and 130 - 6.6ft (2.0m); Perentie 6x6 LRP - 6.0ft (2.0m).
Wheelbases: 90 - 7.9ft (2.4m); 110 - 9.2ft (2.8m); 130 - 10.5ft (3.2m); Perentie 6x6 LRP - 12.8ft (3.9m).

WEIGHTS(GROSS VEHICLE):
90 - 5,621lb (2,550kg); 110 - 6,723lb (3,050kg); 130 - 7,716lb (3,500kg); Perentie 6x6 LRP - 10,670lb (4,840kg).

ENGINES:
A variety: 2.5cc petrol (4 in-line cylinders); 3.5cc petrol (V-8 cylinders); 2.5cc diesel (4 in-line cylinders); 2.5cc Tdi (4 in-line cylinders); Isuzu 4BD1 diesel (4 in-line cylinders)

TRANSMISSION:
Permanent 4-wheel drive through 5-speed manual, all-synchromesh gearbox and 2-speed transfer via central lockable differential; 10 forward, 2 reverse gears; single dry-plate, hydraulically actuated clutch.

SUSPENSION:
Live beam axles and dual-rate coil springs, with telescopic, hydraulic dampers.

ELECTRICS:
12v/0.8kW, or 12/.124v 0.8/2.2kW, or 24v 2.2kW depending on model and user choice.

FORDING DEPTH:
No preparation, Defender range - 2ft (0.6m); with preparation, Defender XD range - 4.9ft (1.5m).

GROUND CLEARANCE:
Defender 90 - 7.5in (191mm); Defender 110/130 - 8.5in (215mm).

FUEL:
Defender 90 - 14.3gal (54 liters); Defender 110/130 - 21 gals (80 liters).

PERFORMANCE:
Maximum slope (grade) - Defender 90/110/130 - 45 degrees.

LEFT: The Defender XD Multi-Role Combat Vehicle (MRCV) is intended for use by rapid deployment and special forces, and can be built on 90, 110 or 130 chassis, with a similar weapons capability to that of the SOV. This particular version is armed with an M2HB 0.5in heavy machine gun.

McDonnell Douglas Helicopters AH-64D Longbow Apache

THE US ARMY'S SEARCH for an attack helicopter lasted so long that an interim machine - the AH-1 (qv) – had to be procured, but the program finally achieved success with the fielding of the AH-64 Apache in 1984. The AH-64 was widely criticized until the 1991 Gulf War, when it was finally given the opportunity to demonstrate its capabilities in combat. During that brief campaign the AH-64 penetrated deep into hostile territory, supporting US special operations forces and attacking Iraqi armor and radars, all of them with great success.

The latest development, the AH-64D Longbow Apache, has the distinctive radome for the Westinghouse Longbow millimeter-wave fire-control radar atop the rotor mast. Inside the radome is a rotating antenna whose output is integrated with the aircraft's avionics and the radio frequency seeker in the Hellfire missiles to provide an outstanding all-weather capability against tracked vehicles, wheeled vehicles, ground air defense weapons sites, and rotary- and fixed-wing aircraft. The

ABOVE: US Army McDonnell Douglas AH-64D Longbow Apache. The millimeter-wave Longbow radar is located in the radome atop the mast and can penetrate rain, fog and smoke, giving 360-deg coverage against airborne targets and 270-deg against ground targets. AH-64Ds for the US Army are being produced by remanufacturing AH-64As.

first prototype flew in March 1991 (with a dummy radome) and the program proceed smoothly to service entry in 1996.

The Longbow radar can penetrate fog, rain, and smoke, all of which defeat conventional FLIR and TV; it scans through 360 degrees for airborne targets and through 270 degrees (in 90 degree segments) for ground targets.

The helicopter's survivability criteria are very demanding, it being required to fly for 30 minutes after being hit by 12.7mm bullets from below the aircraft and by 20mm bullets in many specified areas. The aircraft is fitted with the target acquisition and designation system (TADS) and the pilot night vision system (PNVS). It is armed with a chin-mounted M230 30mm Chain Gun, and carries up to 16 Hellfire missiles or up to 75 2.75in folding-fin aerial rockets (FFAR) or a combination of the two. Air-to-air missiles can also be carried.

The AH-64D Apache Longbow has been ordered by the armies of the Netherlands, the UK, and the USA, all of which will deploy it in support of special operations. It is an outstanding aircraft which will add considerably to the combat potential of its users.

SPECIFICATIONS

ORIGIN:
United States.
TYPE:
Gunship.
DIMENSIONS:
Main rotor diameter 48.0ft (14.6m); length (rotors turning) 58.3ft (17.8m); height 15.3ft (4.7m).
WEIGHT:
Empty - 11,387lb (5,165kg); maximum take-off - 21,000lb (9,5250kg).
POWER PLANT:
Two General Electric T700-GE-701C turboshafts, each rated at 1,800shp (1,342kW).
RANGE:
Internal fuel - 260nm (428km); with drop tanks - 918nm (1,701km).
SPEED:
Maximum level - 197kt (365km/h); maximum cruising - 158kt (293km/h).
CEILING:
Service - 14,765ft (4,500m); hover (in ground effect) - 17,210ft (5,245m).
CREW:
2 (pilot, copilot/gunner).

LEFT: The WAH-64 Apache attack helicopter is on order for the British Army, with 67 in production at the GKN Westland factory at Yeovil, England, the first being due to enter service in 2000. They will be operated by the Army Air Corps (AAC) in both conventional operations and in support of special forces, such as the SAS and SBS.

FAR LEFT: An early production WAH-64 Apache. Weapons comprise a chin-mounted M230 Chain Gun, and a mix of Hellfire missiles, 2.75in folding-fin aerial rockets (FFAR), or air-to-air missiles. This very sophisticated fighting machine is fitted with the Target Acquisition and Designation System (TADS) and the Pilots Night Vision System (PNVS).

MIL MI-24

SPECIFICATIONS

ORIGIN:
Russian Federation.
TYPE:
Gunship.
DIMENSIONS:
Main rotor diameter
56.75ft (17.3m); length
(rotors turning) 64.9ft
(19.8m); height 21.3ft
(6.5m).
WEIGHTS:
Empty - 18,520lb
(8,400kg); maximum take-
off - 27,760lb (12,500kg).
POWER PLANT:
Two Klimov TV3-117 Series
III turboshafts; each
2,200shp (1,640kW).
RANGE:
Internal fuel – 405nm
(750km); combat radius
(max load) - 86nm
(160km); four external
tanks - 155nm (288km).
SPEED:
Maximum level – 168kt
(310km/h); maximum
cruising – 140kt
(260km/h).
CEILING:
Service – 14,765ft
(4,500m); hover (out of
ground effect) – 7,200ft
(2,200m).
CREW:
3 (pilot, copilot, flight
engineer).

THE MIL MI-24, more widely known under its NATO name of "Hind," came as a major surprise to the West when it first appeared in 1974. The Mil design bureau took the existing engines and transmission of the Mil Mi-8 (NATO = Hip) and married them to a new airframe to produce an aircraft whose prime mission was moving an infantry squad of eight men around the battlefield. The airframe was fitted with armor for protection and with weapons to suppress hostile fire. This first production version (Mil 24A = Hind-A) entered service in 1972

The next major version was the Mil Mi-24D (Hind D), which included many changes, most of them resulting from the decision to make its primary role a helicopter gunship, with the infantry-carrying capability reduced to minor importance. This involved fitting a totally new nose, with individual cockpits for the two-man crew, who also received greatly improved protection. Armament was also improved by fitting an undernose, stabilized, 4-barrel 12.7mm gatling, and the hard-points on the stub wings were upgraded. In addition, new engines were installed which resulted in the tail rotor being moved from the starboard side of the tail pylon to the port side.

ABOVE: The latest version of this very effective attack helicopter is the Mil-24P (NATO = Hind-F), which is a Hind-E with the chin-mounted 12.7mm machinegun replaced by a single fixed GSh-30-2 twin-barreled 30mm cannon on the starboard side of the fuselage. The export version is designated Mil-35P.

RIGHT: A frontal view of the same aircraft, showing the cockpit for the two crew, with the twin barrels of the GSh-30-2 protruding forward of the starboard side of the nose. These aircraft are normally deployed in mixed aviation regiments alongside Mil Mi-24V (Hind-E), but are also very suitable for use on special operations.

The Hind-D was a great success and achieved a fearsome reputation during the ill-fated Soviet campaign in Afghanistan, although there was still room for improvement. This resulted in the Mi-24V (Hind-E), which is generally similar to the Hind-D, but is armed with AT-6 anti-tank missiles and revised electronics and avionics. Yet another development is the Mil Mi-24P (Hind-F) which is generally similar to the Hind-E but has a fixed, twin-barreled GSh-23L in the nose instead of the turret-mounted four-barreled JakB.

LEFT: An early model Mil Mi-24 (NATO = Hind-A). This aircraft used the same power-train and dynamic components as the Mil Mi-8 (NATO = Hip) but with a totaly new fuselage and stub wings. It had a low, wide canopy for the 2-man crew and in the passenger compartment the troops could raise the windows to fire their rifles at ground targets.

BELOW: This civilian-looking version is a wolf in sheep's clothing. The Mil Mi-24PS is operated by the Russian Ministry of the Interior special forces and is used for surveillance and to deploy SWAT teams in assault operations against criminals, such as drug gangs and hostage takers.

SIKORSKY UH-60 BLACKHAWK

ABOVE: An MH-53 (left) and an MH-60 Blackhawk (right) approach the refueling drogues deployed by a Lockheed HC-130P Hercules. The USAF's MH-60 is one of the most sophisticated versions of the Blackhawk.

ONE OF THE MOST widely used military helicopters in the world, the UH-60 has taken part in countless special forces operations. The basic helicopter was the winner of the long-running Utility Tactical Transport Aircraft System (UTTAS) competition in the 1970s and has since been produced in large numbers for the US Navy, Marine Corps, Army, and Air Force, as well as many foreign customers. In the transport version there is a crew of three, with seats for 11 passengers, which can be replaced by four litters for the casualty evacuation role. The aircraft is fitted with a winch above the starboard door and a hook beneath the fuselage.

A variety of versions have been produced for the special operations role, of which the US Army's MH-60K is one of the most advanced. This is fitted with a nose-mounted APQ-174 terrain-following radar, AAQ-16B FLIR, night-vision imaging system, and a moving-map display. It has angled stub-wings for fuel pods and armament comprises two pintle-mounted 0.5in M2 machine guns and Stinger air-to-air missiles. The aircraft also carries a comprehensive range of navigation, communications, and electronic warfare equipment.

RIGHT: US Army troops emplane in a line of U-60 Blackhawks. The UH-60 had a long and controversial development period but has now become one of the most extensively used and successful helicopters in the world. It is widely used in special forces operations.

SPECIFICATIONS

ORIGIN:
United States.

TYPE:
Transport/gunship/special operations.

DIMENSIONS:
Main rotor diameter 53.33ft (16.36m); length (rotors turning) 64.9ft (19.76m); height 16.9ft (5.13m).

WEIGHTS:
Empty - 11,284lb (5,118kg); maximum take-off - 20,250lb (9,185kg).

POWER PLANT:
US versions - two General Electric T700-GE-700 turboshafts, rated at 1,550shp (1,151kW) each; export versions -two General Electric T700-GE-701A turboshafts, rated at 1,723shp (1,285kW) each.

RANGE:
Standard fuel - 319nm (292km); ferry range (four fuel tanks) - 1,200nm (2,224km).

SPEED:
Maximum level - 160kt (296km/h); normal cruising - 145kt (268km/h).

CEILING:
Service - 19,000ft (5,790m); hover (in ground effect) - 9,500ft (2,895m).

CREW:
3 (pilot, copilot, crew chief).

PASSENGERS:
11.
(Specifications above are for a typical transport variant; there are many minor variations between different models.)

BELL AH-1W SUPERCOBRA

THE AH-1 HUEYCOBRA was rushed into service as an interim gunship to meet a Vietnam War requirement, using the well-proven UH-1 rotor and transmission system married to a new, slim fuselage. The initial service variant was the AH-1G, but this has been progressively upgraded or replaced, with the latest of the single engine models being the AH-1S. This remains in service with the US Army and at least seven overseas armies/air forces.

The US Marine Corps followed a different path, which led to the AH-1W, which differs from the Army AH-1S, by having twin engines, longer tail boom and forward fuselage, and a larger diameter main rotor. The standard weapon is an M197 cannon in an undernose turret, but a wide variety of other weapons can be carried on the stub wings. These include eight TOWs or eight Hellfires in two pods, 14 2.75in rockets in two pods, Sidewinder air-to-air missiles, and many others. The AH-1W is in service with the US Marine Corps (230), Turkish Army (5), and Thai Army (18).

BELOW: The 'interim' design AH-1 was rushed into service during the Vietnam War and large numbers remain in service with many armies and air forces at the end of the 1990s. This US Marine Corps aircraft is to the latest AH-1W twin-engined standard.

SPECIFICATIONS

ORIGIN:
United States.
TYPE:
Gunship.
DIMENSIONS:
Main rotor diameter 48.0ft (14.63m); length (rotors turning) 58.0ft (17.7m); height 14.2ft (4.32m).
WEIGHTS:
Empty - 10,200lb (4,627kg); maximum take-off - 14,750lb (6,691kg).

POWER PLANT:
Two 1,625shp (1,212kW) General Electric T700-GE-401 turboshafts, limited to a total of 2,032shp (1,515kW) for take-off and 1,725shp (1,288kW) continuous running.
RANGE:
Standard fuel - 343nm (635km).
SPEED:
Maximum level - 190kt (352km/h).
CEILING:
Service - 12,00ft (3,660m); hover (in ground effect) - 14,750ft (4,495m).
CREW:
2 (pilot, gunner).

LEFT: The US Army's AH-1S is generally similar to the AH-1W but has only a single Textron-Lycoming engine, smaller rotor and shorter tail-boom. In addition, the canopy is fabricated from a series of flat armored-glass plates, rather than molded as in the AH-1W.

LOCKHEED C-130 HERCULES

THE LOCKHEED C-130 HERCULES is, quite simply, the greatest military transport ever built; it entered service in April 1955 and will remain in production well into the 21st Century; it combines strategic range with tactical short-field capability; and it can be used in a wide variety of roles, including transport, parachute operations, tanker, surveillance, electronic warfare, and gunship. It is in service with the US Navy, Air Force, Coast Guard, and with many foreign air forces, and is widely used by special forces.

The first gunship, the AC-130A, was a conversion of the first production model, and was armed with 4 20mm Vulcan cannon, 4 7.62mm miniguns and flare-dropping equipment. These served in Vietnam and proved so successful that they were followed by 11 of an enhanced version, AC-130E ("Pave Spectre") which had increased armor protection, improved avionics and greater ammunition stowage; these, less one lost, were later brought up to AC-130H standard, with improved engines. Some of the AC-130As and -Hs were also equipped with a 105mm howitzer (Pave Aegis).

The latest gunship is the Rockwell AC-130U, 13 of which were converted from C-130H standard and assigned to 16th Special Operations Squadron, USAF, where they replaced AC-130Hs; these were then transferred to the Air Force reserve, replacing elderly AC-130As,

Below: Lockheed MC-130E Hercules of the USAF deploys flares to decoy ground-launched infra-red missiles as it comes in over a drop zone. The Hercules is one of the greatest aircraft in aviation history; it entered service in 1955 and will remain in production well into the 21st Century. It is in constant use by special forces around the world.

SPECIFICATIONS

ORIGIN:
United States.

TYPE:
Transport/gunship/special operations.

DIMENSIONS:
Wingspan 132.6ft (39.7m); length 97.75ft (29.3m); height 38.25ft (11.4m).

WEIGHT:
Maximum take-off 155,000lb (69,750kg).

POWER PLANT:
4 Allison T56-A-15 turboprops; 4,300hp per engine.

RANGE:
2,356 miles (2,049nm) with max payload; 2,500 miles (2,174nm) with 25,000lb (11,250kg) cargo; 5,200 miles (4,522nm) with no cargo.

SPEED:
374mph (598km/h) at 20,000ft (6,060m).

CEILING
33,000ft (10,000m) with 100,000lb (45,000kg) payload.

CREW:
Transport role 5 (2 pilots, navigator, flight engineer, loadmaster).

PASSENGERS:
Max 92 troops, or 64 paratroops, or 74 litter patients, or 5 standard freight pallets.

(Specifications above are for a typical transport variant; there are many minor variations between different models.)

which were scrapped. The AC-130U is armed with a single 40mm L60 Bofors cannon, an M102 105mm howitzer, and a single 25mm GAU cannon on a trainable mount. There is a comprehensive targeting package (AN/APQ-180 fire-control radar; Low Light Level TV with laser target designator and rangefinder; and AN/AAQ-117 forward-looking infra-red) which, in combination with advanced navigation systems, enable the AC-130U to engage two targets simultaneously under all weather conditions.

Also supporting special forces operations is the MC-130, the latest version being the MC-130H Combat Talon II, of which 26 are in service. Special-to-role equipment includes: APQ-170 radar in an enlarged nose radome, with a FLIR turret underneath; low-level extraction system; and classified defensive systems. Earlier MC-130s were also fitted with the Fulton recovery system in which a man on the ground released a balloon to carry a wire aloft, which was engaged in special nose hooks. The wire was then automatically transferred to the rear of the aircraft where a winch hauled the man aboard. This system, which must have been extremely exciting for the man involved, was tested but never, as far as is known, used operationally.

Transport variants are used to deliver special forces into hostile territory. This can include landings at airfields, as was done, for example, during the Entebbe raid or into unprepared landing sites; C-130s regularly land on and take-off from 3,000ft (930m) dirt strips. In the paratrooping role, C-130s carry a maximum of 64 fully equipped paratroops over a combat radius of 740nm (1,142km). C-130s also carry out vital resupply missions, by air-landing, parachute or low-level extraction.

Many users of first-generation C-130s are now replacing them by new-build aircraft, either of the basic design (eg, C-130H) or the C-130J, which is virtually a new aircraft, with new engines, propellers, avionics, electronics, fully digitized systems, and a two-man, fully automated cockpit.

In one form or another, the C-130 looks certain to remain in service, particularly on special operations, until the 2020s at least.

ABOVE: Lockheed MC-130E-C Combat Talon - Clamp is a special operations version, with the Fulton STAR equipment and a 'Pinocchio' nose radome. Its task is very low-level penetration of hostile airspace to make very precise delivery of either special operations paratroops or resupply drops.

LEFT: The C-130 makes a versatile and maneuverable gunship and various versions (AC-130A/E/H) have been produced, armed with weapons such as 7.62mm Miniguns, 0.50in heavy machineguns, 20mm Vulcan cannon, 40mm cannon, and even a 105mm howitzer. They also carry sensors to locate and engage hostile targets in the dark.

SUBMARINES FOR SPECIAL FORCES

SPECIFICATIONS
OVERALL LENGTH:
65ft(19.8m).
APPROXIMATE RANGE:
125nm.
SUBMERGED SPEED:
8kt.
DIVING DEPTH:
not known.
PROPULSION:
internal batteries.
CREW: 2.
PASSENGERS:
maximum 16 swimmers,
depending on equipment.

ALL SUBMARINES CAN be used for covert delivery and recovery of special forces to hostile coastlines, although it should be noted that the distance from the shore depends upon the depth of water. The tasks for such special forces can include: attacks by combat swimmers on enemy shipping or installations; reconnaissance, surveillance; infiltration/exfiltration across the beach; and beach reconnaissance in preparation for amphibious landings. Shown here are examples of the most sophisticated submarines operated by the US Navy, and of two North Korean classes, which show what a relatively unsophisticated navy can achieve.

US NAVY SWIMMER DELIVERY SUBMARINES

The high speed, long endurance and stealth of nuclear-powered submarines make them particularly suitable for employment in the swimmer-delivery role. Any US Navy submarine can carry a small number of SEALs, but eight have been converted to carry Dry-Deck Shelters (DDS): six Sturgeon class SSNs - one DDS each: and two much larger Franklin-class former ballistic missile submarines - two DDS each. SEALs or other special forces can join the submarine in port, or can transfer at sea by parachute, by abseiling from helicopters or from surface ships.

The DDS is a watertight cylinder with a large door at the after end and an internal hatch which connects to the submarine's after hatch thus allowing direct access between the two while submerged. The DDS can house, launch and recover one Swimmer Delivery Vehicle (SDV), special inflatable boats, canoes and other stores. A DDS can be installed in about 12 hours and is air-transportable, further increasing special operations flexibility.

The current Swimmer Delivery Vehicle is the SDV Mk8, which is being replaced by the SDV Mk9. These are unpressurized vehicles which carry a maximum of six SEALs in "dry suits." Now under development, however, is the "Advanced Swimmer Delivery System" (ASDS) which will carry a crew of two and 8-16 swimmers inside a pressure hull, thus delivering the swimmers in rather greater comfort than in the current SDV. The captain/helmsman will be a submariner, supported by a SEAL navigator. There will be a lock-in/lock-out chamber in the floor of the craft, which will also be able to mate with a parent submarine, as is done today by deep submergence rescue vehicles (DSRVs). Estimated characteristics of the ASDS are shown in the specifications above.

Six ASDS are to be built and will be transportable by C-5 or C-17 transport aircraft and will be capable of operating with suitably modified Sturgeon/Franklin class SSNs or the New Attack Submarine (NSSN). The latter will also have an integral nine-man lock-out/lock-in chamber for the insertion and recovery of special operations forces. In addition, when fitted with an ASDS-capable Dry Deck Shelter (DDS), the NSSN will be able to deliver many more special operations forces and their equipment.

RIGHT ABOVE: A Sturgeon-class SSN with a Dry-Dock Shelter (DDS) abaft the sail deploys special forces during Exercise Ocean Venture 93. A DDS can accommodate, launch, and recover a single Swimmer Delivery vehicle (SDV) or a number of RIBs or canoes.

BELOW RIGHT: One of various types of SDV used by SEALs for worldwide deployments. These vessels are due to be replaced by the new Advanced Delivery System, in which the swimmers will be accommodated in a pressure-hull.

BELOW: USS Sturgeon (SSN-651). Such nuclear-powered submarines are increasingly used to deliver special forces to hostile shores.

	FRANKLIN CLASS	STURGEON CLASS
NUMBER CONVERTED TO SWIMMER DELIVERY	2	6
ORIGINAL LAUNCH CONVERSION	1965 1992-94	1968-70 1982-89
DISPLACEMENT:		
Surfaced	7,350tons	4,460tons
Submerged	8,250tons	4,960tons
DIMENSIONS:		
Length	425ft (129.54m)	302ft (92.1m)
Beam	33ft (10.05m)	31.8ft (9.7m)
Draught	29.5ft (9.0m)	28.8ft (8.8m)
PROPULSION:		
Nuclear reactor	one	one
Steam turbines	2 sets	2 sets
Propeller	one 7-bladed	one
Power output	15,000shp	15,000hp
PERFORMANCE:		
Max speed	25kt	30kt
Endurance	68 days	n/k
WEAPONS:		
Torpedo tubes	four 21in (533mm)	four 21in (533mm)
CREW:		
Officers	13	13
Enlisted SEALs	107	115
Troops	180	16
DRY-DOCK SHELTERS	2	1

NORTH KOREAN SPECIAL OPERATIONS SUBMARINES

The North Korea Navy has made particular efforts to develop small, swimmer-delivery submarines for use by its special forces. The existence of the latest types was spectacularly revealed on two separate occasions, the first being on 17-18 September 1996 when a | Sang-O (= shark) class boat was captured by South Korean forces while engaged in infiltrating commandos into South Korea. This particular boat had a crew of seven and was carrying 19 commandos. The Sang-O appears to be a North Korean design and some of the class are fitted for employment as conventional attack submarines, but a number are fitted specifically for special forces operations. They have a lock-in/lock-out chamber and swimmers normally transfer while the boat is at periscope depth.

The second incident occurred in June 1998 when one of the much smaller Yugo-class boats became entangled in fishermen's nets in waters south of the border. South Korean frogmen found the hatches sealed from the inside and the boat had to be taken to Donghae, where the frogmen obtained entry via the torpedo tubes. All nine North Koreans inside had been shot, although who shot whom has never been established. The capture of these two boats raises the question of how many missions had been carried out which were not detected by the South Koreans.

ABOVE: This North Korean submarine brought 11 special forces men to South Korea before snagging itself on fishermen's nets and being captured. Such small submarines have been specially developed for these missions and have proved very effective.

	SANG-O CLASS	YUGO
NUMBER IN SERVICE	20	43
LAUNCHED	1991-?	1960-?
DISPLACEMENT:		
Surfaced	256 tons	90 tons
Submerged	277 tons	110 tons
DIMENSIONS:		
Length	116.5ft (35.5m)	65.6ft (20m)
Beam	12.5ft (3.8m)	10.2ft (3.1m)
Draught	2.1ft (3.7m)	15.1ft (4.6m)
PROPULSION:		
Engine	one diesel generator	two diesels
Electric motor	one	one
Propeller	one shrouded	one
PERFORMANCE:		
Max speed	8.8kt	8kt
Endurance	2,700nm at 7kt	550nm at 4kt
Diving depth	590ft (180m):	
WEAPONS		
Torpedo tubes	2/4 21in (533mm)	
CREW:		
Officers	2	1
Enlisted	17	1
Swimmers	6	6-7

INDEX

Page numbers in **bold** type refer to subjects mentioned in captions to illustrations.

PICTURE CREDITS

The publishers wish to thank E. Nevill of TRH Pictures for his research services, and all the private individuals, agencies, various international services, and companies who have provided photographs for this book.

Front cover: US DoD. Back cover: Top, Land Rover; bottom left, DGP-S. Prensa via TRH Pictures; bottom right, Paulo Valpolini via TRH. Endpapers: Salamander. Page 1: Paulo Valpolini via TRH. 2-3: Paulo Valpolini via TRH. 4-5: Canadian Defense Forces. 7: US DoD. 8: US DoD. 9: Left, US DoD; right, Rex/SIPA via Salamander. 10: TRH. 11: Paulo Valpolini via TRH. 12: Rex via Salamander. 14-15: Paulo Valpolini via TRH. 16-17: Australian DoD via TRH. 18: Top, Salamander; bottom, Paulo Valpolini via TRH. 19: Paulo Valpolini via TRH. 20: Salamander. 21: Paulo Valpolini via TRH. 22: Rex/SIPA via TRH. 23: Top, Gamma via Salamander; bottom, Paulo Valpolini via TRH. 24: TRH. 25: Top, Y. Debay via TRH; bottom, Salamander. 26: Salamander. 27: Paulo Valpolini via TRH. 28: Bernard & Graefe Verlag via Salamander. 29: Top, Bernard & Graefe Verlag via Salamander; bottom, Bernard & Graefe Verlag via TRH. 30-31: Rex/SIPA via TRH. 32: Top, Salamander; bottom, TRH. 33: Israel Defense Forces via TRH. 34-35: Paulo Valpolini via TRH. 36: Rex/SIPA via TRH. 38: Y. Debay via TRH. 39: Salamander. 40-41: Paulo Valpolini via TRH. 42: Top, Salamander; bottom, TRH. 43: TRH. 44-45: Salamander. 46: Top, TRH; bottom, Salamander. 47: Top, TRH; bottom, Paulo Valpolini via TRH. 48: Top, TRH; bottom, Salamander. 49: Salamander. 50-51: Salamander. 52: E. Nevill via TRH. 53: Salamander. 54: Salamander. 55: Top, Salamander; bottom, TRH. 56-57: Salamander. 58-59: Salamander. 60: Salamander. 61: Top, Salamander; bottom, E. Nevill via TRH. 62: Top, US Army via Salamander; bottom, US DoD via TRH. 63: Salamander. 64-65: E. Nevill via TRH. 66-67: US Navy via TRH. 68-71: Salamander. 72: Top, US Navy via TRH; bottom, Salamander. 73: Top US Navy via TRH; bottom, Salamander. 77-78: Rex via Salamander. 79: Spooner/Gamma via Salamander. 80-84: Rex/SIPA via Salamander. 86-87: US DoD via Salamander. 88: Top, US DoD via Salamander; bottom, Rex/SIPA via Salamander. 90: Top, London Express News via Salamander; bottom, Rex via Salamander. 91: BBC via Salamander. 92-93 Photo Source via Salamander. 94: London Express News Service via Salamander. 95: Top, London Express News Service via Salamander; bottom, Salamander. 96: Top, London Express News Service via Salamander; bottom, Salamander. 97: Salamander. 98-99: US DoD. 100: Rex/SIPA via Salamander. 101: Top, Rex/SIPA via Salamander; bottom, Salamander. 102-103: Rex/SIPA via TRH. 106: Rex/SIPA via TRH. 107-109: Rex/SIPA via TRH. 110-11: Paulo Valpolini via TRH. 112: Top, Salamander; bottom, TRH. 113: SIG via TRH. 114-115: Heckler & Koch via TRH. 116-121: Salamander. 122: Top and bottom, Salamander; center, TRH. 123: Left, TRH; right and bottom, Salamander. 124-125: GIAT. 126: Top, Steyr via TRH; bottom, Steyr. 127: Top, Steyr via TRH; bottom, Steyr. 128-130: Salamander. 131: Top left, US Air Force via TRH; top right, US Army. 132-133: Israel Defense Forces. 134: Royal Ordnance Factory. 135: TRH. 136-137: Salamander. 138: Top, Paulo Valpolini via TRH; bottom, Salamander. 139: Top, Paulo Valpolini via TRH. 140: Top, Accuracy International; bottom, Accuracy International via TRH. 141: Top, Rex/SIPA via TRH; bottom, US Marine Corps via TRH. 142: US Army. 143: Top, TRH; bottom, G.D. Taylor via TRH. 144-145: FN Herstal via TRH. 146-147: Top, FN via TRH; bottom, US DoD via TRH. 148: Top, E. Nevill via TRH; bottom, TRH. 149: US Marine Corps. 150: Rex/SIPA via Salamander. 151: Salamander. 152: US DoD via TRH. 153: Left, US Air Force via TRH; right, Salamander. 154: McDonnell Douglas via TRH. 155: Top, Salamander; bottom, Westland via TRH. 156-157: E. Nevill via TRH. 158: TRH. 159: Salamander. 160-161: Land Rover. 162: Top, Boeing via TRH; bottom, Westland via TRH. 163: GKN Westland via TRH. 164: Top, M. Roberts via TRH; bottom, G.D. Taylor via TRH. 165: Top, Salamander; bottom, J. Widdowson via TRH. 166: Top, US Air Frce via TRH; bottom, Salamander. 167: Bell Helciopters via TRH. 168-169: US Air Force. 170: Salamander. 171: Top left, US DoD via TRH; top right, Rex/SIPA via TRH; bottom, Salamander.